THE DREAD

A STUDY ON IRRATIONAL FEAR / PHOBIAS

DR. JIPSON LAWRANCE. J

Copyright © Dr. Jipson Lawrance. J
All Rights Reserved.

I Dedicate this book to all those who want to take away the fear of surroundings and those who thought me that it's never too late to chase my passion.

Contents

FOREWORD

Phobia is a condition in which a living thing has a different fear of an event or object. Phobias can not only be a biological phenomenon but also an emotional response to nature. However, there has been controversy over what causes phobias and it is generally accepted that both phobias come from biological and environmental knowledge. The first discourse on phobias was made by Hippocrates, who wrote about one of his patients who was terrified of what some might consider foolish. About 1890 phobias were described as a different attitude by Freud and his researchers. Freud the creator of psychoanalysis said that phobias were just a contradiction within you. Therefore, in order to get rid of their phobia they will have to overcome his part. However, not everyone was willing to agree with Freud, things like behavior for example, formed a system known as mood and stimulus generalization to show that fear is a behavioral disorder created by the use of avoidance.

Fear is the most common and important form of a person's reaction to something dangerous, it keeps the person from getting into danger, because fear is unpopular and the person tries very hard to avoid the object or situation of fear. It causes changes in the body known as the fight-or-flight reaction, which causes the blood pressure to rise and the heartbeat to speed up pumping blood to the large muscles used to escape, to measure this the human body has sweat glands that produce sweat. body cooling.

Young people are often more fearful than older people. When a person has a certain fear, he usually does not spend much time thinking about it, and it only affects him when he is forced to deal with it. Almost everyone is afraid of something. However, phobia can even cause people to risk their lives.

Preface

People with a certain phobia know that their fears are extreme. But they cannot defeat it. The problem is found only when direct fear interferes with the daily activities of institute, work, or home life.

The cause is unknown, although they appear to be running into families. If the object of fear is easy to avoid, people with phobias may not want treatment. In some cases, however, they may make important career or personal decisions to avoid a situation involving the source of the phobia.

The Dread is an asset to those who want to know about the phobias, and a guide to effective work for psychologist, either as a student, teacher, researchers or therapist. Its aim to accompany you throughout the progression in emerging, directing, and broadcasting psychological research on phobias. It can be useful as an supplementary education material in practical psychological assessment studies on phobias.

Acknowledgements

The world is a better place for people who want to develop and lead others. What makes it even better is people who share the gift of their time directing future leaders. Thank you to everyone who is striving to grow and help me grow.

To all the individuals I have had the opportunity to lead, be led by, or watch their growth from afar, I want to say thank you for being the inspiration and foundation for writing books.

Writing a book is more pleasing than I could have ever imagined. I'm eternally grateful to those who stood by me during every struggle and all my successes. Especially to my parents (Dr. D.E. Lawrance & Mrs. Jaya Lawrance) and brother (Lickson Lawrance). Always they are my best friends and mentors.

Writing a book about fear/ phobias is a surreal process. I'm forever indebted to all for their help, keen insight, and ongoing support in bringing my writing to life.

Special thanks to Dr. Stalin K Thomas (international Director, IATA) and IATA International officers from all Continents for encouraging me to distillate on academic writings.

Thanks Notion Press for letting me in, for being a part of amazing world of writers.

Finally, to all those have been the part of my life's journey as the readers.

Thank you

PROLOGUE

We all have fears and anxieties and there are various situations that leave us with the desire to prepare for the danger we have seen. Fear is a natural human experience, and it allows us to judge fairly the safety of the situation. The difference between common fear and phobia is that phobia for the most part, is an irrational fear without tangible evidence that you will be harmed, and the fear will eventually subside and not affect your quality of life on a regular basis.

Phobias are, in fact, an extreme form of fear or anxiety caused by a condition even when there is no danger. For example, you did not know it was safe to be outside on the porch, but you were afraid to go out and enjoy the view or be inside. Similarly, you may know that a snake is not poisonous and will not bite you, but this does not reduce anxiety.

People with phobias may find themselves in a state of constant anxiety about whether they can touch something or a place they are afraid of. In many cases, avoiding certain places or things may make it look worse than it actually is, and many people will begin to fear the normal activities of daily life, leading to unpleasant behavior in control. These debilitating and depressing feelings can make life extremely difficult and can have a detrimental effect on one's health.

Turn the pages to learn more about irrational fears.

I

Fear

Fear is an intensively unwelcome emotion in response to perceiving or feting a peril or trouble. Fear causes physiological changes that may produce behavioral responses similar to mounting an aggressive response or fleeing the trouble. Fear in mortal beings may do in response to a certain encouragement being in the present, or in expectation or anticipation of unborn trouble perceived as a threat to oneself. The fear response arises from the perception of peril leading to a battle with or escape from/ avoiding the trouble (also known as the fight-or-flight response), which in extreme cases of fear (horror and terror) can be a snap response or palsy.

In humans and other creatures, fear is modulated by the process of cognition and literacy. therefore, fear is judged as rational or applicable and illogical or unhappy. An illogical fear is called a phobia.

Fear is nearly related to the emotion anxiety, which occurs as the result of pitfalls that are perceived to be willful or necessary. The fear response serves survival by actualizing applicable behavioral responses, so it has been saved throughout elaboration Sociological and organizational exploration also suggests that individualities' fears aren't solely dependent on their nature but are also shaped by their social relations and culture, which guide their understanding of when and how important fear to feel

Fear is occasionally considered the contrary of courage; still, this is incorrect. Because courage is an amenability to face adversity, fear is an illustration of a condition that makes the exercise of courage possible.

Many physical changes in the body are associated with fear, which is defined as a response to combat or flight. The ingrain of pitfall management, activates rapid respiratory rate (hyperventilation), heart rate, and vasoconstriction of additional blood vessels leading to blood clots, which increases the tension of the connective tissue in each hair follicle to shorten and cause "goosebumps. ", or continuously, piloerection (warming or cold-blooded animal), sweating, increased blood glucose (hyperglycemia), increased serum calcium, increase in white blood cells called neutrophilic leukocyte, sleep-induced sleep apnea and "Butterflies in the stomach" (dyspepsia). This ancient method may help a living creature to run down or to fight a hole. (4) Through a series of physical changes, knowledge perceives feelings of dread.

Strong segregation of terrorism was proposed by Gray; videlicet, obesity, adolescence, special evolutionary problems, incentives arising from social trade, and conditional simulation. Another classification was proposed by Archer, who, in addition to conditional fears, spread the fearsome motives (and attacks) into three groups; videlicet, pain, something new, and frustration, though he also defines "drinking alcohol," which refers to something that is rapidly going to the visual senses of the subject and can be disseminated as "firmness. "Russell explained the effective classification of horror motivation when in a new context it is a dynamic that affects more than one command 1) Bloodsucker instigations (including movement, sudden, collapse, but also learning and incorporating bloodsucker instigations); 2) Physical problems (including thickness and height); 3) motivation associated with an increase in rape problems and other problems (including youth, openness, lightness, and loneliness); 4) Updates from conspecifics (including something new, movement, and distance behavior

); 5) Species- predicted causes of fear and information (special evolutionary problems); and 6) The promotion of fears that are not predictable species (triggers for fear).

Natural fears

Although many fears are learned, the ability to fear is a part of human nature. Many studies have found that certain fears (e.g., animals, heights) are more common than others (e.g., flowers, clouds). This fear is also easy to seduce in the laboratory. This condition is known as readiness. Because the first people who were quick to fear dangerous situations were in danger of surviving and reproducing; readiness is defined as the result of genetic predisposition to natural selection

From the perspective of psychological evolution, a different fear may be a different familiarity that has been useful in the past evolutionary process. They may have been built at different times. Other fears, such as fear of heights, may be common in all mammals and developed during the Mesozoic period. Other fears, such as the fear of snakes, may be common to all simians and developed during the Cenozoic period (a continuous geological period covering the last 66 million years of history). Alternatively, such as fear of rats and insects, may be different from humans and developed during the paleolithic and neolithic periods (when rats and insects become important carriers of infectious diseases that damage plants and stored food).

Learned Fear

Animals and humans create some fear as a result of learning. This has been explored in psychology as a fear correction, beginning with a study by John B. Watson's Little Albert in 1920, which was inspired after looking at a child with irrational dog fear. In the study, an 11-month-old boy was placed in a state of shock in a white laboratory mouse. Increased fear included other white, furry items, such as rabbits, dogs, and even Santa Claus masks with white cotton balls on their beards.

Fear can be learned by encountering or observing a traumatic event. For example, if a child falls into a well and struggles to get out, he may have a fear of springs, elevations (acrophobia), enclosed spaces (claustrophobia), or water (aquaphobia). There are studies that look at the areas of the brain involved in relation to fear. When looking at these areas (such as the amygdala), it was suggested that a person learn to fear whether he or she has experienced adversity, or if he or she has seen the fears of others. In a study completed by Andreas Olsson, Katherine I. Nearing, and Elizabeth A. Phelps, the amygdala was affected both when subjects see another person being moved to a contradictory event, knowing that the same treatment awaits them, and when subjects are included later. a situation that evokes fear. This suggests that fear can develop in both cases, not just in personal history.

Fear is affected by the context of culture and history. At the beginning of the 20th century, for example, many Americans feared polio, a disease that could cause paralysis. There are consistent cultural differences in how people react to fear. The rules of expression affect how people have the opportunity to express facial expressions of fear and other emotions.

Fear of victimization

Fear of abuse is a function of perceived risk and vulnerability. Fear of the unknown or irrational fear is caused by negative thinking (anxiety) arising from the anxiety associated with an independent feeling of anxiety or fear. Nonsense fears share common sense with other fears, a process that involves the nervous system to integrate physical resources in the event of an accident or threat. Many people are afraid of the "unknown". Unreasonable fear can spread to many places the latest, the next decade or so. Persistent irrational fear has harmful consequences as the elicitor stimulus is usually absent or perceived as deceptive. Such fear can cause comorbidity and the umbrella of anxiety disorder. Fear may cause people to feel the expected fear of what might continue with similar planning and testing. For example, many "continuing education" educators see it as a potential risk factor for fear and depression, and they would rather teach what they have taught than do research.

The ambiguity of often uncertain and unexpected situations can cause anxiety in addition to other psychological and physical problems in some communities; especially those who do so, for example, in war-torn areas or in areas where there are conflicts, terrorism, harassment, etc. Parental insecurity, which can lead to fear, may diminish a child's mental or emotional development. For example, parents tell their children not to talk to strangers in order to protect them. At school, they will be encouraged not to be intimidated when speaking to strangers but to be firm and aware of the danger and the environment in which it occurs. Misunderstood and mixed messages like these can affect their self-esteem and self-esteem. Researchers say that talking to strangers is not something to be avoided but to be allowed in front of a parent if necessary. Developing a sense of equality in dealing with various situations is often recommended as a solution to irrational fears and as an essential skill of several ancient philosophies.

Fear of the unknown (FOTU) "can be, or perhaps, a basic fear"

Although the behavior of fear varies from animal to animal, it is generally classified into two main categories; that is, avoidance/flight and immobility. To this end, different researchers added different categories, such as the manifestation of threats and attacks, defensive responses (including alarming and upcoming responses), defensive burials, and public responses (including alarm and alarm). Finally, the inability to walk is often divided into ice and tonic instability.

The decision as to what behaviors to fear is determined by the level of fear and context, such as environmental factors (existing escape route, distance to shelter), the presence of a clear and local threat, the distance between threat and topic, threatening features (speed, size, direction), features of the threatened subject (size, body condition, speed, crypsis rate, morphological protective properties), social conditions (group size), and quantity of information on the type of threat.

Often laboratory studies with mice were performed to assess the detection and disappearance of responses to congenital fear. In 2004, researchers installed mice (Rattus norvegicus) in order to scare away a particular stimulus, an electric shock. Researchers were then able to trigger the disappearance of these conditional fears so that no drugs or drugs could continue to aid in extinction. However, the mice showed signs of avoidance of learning, not fear, but simply avoiding the area that caused pain in the experimental mice. Learning to avoid mice appears to be a conditional response, so the behavior may be unconditional, as supported by previous research.

Species-specific defense reactions (SSDRs) or learning to avoid natural instincts tend to avoid certain threats or motives, the way animals live in the wild. Both humans and animals share in this special defense mechanism, such as flight-or-fight, which also includes artificial rage, false or intimidating anger, and a fixed response to threats, controlled by sensitive sensory systems. These SDRs are learned very quickly through social interactions among some of the same species, other species, and ecosystems. These received responses or responses are not easily forgotten. A heavy animal is an animal that already knows what to fear and how to avoid it. For example, people react when they see a snake, many jump back and forth before realizing why they are running away, and in some cases, it becomes a stick instead of a snake.

Like many other brain functions, there are various brain regions involved in interpreting fear in humans and other non-human species. The amygdala connects both signals between the prefrontal cortex, hypothalamus, sensory cortex, hippocampus, thalamus, septum, and brainstem. The amygdala plays an important role in SSDR, such as ventral amygdaloidal, which is essential for integrated learning, and SDRs are studied in conjunction with nature and other similar species. Emotional reactions are created only after the signals have been transmitted between different regions of the brain and activated sensory systems; who controls the plane, fights, blows, fears, and small reactions. Often a damaged amygdala can cause paralysis in the perception of fear (such as a personal patient S.M.). This degeneration can cause a variety of animals to become fearful, and they can often become overconfident, confront their peers, or move on to predators.

Robert C. Bolles (1970), a researcher at the University of Washington, wanted to understand the specific responses to species defenses and to learn to avoid interbreeding but found that the ideas to avoid learning and the tools used to measure this tendency were outside contact with the natural world.). There are three types of SSDRs: flight, combat (false attack), or snow. Even pets have SSDRs, and in those times the animals seem to return to atavistic values and become "wild" again. Dr. Bolles says responses often depend on the strength of the safety signal, and not on the aversive conditioned system. This safety signal can be a source of feedback or even an encouraging change. Internal response or information from within, muscle movement, and increased heart rate, appear to be more important to SSDR than external response, stimuli from external sources. Dr. Bolles found that many creatures have a specific set of fears, helping to ensure the survival of species. Mice will escape any shocking event, and pigeons will flutter their wings more when threatened. The fluttering of the wings in pigeons and the scattering of rats are considered special protective or behavioral responses. Bolles believed that the SDRRs were organized by Pavlovian conditioning, not operating conditions; SSDRs arises from the link between natural causes and adverse events. Michael S. Fanselow conducted a study, in order to test a specific immune response, noting that mice in two different states of shock react differently, based on natural perception or in a protective environment, rather than contextual information.

Species-specific Defensive responses to certain types are made out of fear and are essential for survival. Mice without a stathmin gene do not show learning to avoid, or lack of fear, and will often go straight for cats and be eaten. Animals use these SSDRs to survive, helping to increase their chances of survival, by living long enough to reproduce. Humans and animals alike have developed a fear of knowing what to avoid, and this fear can be learned by encountering others in a community, or by learning about personal experiences with a creature, species, or situations to be avoided. SDRs are the evolution that has been observed in many species throughout the world, including mice, chimpanzees, prairie dogs, and even humans, adaptations designed to help individual creatures survive in a hostile world.

Learning to fear changes throughout life due to natural changes in cognitive development This including changes in the prefrontal cortex and amygdala.

Visual sensory facial testing does not follow a consistent pattern but corrects emotional facial content. Scheller et al. found that participants pay more attention to the eyes when they see a scary or neutral face, while the mouth is focused on the presentation of a happy face, regardless of job requirements and areas where the face is weak. These findings are repeated when the shocking sight is unveiled and when the face of the sacred face is distorted for the sake of scary, neutral, and cheerful speeches.

Brain structures are the center of many neurobiological events associated with fear of the two amygdalae, located at the back of the pituitary gland. Each amygdala is part of a region of fear learning. They are essential for positive adaptation to stress as well as the direct conversion of emotional learning memory. In the presence of threatening stimuli, the amygdalae produce the production of hormones that influence fear and aggression. When a response to a stimulus in the form of fear or anger begins, the amygdalae may release hormones to the body to put a person in a state of alertness, when he is ready to move, run, fight, etc. This immune response is often referred to as physiology as a response-or-flight response controlled by the hypothalamus, part of the limbic system. Once a person is in safe mode, which means that there are no longer any possible threats around him, the amygdalae will send this information to the medial prefrontal cortex (mPFC) where it is stored for the same future conditions, known as memory consolidation.

Other hormones involved during the fight or flight include epinephrine, which regulates heart rate and metabolism as well as stretching blood vessels and airways, increased norepinephrine, heart rate, blood flow to skeletal muscle, and glucose release. stores, along with cortisol which raises blood sugar, and increases the circulation of neutrophilic leukocytes, and calcium among other things.

In the aftermath of a panic attack, the amygdalae, and hippocampus record an event with synaptic plasticity Stimulation in the hippocampus will cause one to recall many details surrounding the condition. Plastic and memory formation in the amygdala is produced by the activation of neurons in a region. Experimental data support the notion that synaptic plasticity of neurons leading to posterior amygdalae occurs through the nervous system. In some cases, this creates responses to chronic fear such as posttraumatic stress disorder (PTSD) or phobia. MRI scans and fMRI scans showed that amygdalae in people diagnosed with such disorders including bipolar or panic disorder are larger and more likely to have high levels of anxiety.

Microorganisms can suppress amygdala function. Rats infected with the toxoplasmosis parasite are less afraid of cats, sometimes even seeking their own urine. This behavior often leads to cats being eaten. The parasite then breeds inside the cat's body. There is evidence that the parasite focuses on the amygdala of infected mice. In a separate experiment, mice with lesions in the amygdala did not show any fear or anxiety about unwanted stimuli. The rats were feeding on iron rods which at times caused electrical shock. Although they learned to avoid pressure, they did not shy away from this traumatic material.

A few brain structures other than the amygdalae have also been found to be effective when humans are presented with a distinct medial-mediated surface, which is the Occipitocerebellar regions comprising the fusiform gyrus and the lower / temporal-parietal temporal gyri. Terrible eyes, nails, and mouths appear to reproduce these brain responses separately. Scientists from a Zurich study show that the hormone oxytocin, which is related to stress and sex, reduces activity at your brain's fear center.

Pheromones and why fear may be contagious

In threatening conditions, insects, aquatic life, birds, reptiles, and mammals emit odors, formerly called alarm substances, which are chemical signals now called alarm pheromones. This defense also simultaneously informs members of the same type of risk and leads to significant behavioral changes such as egg, immune behavior, or dispersion depending on the conditions and species. For example, depressed mice release odors that cause other mice to move away from the signal source.

After the discovery of pheromones in 1959, alarm pheromones were first described in 1968 by ants and earthworms, and four years later they were found in mammals, both mice, and rats. Over the next two decades, the identification and classification of these pheromones continued in all species of insects and marine animals, including fish, but it was not until 1990 that an additional understanding of mammal pheromones was collected.

Earlier, in 1985, a link between the odor emitted by depressed mice and the perception of pain was discovered: mice exposed to these rats developed opioid-mediated analgesia. In 1997, researchers discovered that bees began to develop mild pains after being stimulated with isoamyl acetate, a banana-smelling chemical, and part of a bee alarm pheromone. Studies have also shown that bee stings caused by fear were associated with endorphins.

Using compulsory swimming experiments on mice as a model of panic intrusion, the first "alarm thing" of mammals was discovered. In 1991, this "alarm system" was shown to fulfill the conditions of pheromones: a well-defined behavioral effect, specificity of species, a small effect of experience, and control of indirect arousal. Experiments on rats' activity with a pheromone alarm, as well as preferences/avoidance of odors from pheromones containing pheromones, have shown that pheromones have very low variability.

In 1993 a link was found between the chemosignals alarm in mice and their immune response. Pheromone production in mice was found to be associated with or associated with the pituitary gland in 1994.

In 2004, it was shown that pheromones mice alarms had different effects on "recipient" mice (mouse detecting pheromone) depending on which region of the body was released: Pheromone production from modified facial behavior in the recipient mouse, e.g. triggers sniffing or movement, while pheromones emanating from the back of the mouse trigger responses to stress of the autonomic nervous system, such as an increase in core body temperature. Further studies showed that when the mouse detected alarm pheromones, it increased its immunity and risk test behavior, and its acoustic startle reflex improved.

It was not until 2011 that the link between acute pain, neuroinflammation, and the pheromones release the mouse in the mice was discovered: real-time RT-PCR analysis of rat brain tissue showed that shocking footpad mouse increased its production of cytokines in -proinflammatory to deep brain structures. , IL-1β, heteronuclear Corticotropin-releasing hormone, and c-fos mRNA expression in both the paraventricular nucleus and the nucleus of the stria Terminalis bed, and increase the levels of stress hormone in plasma (corticosterone).

The neurocircuit of how mice detect alarm pheromones was shown to be related to the hypothalamus, brainstem, and amygdalae, all of which are old evolutionary structures within or in the state of the brain below the cortex, and involved anti-or-response response. -plane, as it happens to humans.

Anxiety caused by alarm pheromones in mice has been used to assess the extent to which anxiolytics can alleviate anxiety in humans. In this case, the change in the acoustic startle reflex of mice with pheromone-induced anxiety (i.e. reduced immunity) was rated. Previous treatment of rats with one of the five anxiolytics used in medical treatment was able to reduce their anxiety: midazolam, phenelzine (nonselective monoamine oxidase (MAO) inhibitor), propranolol, a random beta-blocker, clonidine, i -alpha 2 adrenergic agonist or CP -154,526, a corticotropin-releasing hormone antagonist.

Improper development of odor degradation destroys the perception of pheromones and pheromone-related behaviors, such as aggressive behavior in male mice: The enzyme Mitogen-activated protein kinase 7 (MAPK7) has been implicated in controlling the development of odor and odor discrimination. and is widely expressed in brain development in mice, but is not present in many areas of adult rat brain. Conditional removal of MAPK7ne into mouse neural stem cells impairs a few pheromone-mediated behaviors, including aggression and mating in male mice. This behavioral disorder is not the result of decreased testosterone levels, stagnation, extreme fear or anxiety, or depression. Using rat urine as a natural solution containing pheromones, it has been shown that dehydration was associated with the improper acquisition of related pheromones, as well as changes in their innate preference for pheromones related to sexual activity and reproduction.

Finally, a reduction in the response to panic attacks due to peer pressure (or biological language: affiliative conspecific) tends and befriends is called "social buffering". The term is similar to the 1985 "buffering" theory in psychology, where community support has been proven to reduce the negative health effects of alarm pheromone-mediated distress. The role of "public pheromone" was suggested by the recent discovery that olfactory signals were responsible for mediating "public bathing" in male mice. "Temporary community retention" has also been recognized to reduce the natural reaction of bees. The bee colony posed in the area of high-risk rape did not show increased aggression and aggressive genetic patterns in isolated bees but decreased anger. The fact that bees have not only become accustomed to being threatened suggests that disturbed colonies also reduced their food intake.

Biologists proposed in 2012 that fear pheromones appeared as molecules of "keystone value", a term coined to match key types of keywords. Pheromones may determine the composition of species and affect levels of energy and the exchange of substances in the natural community. Pheromones, therefore, form a structure in the food web and play an important role in maintaining natural systems.

Fear pheromones in humans

Evidence of chemosensory alarm symptoms in humans has emerged little by little: Although alarm pheromones have not been physically isolated and their chemical properties have not been identified in humans to date, there is evidence of their presence. Androstadienone, for example, is steroidal, chronic odor, pheromone candy found in human sweat, axillary hair, and plasma. A closely related androstenone compound is involved in talking about domination, violence, or competition; sex hormones influencing the detection of androstenone in men have shown high testosterone levels associated with high androstenone sensitivity in men, high testosterone levels associated with unhappiness in response to androstenone in men, and high estradiol levels associated with androstenone intolerance in women.

A 2006 German study showed that when a person's sweat was caused by stress and exercise from twelve people was collected and given to seven participants, five of them could not distinguish the sweat caused by exercise in the room, and three could also distinguish between exercise. sweat caused by anxiety. The response of the acoustic startle reflex to the sound when you feel the sweat of anxiety was greater than when you feel the sweat caused by exercise, as measured by electromyography analysis of the surrounding muscle, which is responsible for partial blinking of the eyes. This has shown for the first time that fear chemosignals can change a frightening reflex in humans without emotional intervention; fear chemosignals initiate the recipient's "defensive behavior" before the attention of subjects at the acoustic startle reflex level.

Similar to the social interference of rats and bees in responding to chemosignals, the induction of empathy by another person's "smelly anxiety" is found in humans.

A study from 2013 provided brain scan evidence that people's response to the fear of chemosignals may be gender-sensitive. The researchers collected alarm-sweating sweat and sweat from donors who collected it, assembled it, and gave it to 16 unrelated people who received an active brain MRI. Although men's stress-induced sweating produced a more potent emotional response in both women and men, women's sweat-producing sweat produced significantly stronger arousal in women than men. Statistical tests have identified this gender specification in the right amygdala and strongly in the upper nuclei. Since no significant difference was found in the olfactory lamp, the response to the signals triggered by women's fears is probably based on an explanation of the meaning, i.e. at the emotional level, rather than the strength of chemosensory signals from the other sex, i.e. cognitive level.

The approach to avoiding proximity was stopped when volunteers saw an angry or cheerful cartoon face on a computer screen that pushed or pulled on them with a stick of joy very quickly. Volunteers smelling of androstadienone, combined with the scent of clove oil responded quickly, especially on an angry face than those smelling only clove oil, which is interpreted as an androstadienone-related activity of the nervous system. A possible mechanism of action, however, is that androstadienone alters the "processing of the emotional surface". Androstadienone is known to affect the function of the fusiform gyrus associated with facial recognition.

Hypothetical hypotheses suggest that "when two or more active thought structures do not coincide logically, emotional arousal increases, which activates processes with the expected result of increased instability and decreased arousal." In this context, it has been suggested that the behavior of fear is caused by a conflict between a preferred, or expected state, and a truly imagined situation, as well as activities, to remove inconsistent stimuli in the point of view, for example, in-flight or hiding, respectively. to resolve inconsistencies. This approach puts fear in a wide range of areas, including aggression and curiosity. When the conflict between vision and expected time is minimal, curiosity learns by reducing the time-consuming conflict over time. If the inconsistency is high, fear or aggressive behavior may be used to change the view to match the expected time, depending on the size of the conflict and the specific context. Aggressive behavior is thought to alter the idea by forcefully altering it to fit the expected mood, while in some cases a blocked escape may also trigger aggressive behavior in an attempt to eliminate a disturbing motive.

To improve our understanding of neural and behavioral mechanisms of dynamic and maladaptive fears, researchers used a variety of interpretive animals. These models are very important in research that may be very aggressive in human studies. Mice like rats and mice are examples of common animals, but other species are used. Certain aspects of fear research still require further research such as sex, gender, and age differences.

animal models include, but are not limited to, a state of panic, stress based on predators, single-term stress, chronic stress models, unavoidable leg/tail shocks, immobility or self-control, and improved learning to fear. While the paradigms of stress and fear vary between models, they tend to include features such as discovery, production, extinction, mental control, and reunification.

Fear conditioning, also known as Pavlovian or Classical conditioning, is a learning process that involves pairing a medium and unconditional motive (US). Neutral motivation is something like metal, stone, or room that does not block the response in general when the US is the motive that leads to a natural or unconditional response (UR - in Pavlov's famous study and US effects on UR can occur not only in the US but also with moderate motivation. antagonistic such as shock, tone, or bad smell.

Predator-based (PPS)-based mental stress involves a natural way of learning to fear. Predatory animals such as cats, snakes, or fox or cat urine are used along with other stressors such as immobilization or self-control to obtain responses to natural fears.

Examples of chronic stress include chronic bipolar disorder, chronic social failure, and chronic stress. These models are often used to study how long-term stress/pain can change learning from fear and anxiety.

Single prolonged stress (SPS) is a fear model commonly used to study PTSD. Its paradigm includes many pressures such as the inability to move, swim in power, and exposure to others that are simultaneously delivered to the subject. This is used to study non-natural, uncontrollable situations that can trigger responses to negative fears that are manifested in many anxiety and trauma-based disorders.

Stress-enhanced fear learning (SEFL) studies such as SPS are often used to study the negative fears associated with PTSD and other trauma-based disorders. SEFL involves one extreme stress such as a large number of feet mimicking single intense stress that somehow develops and alters the study of future fears.

Pharmaceutical

Treatment of panic disorder and phobias with amygdalae use of glucocorticoids. In another study, glucocorticoid receptors in the central nuclei of the amygdalae were disrupted to better understand the mechanisms of fear and nervousness. Glucocorticoid receptors were blocked using lentiviral vectors containing Cre-recombinase injected into mice. The results showed that disruption of glucocorticoid receptors prevents behavioral panic disorder. Mice had hearing symptoms which caused them to freeze normally. However, a decrease in freezing was observed in mice that inhibited glucocorticoid receptors.

Psychology

Behavioral therapy has been effective in helping people overcome their fears. Because fear is more complex than simply forgetting or erasing memories, a more effective and efficient way is to get people to deal with their fears over and over again. By dealing with their fears in a safe way one can suppress "fearful memories" or motivations.

Exposure therapy is known to have helped 90 percent of people with specific phobias significantly reduce their fears over time.

Another form of psychotherapy is systematic desensitization, which is a form of behavioral therapy that is used to completely remove fear or produce an offensive response to this fear and its replacement. The change that happens will be a relief and it will happen in a correction. With cooling therapy, muscle strength will decrease and deep breathing techniques will help reduce stress.

Other treatments

There are other ways to treat or deal with a person's fears, such as writing down specific thoughts about fear. Journal entries are a healthy way to express a person's fears without endangering the safety or causing uncertainty. Another suggestion is a fear ladder. To build a ladder of fear, one has to write down all their fears and note them on a scale of one to ten. Next, the person talks about his phobia, starting with the lowest number.

Finding comfort in religion is another way to cope with one's fears. Having something to answer your questions about your fears, such as, what happens after death or if there is an afterlife, can help reduce one's fear of death because there is no room for uncertainty as their questions are answered. Religion provides a way to understand and make sense of human fears rather than ignore them.

Inability to feel fear

People with damage to their amygdalae, which can be caused by a rare genetic disease known as Urbach – Wiethe disease, are unable to feel fear. The disease destroys both amygdalae by the end of the baby. Since the outbreak, there have been only 400 recorded cases. This is not discouraging; however, a lack of fear can allow a person to get into a dangerous situation that he could have avoided. For example, those who are fearless may approach a well-known poisonous snake while those who are fearless, and imperfect, often try to avoid it.

Society and culture

Death

Fear of the end of your life and existence, in other words, fear of death. Historically, efforts have been made to allay such fears by making cultures help to gather the cultural ideas we now have. These practices also helped to preserve cultural ideas. The effects and mechanisms of human existence have been changing as the structure of society has changed.

When people face their thoughts of death, they admit that they are dying or that they will die because they have lived a full life or they will face fear. The theory was developed in response to this, called terrorism theory. The theory states that a person's perceptions of culture (religion, values, etc.) will reduce the fear associated with the fear of death by avoidance. To help control their fears, they found solace in their death-defying beliefs, such as their religion. One way people deal with the fear of death is to push aside any thoughts of death in the future or to avoid all these distractions. While there are ways to deal with the fear of death, not everyone is affected by the same uncertainty. People who believe they have lived a "very full" life are usually not afraid of death.

Fear of death

Mortality in multidimensional death; includes "fear related to the death of a person, death of others, fear of the unknown after death, fear of extinction, and fear of the process of death, which includes the fear of slow death and painful death". uncertainty about death. However, there is a more serious form of fear of death, known as Thanatophobia, which is the fear of death that weakens or impairs one's ability to live one's life.

Yale philosopher Shelly Kagan explored the fear of death in an open Yale study in 2007 by examining the following questions: Is the fear of death the right answer? What conditions are needed and what are the proper conditions for feeling the fear of death? What does fear mean, and how much is it worth fearing? According to Kagan for the general fear of making sense, three conditions must be met:

1. something to fear needs to be a "bad thing"
2. there should be an unparalleled chance that a bad situation will happen
3. there needs to be some uncertainty about the negative state of affairs

The amount of fear should be appropriate for the "bad" size. If these three conditions are not met, fear is a negative emotion. He says, that death does not meet the first two ways, even if death is "deprived of good things" and even if one believes in the afterlife there is a painful death. Because death is certain, it also does not meet the third condition but offers that uncertainty, when a person dies, maybe a cause for fear.

In a 2003 study of 167 women and 121 men, aged 65-87, dysfunction predicted unknown post-mortem and fear of dying for women and men better than demographics, social support, and physical health. Fear of Death is rated as the "Multidimensional Fear of Death Scale" which includes 8 subscales Fear of Death, Fear of the Dead, Fear of Destruction, Fear of Destruction, Fear of the Unknown, Fear of Death Known, and Fear of Destruction. Body After Death, And Fear Of Premature Death. In many consecutive retrospective analyzes, the strongest predictions for the fear of death were low "spiritual well-being," defined as beliefs related to man's imagined ability to produce spiritual strength and inner strength, and low "metallic efficiency", defined as human-related perceptions.

Psychologists have explored theories that the fear of death inspires religious commitment, and that assurances about life after death allay fear; however, research conducted on this topic has been equally relevant. Religion may be associated with the fear of death when the afterlife is portrayed as a time of punishment. "Intrinsic religiosity", as opposed to "official religious involvement", has been found to be negatively associated with death concerns. In a 1976 study of people of various denominations, those who were very strong in their faith, attending weekly church services, were not too afraid to die. The study found a negative link between fear of death and "religious anxiety".

In a 2006 study of white Christian men and women, the theory was put to the test that traditional religion, church-centered, and the pursuit of spiritual purity were ways of approaching death in adulthood. Both religion and spirituality had to do with the sanctity of the mind, but only a church-centered religion that protected people from the fear of death.

Religion

From a religious point of view, the word fear involves more than simple fear. Robert B. Strimple states that fear includes "... a combination of fear, reverence, praise ...". Some Bible translations, such as the New International Version, have at times replaced the word with fear.

Fear of religion is evident in all ages; however, an outstanding example would be the Crusades. Pope Urban II allowed Christian mercenary soldiers to be sent to work to restore the Holy Land to Muslims. However, the message was misinterpreted and, as a result, innocent people were killed. Although the Crusades were aimed at incorporating Muslims and Christians, hatred spread to Jewish culture. The Jews who feared for their lives accepted the forced conversion to Christianity because they believed that this would protect their security. Some Jewish people were afraid to betray their God by agreeing to repent, and instead, they defended their destiny, which was death.

Deception

Further information: Culture of fear, Fear mongering, Fear appeal, psychological warfare, Tactics of terrorism, and List of causes of death by rate

Fear can be used politically and culturally to entice citizens with ideas that would not be strongly rejected or drive citizens away from ideas that were not widely supported. In the event of a disaster, states-states control fears not only by giving their citizens an explanation about the event or blaming a few individuals but also by correcting their previous beliefs.

Fear can change the way a person thinks or reacts to situations because fear has the power to prevent a person from thinking logically. As a result, fearless people are able to use fear as a tool to deceive others. People who are scared, want to be safely protected and can be used by the person present to provide the desired security. "If we are afraid, the deceiver may speak the truth that we see in front of us. let us believe and trust in their truth. Politicians are notorious for using fear of manipulating people to support their ideals.

Fiction and Mythology

Fear is also found in myths and legends and in fairy tales such as novels and films.

The dystopian activities and (posts) of apocalyptic mythology convey the fears and anxieties of societies.

Fear of the end of the world is almost created as civilization itself. In a 1967 study, Frank Kermode suggested that the failure of religious prophecy led to a change in society's attitude toward this ancient state. Scientific and critical thinking that replaces religious thought and myth and social liberation may be the cause of eschatology being replaced by realities. That, in turn, could lead to constructive discussions and steps that could be taken to prevent the catastrophe that has been identified.

An Adult Youth Story Will Learn What Fear Was A German mythology about the subject of fearlessness. Many stories include characters who are afraid of a building opponent. One important feature of the historical and mythological heroes of all cultures is fearlessness in the face of great and often deadly enemies.

Athletics

In the world of athletics, fear is often used as a barrier to success. This condition involves the use of fear in a way that increases the likelihood of a positive outcome. In this case, the fear created initially is a state of mind for the recipient. This first situation is what creates the athlete's first response, this response creates an opportunity to fight or react to the flight with the athlete (receiver), which will increase or decrease the chances of success or failure in a particular athlete's situation. . The time an athlete has to make this decision is short but there is still enough time for the recipient to make a determination using common sense. Although the decision is made quickly, the decision is based on past incidents that the athlete has experienced. The results of these past events will determine how the athlete will make his or her decision based on the preconceived notion of a second.

Fear of failure as described above has been studied many times in the field of sports psychology. Many experts have tried to determine how often fear of failure affects athletes, as well as what characteristics of athletes often choose to use this type of motivation. Research has also been done to determine the effectiveness of this approach.

Murray's Exploration in Personal (1938) was one of the first studies to identify fear of failure as the real motivation for avoiding failure or achieving success. His research suggested that in avoidance, the need to avoid failure was found in many college men during his study period in 1938. This was a milestone in the history of psychology because it allowed some researchers to better explain how fear is. failure can actually be a decision to create goals for success and how it can be applied to real action success.

In terms of sports context, the model was created by R.S. Lazarus in 1991 using the cognitive-motivational-relational theory of emotion.

It holds that Fear of Failure results when beliefs or schemes of understanding about the distorted consequences of failure are made effective in situations where failure is possible. These belief systems predict that a person should make threatening measures and feel the state of anxiety associated with Fear of Failure in experimental situations.

Another study conducted in 2001 by Conroy, Poczwardowski, and Henchen produced five contradictory failure results over time. The five categories include (a) shame and embarrassment, (b) undermining one's self-esteem, (c) having an uncertain future, (d) the importance of others who lose interest, and (e) irritating others who are important. These five stages can help one to think that it is possible for a person to associate failure with one of these threatening stages, which will lead them to fear failure.

II

Phobia or Irrational Fear

The word phobia comes from the Greek: φόβος (phóbos), meaning "hate", "fear" or "terror". The common form of naming certain phobias uses prefixes based on the Greek word for fear, as well as the suffix -phobia. Benjamin Rush's 1786 satyrical inscription, 'On the Different Species of Phobia', introduced the dictionary concept of this word of horror. However, many phobias are rarely named after Latin, such as apiphobia instead of Melissaphobia (fear of bees) or aviophobia instead of ornithophobia (fear of birds). Creating these words is a game of words. Such fears are psychological in nature, and few of these terms are found in medical textbooks. In ancient Greek mythology, Phobos was the twin of Deimos (terror).

The word phobia may refer to situations other than true phobias. For example, hydrophobia is an old term for rabies, as dehydration is one of the symptoms of the disease. A specific phobia of water is called aquaphobia instead. Hydrophobic is a combination of chemicals that repel water. Similarly, photophobia usually refers to a physical complaint (dislike of light due to swollen eyes or very open pupils), rather than a fear of irrational light.

Phobia is an anxiety disorder characterized by persistent and extreme fear of an object or situation. Phobias often lead to a rapid onset of fear and usually last for more than six months. Those affected do their best to avoid the situation or the object, to a greater degree than the real danger posed. When an object or situation is unavoidable, they become deeply depressed. Other symptoms may include fainting, which may be due to fear of blood or injury, and panic attacks, which are commonly found in agoraphobia. About 75% of those with phobias have multiple phobias.

Phobias can be classified into specific phobias, social anxiety disorder, and agoraphobia. Certain phobias are also classified to include specific animals, natural habitats, blood or injury, and specific conditions. The most common are fear of spiders, fear of snakes, and fear of heights. Some phobias may be caused by a bad feeling about something or a situation in childhood. Social phobia is when a person fears a situation because of the worry that others are judging him or her. Agoraphobia is a fear of the situation due to perceived difficulty or inability to escape.

It is recommended that certain phobias be treated with exposure treatment, in which a person is introduced to the condition or substance in question until the fear is resolved. Medications are not helpful for certain phobias. Social phobia and agoraphobia may be treated with counseling, medication, or a combination of both. Medications used include antidepressants, benzodiazepines, or beta-blockers.

Some phobias affect about 6-8% of the population in the Western world and 2-4% in Asia, Africa, and Latin America at some point. Social phobia affects about 7% of the population in the United States and 0.5-2.5% of the world population. Agoraphobia affects about 1.7% of the population. Women are affected by phobias almost twice as often as men. The typical onset of phobia is around 10-17, and rates are lower with age. Those with phobias often attempt suicide.

Fear of reacting emotionally to a perceived danger right now. This is in contrast to the anxiety that is a response to preparing for a future threat. Fear and anxiety often accumulate but these differences can help to identify subtle differences between disturbances, as well as distinguish between responses that can be expected in terms of a person's stage of growth and culture.

International Classification of Diseases (version 11: ICD-11) is a widely used diagnostic tool for epidemiology, health management, and clinical purposes maintained by the World Health Organization (WHO). ICD classifies phobic disorders under the category of psychiatric, behavioral, or neurodevelopmental disorders. ICD-10 distinguishes between Phobic anxiety disorders, such as Agoraphobia, and other anxiety disorders, such as Generalized Anxiety Disorder. ICD-11 binds both groups together as an anxiety or anxiety disorder.

Most phobias are divided into three categories. According to the Diagnostic and Statistical Manual of Mental Disorders, Fifth Edition (DSM-V), such phobias are considered minor forms of anxiety disorder. The categories are:

1. Specific phobias: Fear of certain things or situations that lead to anxiety and avoidance. It can lead to panic attacks if a feared alarm is released or is expected to reunite. Specific phobia can also be divided into five categories: animal, natural environment, condition, injection damage, and more.

2. Agoraphobia: a common fear of leaving home or a small 'safe' place and the panic attacks that may follow. Certain types of fears can also cause, such as fear of open spaces, social stigma (social agoraphobia), fear of pollution (fear of germs, which may be severe due to obsessive-compulsive disorder), or PTSD (post-traumatic stress disorder). without.

3. Social Anxiety Disorder (SAD), also known as social phobia, is when a condition is feared because of anxiety about being judged by others. Working alone is a small form of social anxiety.

Phobias vary in size among people. Some people may be able to avoid the topic and get a little worried about that fear. Others experience a complete panic attack with all the symptoms that go along with it. Most people understand that their fears are irrational but they cannot escape their panic response. These people often report dizziness, bladder loss or diarrhea, tachypnea, feelings of pain, and shortness of breath.

There are many theories about how phobias grow and how they can occur due to a combination of natural and genetic factors. The degree to which the environment or genetic influence plays a significant role varies in nature, with social anxiety disorder and agoraphobia with a mortality rate of 50%.

Rachman proposed three ways to develop phobias: direct or indirect behavior (exposure to phobic stimulus), sudden gains (seeing others receive phobic stimuli), and acquisition of knowledge/teaching (learning about phobic stimuli for others).

Classical conditioning: Much of the progress in understanding the detection of frightening responses to phobias can be attributed to classical conditioning (Pavlovian model). If negative and neutral motivations are paired together, for example, when an electric shock is given to a particular room, the subject may begin to fear not only the shock but also the room. Morally, the room is a conditional motive (CS). When paired with aversive unconditioned stimulus (UCS) (panic), it creates a conditional response (CR) (room fear) (CS + UCS = CR). For example, in the event of panic attacks (acrophobia), CS is high. Similar to a balcony on the upper floors of a high-rise building. UCS can arise from a traumatic or traumatic event in a person's life, such as a fall from a high point. The initial fear of falling almost is associated with height, which leads to fear of heights. In other words, the CS (height) associated with the opposing UCS (almost collapsed) leads to CR (fear). Although historically it had an impact on the perception of fear, this model of setting a positive attitude is not the only proposed way to detect phobia. This theory actually has its limitations as not everyone who has ever experienced a traumatic event develops phobia and vice versa.

Vicarious conditioning: Discovering a traumatic fear is learning a certain fear, not by personal knowledge of fear, but by looking at others, often a parent (reading with caution). For example, when a child sees a parent reacting to fear of an animal, the child may fear the animal. By reading carefully, humans can learn to fear what may be dangerous — a reaction that is evident in other chimpanzees. A study of non-human animals showed that monkeys learned to fear snakes soon after observing their parents' fears. An increase in horrible behavior was observed as non-human chimpanzees observed their parents' fearful reactions. Although observational studies have been shown to be effective in creating fear and anxiety reactions, it has also been shown that experiencing a physical event, increases the risk of behavioral fear and discrimination. M In some cases, having a physical event may increase fear and phobia in addition to seeing a horrible or non-human reaction.

Informational/Instructional acquisition: Informational/Instructional acquisition is to learn to fear certain fears through access to information. For example, the fear of electrical wires after hearing that touch them causes an electric shock

A fearful reaction to an object or situation is not always phobia. There should also be signs of disability and avoidance. Corruption is defined as the inability to complete routine tasks, whether occupational, educational, or social. For example, a work disability may be caused by acrophobia, due to not taking a job simply because of your location on the upper floor of a building, or not participating in a community event at a theme park. The avoidance of behavior is defined as the behavior that leads to the release of a potential adverse event, intended to prevent anxiety.

With the completion of the Human Genome Project in 2003, more and more studies have been completed looking at genes that may cause or influence medical conditions. Candidate genetics were the focus of many of these studies until the last decade when the cost and ability of genome-wide analysis were widely available. The gene GLRB has been identified as a potential target for agoraphobia. The genetic site reviews epigenetic components or environmental interactions in genes through methylation. The number of genes being assessed by this epigenetic lens may be linked to social anxiety disorder, including MAOA, CRHR1, and OXTR. Each phobia-related disease has a specific genetic predisposition. Those with certain phobias are more likely to have first-degree relatives with the same phobia. Similarly, social anxiety disorders are found two to six times more often in those with first-degree relatives than in those without. Agoraphobia is believed to have a very strong genetic relationship.

Instruments

Limbic System: Below the lateral fissure in the cerebral cortex, insula, or insular cortex, the brain is identified as part of the limbic system, as well as the cingulated gyrus, hippocampus, corpus callosum, and other -cortices nearby. This system has been found to play a role in emotional processing, and insula, in particular, can contribute to maintaining independent functions. The studies of Critchley et al. identify the insula as being involved in an emotional experience by identifying and interpreting threatening motives. The same study that monitored insula function showed an association between increased insular activity and anxiety.

In the frontal lobe, some cortices are involved in phobia and fear of the anterior cingulate cortex and the medial prefrontal cortex. In the study of emotional stimulation, studies of facial phobia have shown that these areas are involved in analyzing and responding to negative stimuli. The ventromedial prefrontal cortex is said to influence the amygdala by monitoring its response to emotional stimuli or even frightening memories. Specifically, the medial prefrontal cortex is active during the elimination of fear and is responsible for long-term extinction. The promotion of this area reduces the responses to congenital fear, so your role may be in preventing the amygdala and its reactions that trigger horror.

The hippocampus is a shoe-shaped structure that plays an important role in the nervous system of the brain. This is because they create memories and connect them with feelings and emotions. In the face of fear, the hippocampus receives impulses from the amygdala that allows it to associate fear with a specific emotion, such as smell or sound.

Amygdala: The amygdala is a cluster of almond-shaped nuclei located deep in the temporal lobe of the brain. It considers incidents associated with fear and is linked to social phobia and other anxiety disorders. The amygdala's ability to respond to frightening stimuli occurs through the state of fear. Like the old conditioning, the amygdala learns to associate a conditional stimulus with negative or avoidable motivation, creating a state-of-the-art response that is often seen in people with phobics. The amygdala is responsible for identifying certain motives or symptoms as dangerous and plays a role in the retention of threatening motives in memory. The basolateral nuclei (or basolateral amygdala) and the hippocampus interact with the amygdala to store memory. These connections suggest why memories are often more vividly remembered when they have emotional significance.

In addition to memory, the amygdala also triggers the release of hormones that affect fear and violence. When a response to fear or anger is triggered, the amygdala releases hormones from the body to keep the human body in a state of "vigilance", which prepares a person for movement, running, fighting, etc. known as the combat-or-flight response.

However, within the brain, this stress response can be seen in the hypothalamic-pituitary-adrenal axis (HPA). This cycle involves the process of identifying, defining, and releasing certain hormones into the bloodstream. Parvocellular neurosecretory neurons of the hypothalamus release corticotropin-releasing hormone (CRH), which is secreted into the pituitary gland. Here the pituitary releases the adrenocorticotropic hormone (ACTH), which in turn stimulates the release of cortisol. In terms of anxiety, the amygdala opens this circuit, while the hippocampus is responsible for compressing it. Glucocorticoid receptors in the hippocampus monitor the amount of cortisol in the system and with a negative response may tell the hypothalamus to stop producing CRH.

Studies in mice designed to have high concentrations of CRH showed higher levels of anxiety, whereas those designed to have low or low CRH receptors were less sensitive. In people with phobias, therefore, high levels of cortisol may be present, or there may be low levels of glucocorticoid receptors or serotonin (5-HT).

Injury disturbances: In areas of the brain involved in emotions — especially fear — the processing and response to emotional stimuli can be altered when one of these regions is damaged. Damage to the cortical areas involved in the limbic system, such as the cingulate cortex or frontal lobes, has caused serious changes in mood. Other types of damage include Klüver – Bucy syndrome and Urbach – Wiethe syndrome. In Klüver-Bucy syndrome, a temporary lobectomy, or removal of the temporary lobe, causes changes that include fear and aggression. Clearly, the removal of these lobes causes a diminished fear, which confirms its role in the alarming response and response. Injuries on both sides (bilateral injuries) of the intermediate temporal parts are known as Urbach – Wiethe disease. It shows similar symptoms of decreased fear and anger but with the addition of not being able to detect emotional manifestations, especially angry or nervous faces.

The role of the amygdala in learning fear involves interacting with other regions of the brain in the emotional cycle of fear. Although damage to the amygdala may impair its ability to detect shocks, other areas such as the ventromedial prefrontal cortex and basolateral nuclei of the amygdala may affect the region's ability to not only have a state of alertness but eventually extinguish itself. By receiving stimulant information, the basolateral nuclei undergo synaptic changes that allow the amygdala to develop a response that triggers fear. The damage, therefore, in this area, has been shown to interfere with the finding of learned responses to fear. Similarly, damage to the ventromedial prefrontal cortex (the area responsible for monitoring the amygdala) has been shown to reduce the rate of extinguishing the response to the studied fears and how extinction works. This suggests that there is a pathway or region between the amygdala and nearby cortical areas that process emotional stimulation and influence emotional expression, all of which can be disrupted in the event of damage.

Diagnosis

It is recommended that the terms depression and disability take into account the context of a person's environment at the time of diagnosis. The DSM-IV-TR states that if a traumatic event, no matter what the object or situation, is completely out of place, a diagnosis cannot be made. An example of this would be a person who is afraid of rats but who lives in a place where there are no rats. Even if the rat mind causes significant stress and paralysis in the individual, because a person does not normally come in contact with rats, no real stress or damage occurs. It is recommended that proximity, as well as the ability to escape, and the motive are also considered. As the nervous person approaches the dreaded stimulus, anxiety levels increase, and the level at which the person perceives that he or she may escape from the stimulus affects the intensity of fear in situations such as elevating (e.g., anxiety increases between the floor and the floor decreases when access is reached and doors open). The DSM-V has been revised to show that a person is likely to change his or her daily activities in relation to a frightening motive in such a way that he or she can completely avoid it. A person may meet diagnostic criteria if he or she continues to avoid or refuses to participate in activities that may involve exposure to potential phobic motivation.

A particular phobia is a marked and persistent fear of an object or situation. Some phobias may also include fear of losing control, panic, and fainting when you experience phobia. Specific phobias are defined in relation to objects or situations, while social phobias emphasize social fears and potential explorations.

The DSM divides certain phobias into five subtypes: animal, natural environment, injection damage, condition, and more. In children, blood-injection-injury phobia, animal phobias, and natural fears usually develop between the ages of 7 and 9 which show normal growth. In addition, certain phobias are more common in children between the ages of 10 and 13. Situational phobias are commonly found in older children and adults. [1]

There are a variety of methods used to treat phobias. These methods include structured conflict, continuous relaxation, visual acuity, modeling, medication, and addictive therapy. Over the past few decades, psychologists and other researchers have developed effective behavioral, pharmacological, and technical interventions in the treatment of phobia.

Cognitive Behavioral Therapy (CBT) can be beneficial in allowing a person to refute negative thoughts or beliefs by recognizing his or her feelings to see that their fears are unreasonable. CBT can occur in a group setting. The gradual treatment of desensitization and CBT is usually effective, as long as one is willing to tolerate certain discomfort. In one clinical study, 90 percent of people no longer had a severe reaction after successful CBT treatment.

Evidence supports that eye movement desensitization and reprocessing (EMDR) is effective in treating some phobias. Its effectiveness in treating complex or related phobias has not yet been officially established. Mainly used to treat post-traumatic stress disorder, EMDR has been shown to reduce the symptoms of phobia following certain trauma, such as fear of dogs following dog bites.

Systematic desensitization is a process in which people who seek help gradually become accustomed to their fears, and eventually overcome them. Traditional systemic instability involves exposure to something they are afraid to do over time so that fear and discomfort are lessened. This controlled exposure to stressful motivation is key to the success of exposure treatment in the treatment of certain phobias. It has been shown that humor is a very effective means when formal cultural anger does not work. Strangely planned sensitivity involves a series of humorous therapeutic activities that are feared. Previously learned procedures for continuous muscle relaxation can be used as the tasks become more complex. Continuous muscle relaxation helps people to relax before and during exposure to the feared stimulus.

Virtual reality therapy is another way of helping people with phobic to deal with something scary. It uses virtual reality to produce scenes that may or may not have happened in the physical world. It works equally well as traditional exposure treatment and offers additional benefits. This includes controlling the scenes and making the person with a phobic tolerate more exposure than they can actually deal with.

Medication is a treatment commonly used in conjunction with CBT or if CBT is intolerable or ineffective. Medications can help control the fear and dread of something terrible or a situation. There are a variety of treatment options available for both social anxiety disorder and agoraphobia. Drug use for specific phobias, with the exception of the limited role of benzodiazepines, currently has no established guidelines due to limited supporting evidence.

Anti-depressant medications such as selective serotonin reuptake inhibitors (SSRIs), serotonin-norepinephrine reuptake inhibitors (SNRIs), or monoamine oxidase inhibitors (MAOIs) may be helpful in some cases. SSRIs / SNRIs work on serotonin, a neurotransmitter in the brain. Because serotonin has a positive effect on the air, antidepressants may be given and prescribed as a treatment. For public concern, SSRIs sertraline, paroxetine, fluvoxamine, and SNRI venlafaxine are FDA approved. The same drugs may be prescribed for agoraphobia.

Benzodiazepines Sedatives like benzodiazepines (clonazepam, alprazolam) are another treatment, which can help people to relax by reducing the amount of anxiety they feel. Benzodiazepines may be helpful in the complex treatment of severe symptoms, but the risk-benefit ratio often contradicts their long-term use in phobia disorders. This class of drugs has recently been shown to be effective when used with unhealthy behaviors such as alcohol abuse. Despite these positive findings, benzodiazepines are used with caution because of the side effects and the risk of developing symptoms of withdrawal or withdrawal symptoms. In a particular phobia for example, if phobic motivation may come together as often as flying a short lesson can be given.

Beta-blockers (propranolol) is another treatment option, especially for those with a low-dose type of social anxiety disorder. They may trigger adrenaline-stimulating effects, such as sweating, increased heart rate, high blood pressure, tremors, and a pounding heartbeat. By taking beta-blockers before a phobic event, these symptoms subside, making the event less intimidating. Beta-blockers do not work in the treatment of generalized social anxiety.

Hypnotherapy can be used alone and in conjunction with systematic resistance to treat phobias. With hypnotherapy, the underlying cause of phobia may be identified. Phobia can be caused by a past memory, a condition known as depression. The mind suppresses painful memories from the mind that you know until one is ready to deal with them.

Hypnotherapy can also remove conditional responses that occur during a variety of conditions. People are first put into a hypnotic trance, a very relaxed state in which the unconscious can be restored. This situation makes people more open to suggestions, which helps to bring about desirable change. Dealing with old memories helps individuals understand the event and see it in a threatening way.

Outcomes vary widely between phobic anxiety disorders. There is a possibility that forgiveness occurs without intervention but relapse is common. The rate of response to treatment and remission and recovery is affected by the severity of the illness and the severity of the symptoms. For example, in the case of social phobia, most people will receive a remission within the first few years of symptoms without any specific treatment. On the other hand, in Agoraphobia as little as 10 percent of people are seen achieving complete remission without treatment. A study looking at 2-year remission rates for anxiety disorders found that those with more anxiety were less likely to receive forgiveness.

Most those who develop a certain phobia begin to experience symptoms in childhood. Usually, people will have symptoms from time to time during the remission period before a full remission occurs. However, some phobias continue until adulthood and may have a chronic course. Certain phobias in older adults are linked to declining quality of life. Those with certain phobias are at increased risk of suicide. Severe disability is found in those with multiple phobias. The response to treatment is very high but many do not seek treatment because of the inability to access, the ability to avoid panic, or unwillingness to deal with something feared during repeated CBT sessions.

Most of those with phobia tend to have more than one phobia. There are also a number of psychological and physical problems that often occur or coexist in high numbers within this figure. As with all anxiety disorders, the most common attitude to phobia is a major depressive disorder. Adding bipolar disorder, substance dependence disorder, obsessive-compulsive disorder, and post-traumatic disorder have been found to occur in those with high phobias.

Phobias are a common form of anxiety disorder, and distribution varies according to age and gender. An American study by the National Institute of Mental Health (NIMH) found that between 8.7 percent and 18.1 percent of Americans have phobias, making it the most common mental illness among women of all ages and the second most common disease among older men than 25. . Between 4 and 10 percent of all children experience some form of anxiety during their lifetime, and social anxiety occurs in 1 to 3 percent of children.

A Swedish study found that women had a higher rate of cases per year than men (26.5 percent for women and 12.4 percent for men). Among adults, 21.2 percent of women and 10.9 percent of men have some form of phobia, while most phobias occur in 5.4 percent of women and 1.5 percent of men. Women are four times more likely than men to be afraid of animals (12.1 percent for women and 3.3 percent for men) - the highest dimorphic for certain or common phobias or social phobias. Social phobias are more common in girls than boys, whereas phobia occurs in 17.4 percent of women and 8.5 percent of men.

Prior to the development of pharmacotherapy, the treatment of phobias and psychiatric disorders relied solely on treatment such as CBT. Although treatment may be incredibly effective for most people, it does not always achieve the desired result. Interventional psychiatry is an additional medical branch that has expanded its treatment options, and further research is ongoing to evaluate efficacy and applications. Electroconvulsive Therapy (ECT) and Transcranial Magnetic Stimulation (TMS) are two examples of widely used device-based interventions. With regard to its use in the treatment of phobias and general anxiety disorders, TMS is considered an extension option for those who do not have the desired response to other treatments or side effects from medications. Numerous studies have been conducted examining the use of TMS in PTSD and generalized anxiety disorder. A meta-analysis conducted in 2019 found only two clinical trials on the use of TMS in certain phobias, one of which assessed anxiety and avoidance levels in people with acrophobia. Although the study found reduced levels of both anxiety and avoidance after two TMS sessions due to the limited number of subjects and the small sample size, few conclusions can be drawn. D-cycloserine (DCS), a component of the N-methyl-D-aspartate agonist, is an additional research method to increase certain phobias whose proposed meta-analysis had better results and less symptom severity when used before starting CBT.

III
Specific Phobia

Specific phobia is a disorder of anxiety, characterized by excessive, irrational, and irrational fear associated with something, a situation, or an idea that causes little or no harm. A particular phobia can lead to avoidance of an object or situation, persistent fear, and significant depression or functional problems related to fear. Phobia can be the fear of anything.

Although fear is common and commonplace, the phobia is an extreme form of fear when it is taken too long to avoid exposure to a particular danger. Phobias are considered to be the most common mental illness, affecting about 10% of the world's population, according to the Diagnostic and Statistical Manual of Mental Disorders, Fifth Edition (DSM-5), (among children, 5%; among adolescents, 16%). About 75% of patients have more than one phobia.

It can be defined as when patients are concerned about a particular condition. It creates a heavy burden of hardship in life. Patients suffer from major depression or anxiety as they go about their daily life. An irrational or irrational fear disrupts daily routines, work, and relationships as a result of the patient's effort to avoid the frightening emotions associated with fear.

Women are twice as likely to be diagnosed as men with phobia (although this may depend on motivation).

Children and adolescents diagnosed with certain phobias are at increased risk of developing additional psychopathology later in life.

Fear or anxiety can be triggered by both the presence and the desire for something or a situation. For many adults, a person may be rationalizing that fear is unreasonable but that they find it difficult to control their anxiety. Thus, this condition can seriously affect a person's performance and even physical health.

A person who experiences this fear will often show signs of fear or express discomfort. In some cases, it can cause panic attacks. The fear or anxiety associated with a specific phobia can indicate physical symptoms such as heart palpitations, shortness of breath, muscle tension, sweating, or a desire to escape the situation.

The cause of certain phobias may vary depending on the phobia itself but may include genetics, environmental influences, status, and other indirect mechanisms. The causes can be both experience (i.e., a specific phobia that begins after experiencing a situation/thing) and non-experience (a person has never experienced a situation or been exposed to something). For example, there appears to be a stronger genetic component in blood-injection-injury phobias compared to animal phobias, which may be due to experience. The most common classical conditioning model suggests that phobia will develop when an event that causes fear or anxiety response is paired with a neutral event. An example of this model is that being close to a dog (a neutral event) is paired with the emotional experience of being bitten by a dog, leading to a constant fear that is described as a certain fear for dogs. Another proposed way to engage is by reading through observation. A person may instill in others fear of something or a situation by considering their reaction. In non-experiential phobia, the normal functioning of the amygdala in response to stimuli may be exacerbated by pathological changes. Lack of familiarity with the amygdala may also contribute to the persistence of inexperienced phobia. Some less deadly phobias (e.g. dogs) seem to be more commonly seen and easily detected compared to potentially dangerous fears that are very important in our current society (e.g. cars and guns). This may be due to the biological adaptation of the evolutionary process that makes recent threats less readily available.

The object or situation the patient is afraid of should not actually be dangerous to the frightened patient. A person should be afraid for more than 6 months to be diagnosed with a Specific Phobia. It should interfere with their school, work, or personal life.

- For example, patients who are afraid of getting up or flying will not be willing to fly to see a loved one, or who may miss out on a job opportunity elsewhere.

- Patients who are afraid of bedbugs or spiders refuse to go on a camping trip with family or friends to avoid any bugs found in the environment.

The patient may change his lifestyle to avoid contact with the object or situation. It is common for a patient to know that their fears are irrational or unreasonable, but they simply cannot control their emotions about it. Symptoms may not be the result of other medications, illicit substances, or other medical conditions.

Children with phobia experience emotions that are different from those seen in adults. In children, fear/anxiety can be manifested by crying, irritability, chills, or holding. For this reason, there are certain types of treatments for children, adolescents, and adults who have that particular phobia.

- A phobic object or state almost always arouses immediate fear or anxiety
- A phobic object or state is avoided or tolerated with great fear or anxiety
- Fear or anxiety is not equated with the actual danger caused by something or the situation and the social situation.
- Fear, anxiety, or avoidance persists, usually lasting 6 months or more
- Fear, anxiety, or avoidance causes severe clinical stress or disability in the community, workplace, or another important workplace.
- Disorders are not best described by the symptoms of other mental disorders, including fear, anxiety, and avoidance associated with symptoms such as panic or other symptoms that lead to disability; objects or situations related to infatuation; reminders of tragic events; separation from home or attachment figures; or social conditions.

According to the fifth review of the Diagnostic and Statistical Manual of Mental Disorders, phobias can be classified under the following general categories:

- Animal species - Fear of spiders (arachnophobia), insects (entomophobia), or dogs (cynophobia).
- Nature of the environment - Fear of water (aquaphobia), altitude (acrophobia), lightning and thunder (astraphobia), or aging (gerascophobia).
- Type of condition - Fear of small closed spaces (claustrophobia), or darkness (nyctophobia).
- Blood type/injection/injury - this includes the fear of treatment procedures, including needles and injections (trypanophobia), fear of blood (hemophobia), and fear of trauma (traumatophobia).
- Alternative - children's fear of loud noises or letters of costume.

There are a variety of treatment options available for certain phobias, most of which focus on psychological interventions. Different psychiatric treatments have different levels of effects depending on the particular phobia mentioned.

Short-term psychotherapy and skills-oriented therapy are aimed at helping people disseminate negative emotional responses by helping people to think differently or change their behavior. CBT represents the gold standard and the first line of treatment for certain phobias. CBT is effective in treating certain phobias, especially with exposure and cognitive strategies to overcome human anxiety. Computer-assisted treatment programs, self-help books, and professional service delivery are all ways to access CBT. One CBT session in one of these modes may be effective for people with a specific phobia.

Exposure therapy is the most effective CBT modality for many specific phobias, however, treatment acceptance and high drop-out rates have been noted as a concern. Additionally, a third of people who complete exposure to exposure to treatment as a treatment for a specific phobia may not respond, regardless of the type of exposure treatment. Other interventions have been successful in certain types of anxiety, such as virtual reality exposure therapy (VRET) for spiders, dentistry, and high phobias, application of muscle tension (AMT) for needle phobia, and psychoeducation for a relaxation exercise. for fear of giving birth. With exposure to exposure, a form of psycho-behavioral therapy, clinically significant improvements have been found in up to 90% of patients. Although the long-term effects remain unknown, many of the benefits of exposure treatment persist after one year. Treatment may be more effective in reducing symptoms in people with low-grade anxiety, and high motivation, and better efficacy in people exposed to exposure treatment. In addition, high cortisol levels, elevated heart rate, arousal irritability, avoidance of rest, the concentration of mood swings, mood swings, insomnia, and memory-enhancing drugs can also reduce symptoms following exposure treatment.

Exposure can be "live" (in real life) or figurative (in one thought) and may include:

• **Systematic desensitization** — A treatment that produces a person with increasing levels of clear stimuli gradually and consistently, while being instructed to relax.

• **Floods** - A treatment that produces a person with a certain fear of waking up first (i.e., the strongest part of fear). Patients are at greater risk of stopping treatment as this approach also exposes the patient to the public.

• **Modeling** — This technique involves the doctor approaching the objects while the patient is watching and trying to repeat the procedure.

Exposures that are imaginal are less effective. Particularly with acrophobia, in-vivo exposure (exposure to real-world height while keeping anxiety at controlled levels) has been shown to significantly improve anxiety measures in the short term, but this effect decreases over the long term. Similarly, exposure to nonlinear matter was statistically significant in some measures to reduce anxiety, but not in others.

Since the end of 2020, there has been limited evidence for the use of pharmacotherapy in the treatment of certain phobias. Pharmacological therapy is often used in combination with behavioral-focused psychotherapy, as introducing independent drug interventions may result in symptom recurrence. Alternative therapies are best suited for certain types of phobia. For example, beta-blockers are useful for those with performance concerns. Selected serotonin retakes inhibitors (SSRIs), paroxetine, and escitalopram showed early success in small randomized controlled clinical trials. However, these trials were too small to show any direct benefits of anxiolytic drugs alone in the treatment of phobia. There are other findings suggesting that the adjuvant use of NMDA receptor partial agonist, d-cycloserine, with virtual reality exposure therapy may improve certain symptoms of phobia in addition to the treatment of viral exposure only. As of 2020, studies on the use of adjunct d-cycloserine do not include.

Prognosis: Most those who develop a certain phobia begin to experience symptoms in childhood. Usually, people will have symptoms from time to time during the remission period before a full remission occurs. However, some phobias continue until adulthood and may have a chronic course. Certain phobias in older adults are linked to declining quality of life. Those with certain phobias are at increased risk of suicide. Severe disability is found in those with multiple phobias. The response to treatment is very high but many do not seek treatment because of the inability to access, the ability to avoid panic, or unwillingness to deal with something feared during repeated CBT sessions.

Some phobia affects up to 12% of people at some point in their lives. There may be a large number of reported cases of certain phobias as most people do not seek treatment, with a US study finding that 70% of people report having one or more irrational fears.

Some phobias have a lifetime prevalence rate of 7.4% and a one-year spread of 5.5% according to data collected in 22 different countries. The first normal years from childhood to adolescence. During childhood and adolescence, the incidence of new phobias is much higher for women than for men. The highest incidence of certain phobias among women occurs during childbirth and in childbirth, which may indicate the benefits of evolution. There is an even higher number of cases, reaching about 1% per year, during the aging of both men and women, which may indicate recent physical conditions or serious health events. The development of phobias varies according to the species, and the sensation of injecting animals and blood usually begins in childhood (5-12 years), and the development of specialized fears of the condition (i.e., fear of flying) usually occurs in late adolescence and adulthood.

In the USA, the life expectancy rate is 12.5% and the one-year spread rate is 9.1%. It is estimated that 12.5% of U.S. adults have a certain phobia at some point in their lives and the increase is almost double that of women compared to men. An estimated 19.3% of teens suffer from some form of phobia, but the difference between men and women is not so.

1 Animal Types

Zoophobia

Zoophobia, or animal phobia, is an irrational fear or hatred of animals (other than humans). Zoophobia is a common adverse reaction of animals but is usually divided into small groups, each with a specific type of zoophobia. Although total zoophobia is rare, types of fear are common. As previously mentioned by Sigmund Freud, an animal phobia is one of the most common mental illnesses in children. Zoophobia does not usually refer to mammals, but to non-mammals.

Ailurophobia

Ailurophobia is a type of phobia. In particular, rare animal phobia is characterized by the persistent fear of cats. Like other phobias, the real cause of ailurophobia is unknown and any possible treatment usually involves treatment. The word comes from the Greek words αἴλουρος (ailouros), 'cat' and φόβος (phóbos), 'fear'. Other names for ailurophobia include Felinophobia, elurophobia, Gatophobia, and cat phobia. A person with this phobia is known as an ailurophobe.

Ailurophobia is a rare phobia compared to other species of animals, such as ophidiophobia or arachnophobia. Ailurophobes may be scared and frightened when they think of cats, think of meeting a cat, contact a cat unknowingly, or see pictures of cats in the media. Fear can also prevent an airline from doing certain activities, such as visiting friends' homes, for fear of encountering a cat. They may experience intense anxiety and fear when they hear meowing, howls, or other sounds ailrophores associate with cats. In one case, it was reported that a patient with ailurophobia was unable to touch clothing that had soft hair, similar to hair possibly due to the similarity of the material with cat hair.

Although the exact cause of ailurophobia is unknown, ailurophobes often trace their fears from an early age. This is a practice seen in many other phobias, especially those involving animals. One theory is that a single traumatic event, such as a cat attack or a cat attack on another person, could lead to the development of this fear. Other ideas about the onset of ailurophobia include a person who watches another person's fears or is filled with worrying information about the danger of cats.

Another explanation could be that humans have conditions for fear of deer because the ancestors of the big cats ate human ancestors. These may be the root cause of leophobia (fear of lions), tigriphobia (fear of tigers), leopardaliphobia (fear of leopards), and acynonixphobia (fear of leopards). The fear of these predators makes sense because of the danger they can represent, yet the fear of domestic cats is absurd, given their small size.

It is widely believed that one of the best treatments for animal phobia is exposure treatment. A type of exposure treatment called systematic desensitization has been successful in ailurophobes in the past. Exposure therapy is performed by exposing the patient to stimuli that have increased fear while continuing only when the patient is relieved of the previous motivation. For example, one patient with an ailurophobia was treated for exposure to her fear of exposure to a cloth-like fabric, pictures of cats, a toy cat, and finally a friendly live cat, which the patient later took. As the kitten grew and remained friendly, the patient was able to fear the fully grown cats. This method is used to help patients with both ailurophobia and cynophobia.

There is no prescriptive drug that will stop the flow of emotions, though their effects can be curtailed. However, anti-anxiety and anti-depressant medications, such as beta-blockers and benzodiazepines, can help reduce symptoms. D-cycloserine has been linked to the effects of exposure.

In a special 1965 animated television series A Charlie Brown Christmas, the character Lucy counts the number of phobias in Charlie Brown and incorrectly says, "If you are afraid of cats, you have ailurophasia." The form of the word "-phasia" is a Greek suffix used to form words and problems related to words and expressions, such as cryptophasia, aphasia, dysphasia, and schizophasia.

In the horror film 1934, The Black Cat, the main character portrayed by Bela Lugosi has a grim version of phobia.

In the horror film 1969, Eye of the Cat, in which the main character who plans to kill the old cat is afraid of cats.

In the series The Mummy, the main protagonist Imhotep fears cats, as they are living corpses, and cats have organizations as guardians of the land of Egyptian mythology.

In the episode of the television series Ipractical Jokers, Sal Vulcano, who has ailurophobia, had to carry out punishment for exposure to several cats.

In Big Nate, the main character Nate Wright has ailurophobia, as he puts it, "Ailurophobia is very common".

Respected character in the anime and manga series Ranma ½ has ailurophobia, returning to a childhood where her father wrapped her in fish sausages and threw her into a large number of hungry cats.

Arachnophobia

Arachnophobia is a specific phobia caused by the irrational fear of spiders and other arachnid-like scorpions. People with arachnophobia often feel uncomfortable in any environment that they believe may have spiders or have visible signs of their presence, such as webbing. If the arachnophobe spots a spider, it may not enter the normal environment until it has overcome the panic attack that is often associated with its phobia. Some people scream, cry, irritate, have trouble breathing, sweat, and experience increased heart rate when they come in contact with spider webs. In some extreme situations, even a picture, a toy, or a real spiderweb can cause great fear. Arachnophobia may be an exaggeration of the natural response that helped the first humans to survive or that is a common cultural phenomenon in European societies.

The evolutionary cause of phobia has not been resolved. Another theory, especially one held by evolutionary theory, is that the presence of poisonous spiders led to a change in the fear of spiders, or made the discovery of fear of spiders easier. As with all aspects, there are variations in the size of fear spiders, and those with the most fear are considered phobic. Being relatively small, spiders do not adhere to the normal threat to animals where size is a factor, but they can be medically important and/or cause skin irritation with their setae. However, a phobia is an irrational fear as opposed to rational fear.

By ensuring that the environment was free of spiders, arachnophobes would have a reduced risk of being bitten on ancestral sites, giving them less profit than arachnophobes in life. However, the greater fear of spiders compared to other, potentially dangerous creatures that existed during Homo sapiens' evolutionary evolution may be problematic.

In The Handbook of the Emotions (1993), psychologist Arne Öhman learns to equate the unconditional motive with the neutral motive (snakes and spiders) associated with evolution with fear (snakes and spiders) comparing the evolution-unimaginable evolutionary response of random response, flowers, guns, and electronics stores) in human studies and found that ophidiophobia and arachnophobia require only one pair to develop a positive response while Mycophobia, anthophobia, phobias representation of polyhedra, guns, and locations of electrical outlets require a lot of pairing and ended up without further ado. condition while acute ophidiophobia and arachnophobia are permanent.

Psychologist Randolph M. Nesse notes that although responses to panic attacks in the emergence of dangerous objects such as electrical outlets are possible, the situation is slow because these symptoms are not linked to fear, noting that despite the emphasis on the dangers of running and getting drunk. driving with a driving education, alone does not provide reliable protection from road accidents and that about a quarter of all deaths in 2014 people aged 15 to 24 in the United States were at risk of a head-on collision. Nesse, psychiatrist Isaac Marks, and evolutionary biologist George C. Williams have noted that people with systematically defective responses to a variety of adaptive phobias (e.g. arachnophobia, ophidiophobia, basophobia) are not tired psychologically and may end up in fatal danger and they have proposed. that such a deficient phobia should be described as "Hypophobia" because of the selfish genetic effects.

A 2001 study found that people were able to identify spider webs between flowers and mushrooms faster than they could detect flower or mushroom pictures among spider webs. Researchers suggest that this was because of the rapid evolution of spider mites, which were closely related to human evolution.

Another theory is that the dangers, such as spiders, are overwhelming and not enough to influence evolution. Instead, getting phobias can have preventative and depressing effects on survival, rather than being helpful. In some communities such as Papua New Guinea and Cambodia, spiders have been included in the traditional diet. This suggests that arachnophobia, at least in part, may be cultural, rather than genetic.

Fear of spiders can be treated with any common techniques suggested by certain phobias. The first line of treatment is systemic resistance - also known as exposure to exposure. Before engaging in a systematic elimination of sensitivity, it is common to train a person with arachnophobia with relaxation techniques, which will help keep the patient calm. Eliminating structured allergies can be done in vivo (with live spiders) or by making one imagine situations involving spiders, and then modeling spider interactions on the affected person and ultimately engaging with real spiders. This process can work in just one session, although it usually takes a lot of time.

Recent advances in technology have allowed the use of virtual or unpopular spiders for the tax collectors we see to be used in medicine. These strategies have proved to be effective. It has been suggested that exposure to short clips from Spider-Man movies may help reduce a person's arachnophobia. Arachnophobia affects 3.5 to 6.1 percent of the world's population.

Batrachophobia

Frog fear is both a form of phobia, known as frog phobia or ranidaphobia (from Ranidae, a family of frogs) and a common superstition in many traditional houses. Books by psychologists use the simple word "fear of frogs" more than any other special word. The word batrachophobia was also coined in the 1953 dictionary of psychology. Also, a common myth is that touching frogs and frogs may give warts. (In many other cultures, frogs are considered a good indicator.) A study by researchers at the Johannesburg Zoo has shown that in modern times superstitions play a small role and modern children are increasingly concerned about whether frogs are toxic or harmless. Phobia against frogs usually occurs after seeing frogs die violently. One case of severe frog fear was reported in the Journal of Behavior Therapy and Experimental Psychiatry in 1983: a woman became terrified of frogs after a tragic incident when her lawn mower ran over a group of frogs and killed them.

Portuguese shopkeepers used ceramic frogs to ward off Roma. Another thought is fear develops after a negative interaction with the rest. In a conversation, he suddenly jumped on a child who had frightened them since childhood.

Chiroptophobia

Chiroptophobia (from the Greek cheir, "hand", and pteron, "wing") scares bats. People are afraid of bats because bats can attack them to get blood or give them rabies. Although in reality, there are only three species of blood-sucking bats, all in Latin America, and 0.5% of all vampire bats carry rabies.

This Phobia can occur even if a person does not have the known knowledge of seeing bats or just seeing a picture that shows bats. Many people with this fear often want to avoid going to caves, ponds, parks, and sometimes even trees depending on the severity of the fear.

Because this phobia usually does not change a life, especially because patients do not live near bat areas, chiroptophobia can be left untreated.

Many people are afraid of bats. They think that bats are infected with diseases, and blood-suckers hide in the dark so that you cannot see them coming. They think that bats exist simply to spread germs.

This fear of bats is driven by a lack of understanding of the real nature of animals. Let's take a closer look at why people are afraid of bats and see if we can resolve some misunderstandings.

When people have a complete phobia about bats the condition is called "Chiroptophobia" Although this condition is real and painful for those who suffer from it, this is not the focus of this article.

Instead of the fear that comes from a phobia, we will be looking at fears that are produced by a lack of understanding. This fear stems from anxiety over attacks, infections, and just the fear of the dark.

Dawn of Bat Mythology: Mayan civilization is one of the earliest known myths about bats. Camazotz, also known as the "God of the Bat of Death", was a symbolic representation of the Mayan art and culture dating back to 2,000 BC. Therefore, we know that even the Mayans had a weak point of view of bats, reaching the point of association with them and death.

When we examine the behavior of many species of bats, it is not surprising that the first humans had such a negative view of them. Bats prefer to stay in the shade or in the dark, fly down into the sky at times when we can't see them well, and are nowhere to be found during the day unless you are wandering in a cave and finding a place to rest. a bat colony that lives on the roof.

However, not all myths about bats are actually negative.

For example, the goddess Evil of ancient Native American mythology is often described as a bat and is associated with sleep and dreams. According to this legend, Evaki is obliged to take the sun out of the pot every morning and return it every evening, contributing to the normal functioning of the universe. However, Evaki is shrouded in a dark, secretive nightmare and emptiness.

Bat bite is something people are afraid of but it is not something they should worry about. Although bats bite humans, they remain defensive.

It is difficult to pinpoint exactly how many people are bitten by bats but some Philadelphia city numbers help put things in perspective. Over the past five years, the city has reported about 500 bat bites compared to 6,900 cat and dog bites.

The most common way people get bitten by a bat is when they try to catch a bat by holding it in their hands. This often happens when a bat is trapped in a house and the wise host tries to control it. Other bites occur when people carry or try to release a sick bat that they have found on the ground.

Bats will not need you to keep biting you. Many bats eat flying insects or fruits and seeds and do not see humans as sources of food. The best way to prevent itching is to leave the bats alone.

Bats are associated with deadly or deadly diseases, such as rabies and humans. In fact, the Center for Disease Control says that most cases of rabies in humans between 1997 and 2006 are from bats and it is understandable that people are concerned.

On the other hand, during that decade there were only 19 cases of rabies in the United States. Put another way, at least two cases of rabies occur in bats per year.

Bats can carry other diseases than rabies. Whatever disease people are concerned about in the top direction is the same:

Do not try to handle the bat. It doesn't matter if you are trying to help an injured bat or trying to get a bat out of your room. Do not try to handle the bat.

What really puzzles people is the thought of a bat flying in the sky, sitting on its neck, and sucking blood.

The perception of people being attacked by blood-sucking bats makes for great horror films but is not something to worry about in the United States. The only bats that can eat the blood of other animals are vampire bats. Although existing vampire bats are found only in Central and South America where their favorite food is sleeping animals

Some people think that bats are flying mice and that as bad mice there should be bats as well.

The good news is that bats and mice have very little in common. Bats are not rodents like mice as they do not have front-growing incisors. Bats often avoid humans when possible while rats thrive in front of us.

The only thing the rats and bats have in common is that they both roam at night, are about the same size, and sometimes live in trees.

If it makes you feel better, bats are more like sugar gliders than mice!

Last on the list of why people are puzzled by bats is that bats often come out at night.

If a person is already afraid of the dark, any sudden movement he feels will increase his levels of anxiety. The thing about bats is the sudden movement that airborne acrobat bats can open a dime and fly at an astonishing speed. So yes, if you are afraid of the dark the bats may scare you even more!

This is one of those crazy situations that you can make even worse if you try to solve it! An easy way to deal with the fear of the dark is to hold a flashlight or to sit in bright areas, such as under a light bulb. The problem is that light will attract moths and moths are one of the favorite eating bats!

Cynophobia

Cynophobia (from the Greek: κύων kýōn "dog" and φόβος phóbos "fear") is common in dogs and dogs. Cynophobia is classified as a specific phobia, under the subtype "animal phobias". According to Timothy O. Rentz of the University of Texas Anxiety Disorders Laboratory, animal fear is among the most common causes of anxiety, and 36% of patients seeking treatment report fear. dogs or scared of cats. Although ophidiophobia or arachnophobia are common fears of animals, cynophobia is debilitating mainly due to the increase in dogs (for example, there are an estimated 25 million missing dogs in India, as well as an estimated 62 million domestic dogs in the United States) and pets. common ignorance of dog owners in phobia. The Diagnostic and Statistical Manual of Mental Disorders (DSM-IV-TR) reports that only 12% to 30% of those with a specific phobia will seek treatment.

DSM-IV-TR offers the following diagnostic methods for a particular phobia:
· the constant fear of an object or situation
· Exposure to a substance triggers an immediate reaction to anxiety
· Elderly patients recognize that fear is excessive, irrational, or unreasonable (not always in children)
· Exposure to a substance is often completely avoided or tolerated by fear
· fear greatly disrupts daily activities (social, family, work, etc.)
· Young patients (those under the age of 18) have symptoms that last for at least six months
· Anxiety, fear or avoidance cannot be counted on other mental disorders

The book Phobias describes the panic attack as "an instantaneous terror that lasts only a few minutes with the usual symptoms of panic attacks". These symptoms may include palpitations, sweating, tremors, shortness of breath, desire to run, fainting or dizziness, dry mouth, nausea, and/or a few other symptoms. As with other phobias, patients with cynophobia may exhibit a variety of these reactions when confronted with a live dog or even when imagining or being presented with a picture (standing or engraved) of a dog. In addition, common avoidance behaviors are also common and may include staying away from areas where dogs may be present (e.g., park), crossing the street to avoid a dog, or avoiding the homes of friends and/or family with a dog.

Jeanette M. Bruce and William C. Sanderson, in their book Specific Phobias, conclude that the first years of fear of animals are usually childhood, between the ages of five and nine. A study conducted in South Africa by Drs. Willem A. Hoffmann and Lourens H. Human continued to confirm this conclusion in patients with cynophobia and found that the dog began to hate after 20 years.

Bruce and Sanderson also claim that animal discrimination is more common among women than men. In addition, B.K. Wiederhold, a psychiatrist who specializes in physical therapy as a possible treatment for anxiety disorders, continues to provide data that although common in both men and women, 75% to 90% of patients report certain small animal phobias in women.

The current theory of fear detection presented by S. Rachman in 1977 emphasizes that there are three instances in which fear is built. This includes accurate personal information, alert information, and informative or educational information. For example, specific personal information involves having a bad contact with a dog such as a bite. In contrast, seeing a friend being attacked by a dog and thus developing a fear of dogs can be a sensible experience. Although both types of experiences involve a live dog, knowledge or educational experience includes simply being told directly or indirectly (i.e., information read in a book, film, parental clues such as avoidance or dislike, etc.) that dogs should be intimidated.

A study was conducted at New York State University to determine the significance of these three conditions in the development of cynophobia. Thirty-seven women aged 18 to 21 were first classified into two groups: dog and non-dog. Next, each woman was given a list of questions that asked if she had ever experienced a frightening and/or traumatic dog, what she expected when she met the dog (pain, fear, etc.), and humbly, what were the prospects for what actually happened. The results showed that, although non-threatening subjects had different expectations of what would happen when they met a dog, traumatic experiences with dogs were common between both groups; therefore, the study concluded that other factors should influence whether these traumatic experiences develop into dog phobia or not.

Although Rachman's theory is an accepted model of panic disorder, cases of cynophobia have been cited where none of the three underlying causes work in a patient. In a speech delivered at the 25th Annual Meeting of the Association for Psychological Research, Arne Öhman suggested that animal fear in particular may be a natural evolutionary necessity of the need to "escape and avoid becoming a victim of predators". Moreover, in his book

Overcoming Animal / Insect Phobias, Martin Antony suggests that in the absence of Rachman's three causes, as long as the patient's memory is healthy, biological factors may be the fourth cause of fear — that is, genetic predisposition. . In any case, these causes may actually be the production of a complex combination of both your learning and genetics.

Treatment

The most common treatments for certain phobias are systemic resistance and in vivo or exposure treatment.

Treatment of systematic desensitization

The planned treatment for alcoholism was introduced by Joseph Wolpe in 1958 and uses relaxation techniques and imaginative situations. In a controlled environment, usually a physician's office, the patient will be instructed to visualize a threatening situation (i.e., being in the same room with a dog). After determining the patient's level of anxiety, the therapist then trains the patient with breathing exercises and relaxation techniques to reduce their anxiety level to normal. Treatment continues until the suspected condition no longer triggers a response to anxiety.

This method was used in the above-mentioned study by Drs. Hoffmann and Human where twelve female students on the Arcadia campus at Technikon Pretoria College in South Africa were diagnosed with symptoms of cynophobia. These twelve students were provided with systematic desensitization therapy one hour a week for five to seven weeks; after eight months, students were contacted again to evaluate the effectiveness of the treatment. The final results showed that the study was successful as 75% of participants showed significant improvement within eight months after the study.

However, in his book, Virtual Reality Therapy for Anxiety Disorders, Wiederhold casts doubt on the effectiveness of systematic resistance as the severity of the perceived threat depends on the patient's imagination and therefore may elicit a false response to the patient's level of anxiety. His research on the latest technological advances has made it possible to integrate virtual reality into systematic anesthesia treatment in order to accurately recreate a threatening condition. At the time of publication, no research had been done to determine its effectiveness.

In vivo or exposure treatment

In vivo treatment or exposure is considered the most effective treatment for cynophobia and involves systematic and long-term exposure to the dog until the patient is able to feel the condition without a negative response. This treatment can be done several times or, as Lars-Göran Öst points out in a 1988 study, can be done in one-hour sessions. The study used 20 female patients with different conditions ranging in age from 16 to 44 years. Patients were given each treatment period when Öst combined exposure and modeling therapy (when someone else showed how to deal with a feared object) to reduce or completely cure the phobia. As each patient was gradually exposed to the feared stimulus, he was encouraged to approach and eventually contact him as his anxiety subsided, culminating in a session in which fear had been reduced by 50% or eliminated. At the end of the session, the patient had to continue working with the object alone in order to reinforce what he had learned from the treatment session. Öst results were collected over a seven-year period and concluded that "90% of patients had significantly improved or fully recovered after an average of 2.1 hours of treatment".

Self-help

Although it is usually performed with the help of a therapist in a professional setting, exposure to dogs is also possible as a form of self-help. First, the patient is advised to seek the help of an assistant who can help set the scene for exposure, assist in handling the dog during the session, and demonstrate modeling behavior. It should also be a person the patient trusts and does not fear dogs. Then, the patient classifies the category of annoying conditions based on his or her rating of each condition. For example, on a scale from 0 to 100, a patient may feel that looking at pictures of dogs may cause only 50 panic attacks, however, stroking a dog's head may trigger a 100-item panic response. With this list of conditions from the least to the most frightening the assistant helps the patient identify the common factors that contribute to the fear (i.e., dog size, color, how it moves, noise, whether it is blocked or not, etc.). Next, the facilitator helps the patient to recreate the most frightening situation in a safe, controlled environment, continuing until the patient has had a chance to let the fear subside and thus strengthen the awareness that fear is unfounded. Once the situation has been overcome, the next frightening situation is re-created and the process is repeated until all positions are replaced.

Whether using standardized desensitization treatment or exposure treatment, a few factors will determine how many times it will be necessary to completely eradicate phobia; However, other studies (such as the Öst study conducted)st in 1996) have shown that those who overcome their fears are often able to maintain long-term progress. Since avoidance contributes to the progression of phobia, consistent, but secure communication, in the real world is recommended during and after treatment to strengthen positive exposure to the animal.

Entomophobia

Entomophobia is a specific phobia that is characterized by an excessive or irrational fear of one or more insect categories and is classified as a phobia by the DSM-5. The most specific conditions included katsaridaphobia (fear of cockroaches), Melissophobia (fear of bees), myrmecophobia (fear of ants), and lepidopterophobia (fear of moths and butterflies). One source states that 6 percent of all US citizens have this phobia.

Entomophobia can be developed in a number of ways. One of them is to have a scary experience or if one believes that an insect is dangerous. For example, if a person thinks a butterfly is poisonous, he will do anything to avoid getting too close to it.

Entomophobia may begin after a person has been exposed to the parasites and insects mentioned. It may develop early or later in life and is very common among animal phobias. A person is usually afraid of some kind of insect, but in some cases, this may include most, if not all other insects, and perhaps other animals of the phylum Arthropoda. Entomophobia leads to behavioral changes: a person with entomophobia will avoid situations in which they may come in contact with a particular insect species. Behavioral therapy is considered an effective treatment.

Melissophobia

Fear of bees (or bee stings), technically known as elissophobia (from Ancient Greek: μέλισσα, melissa, "honey bee" +, ancient Greek: φόβος, phobos, "fear") and also known as apiphobia (from in Latin: apis "honey bee" + Ancient Greek: φόβος, phobos, "fear"), is one of the most common fears among humans and is a form of phobia.

Many people have been stung by bees or by friends or family members. A child may fall victim to a bee sting while playing outside. Itching can be very painful and in some people results in inflammation that can last for a few days and may cause an allergic reaction such as anaphylaxis, so the development of a bee sting is normal.

The common (non-phobic) fear of bees in adults is often associated with ignorance. The general public is not aware that bees are attacking to protect their hive, or when they are accidentally digested, and the bees occasionally in the field are harmless. In addition, many stinging insects in the United States are caused by yellow wasps, which are often mistaken for bees.

The irrational fear of bees in humans can also have a detrimental effect on ecology. Bees are important pollinators, and when, in their fear, humans destroy wild bee colonies, they contribute to the damage to the environment and may be the cause of extinct bees.

The hiring of bee colonies to pollinate crops is a major source of income for beekeepers in the United States, but as the fear of bees spreads, it becomes increasingly difficult to locate colonies due to growing local opposition.

Widespread fear of bees has been fueled by rumors about "deadly bees". In particular, the African bee is greatly feared by American society, a reaction that has been intensified by provocative movies and certain media reports. African bee stings kill one to two people a year in the United States, a rate that makes them less dangerous than venomous snakes, especially since, unlike venomous snakes, they are found in a small part of the country.

As the bees spread across Florida, a densely populated country, officials are concerned that public fears could compel false efforts to combat them. The Florida African Bee Action Plan states,

News reports of the stabbing attacks will promote anxiety and in some cases panic and anxiety, and prompt citizens to call for responsible organizations and organizations to take action to help ensure their safety. We expect increased public pressure to ban beekeeping in urban and urban areas. This action will be counterproductive. Beekeepers who keep European bee colonies are our best protection in the AHB-filled area. These controlled bees fill an area that could be taken over by less desirable colonies if it were not inhabited. "[

Exposure treatment has been proven to be an effective treatment for people who are afraid of bees. It is recommended that people place themselves in a relaxed open space, such as a park or garden, and gradually move closer to the bees.

Using a camera or smartphone to capture bees has also been shown to be helpful; as watching the bees from a distance (on-screen) provides a comfortable way to build confidence. Over time, people may find themselves getting closer to bees for better images.

This process should not be rushed, it could take months to watch the bees before people feel comfortable where they are. Learning about bees also helps to build an understanding of their nature, to dispel fears and appreciation that they do not want to harm humans.

A recommended way to overcome the fear of baby bees is training to deal with fear (a common way to treat certain phobias); plans vary.

Katsaridaphobia

It is true that cockroaches will live longer than humans as they can withstand radiation levels 2000 times higher than us and can survive for days without food. Such facts will not encourage people suffering from extreme cockroach phobia. The name given to such fear of cockroaches is Katsaridaphobia.

Phobia or fear of cockroaches can be debilitating. The teacher had to resign from her job as she could not even tolerate her students calling her 'cockroaches'. It can make her "suddenly fall asleep or sweat cold". One day when she came out of the shower undressed, she heard screams coming into the bathroom.

Thus, excessive, persistent, and unnecessary fear of cockroaches can literally turn a patient's life into a nightmare.

Many people feel uncomfortable or afraid of insects and critics like cockroaches. Cockroaches are known to live in dark, warm places full of food. Often, at night or when the lights are gone, they crawl by accident or mix in our skin. This can evoke deep fear or a disgusting response. Such disgusting reactions are often the result of evolution; our prehistoric ancestors were organized to remain vigilant for these crawling creatures as they slept in caves and out in the open.

Most of the time, a person with Katsaridaphobic may have had a bad or painful experience with cockroaches in the past. Children could be punished or confined in cells or in dark dormitories where such creatures often hide. Such children are more likely to develop cockroach phobia. Adults who express strange fears when they see the end may pass on to their children what they see without realizing it.

Many cases of children's Katsaridaphobia resolve over time. In some cases, however, it may continue until adulthood.

Fear of cockroaches often leads to a depressing situation. The phobic tries to clean its house thoroughly to ensure that the animals stay outdoors. Frequent spraying of pesticides in the house and car, sweeping and brushing carpets and rugs, cleaning kitchens and toilets, etc. to prevent ravens are some of the symptoms of Katsaridaphobia.

Myrmecophobia

Myrmecophobia is a major fear of ants. This fear belongs to the general category of Entomophobia (fear of insects). But the fear of bees and the fear of ants are even clearer as patients fear only those types of insects.

Myrmecophobia is derived from the Greek word Myrmex meaning 'ants' and phobos representing "the God of the Greeks feared". The Myrmecophobic individual, in a sense, is similar to the Arachnophobes- (people who are afraid of spiders) in that; they may shudder or cry at the sight of ants just as much as they do when they see spiders. People with ants often believe that the insects can invade their homes, contaminate their food supply, or cause great destruction, damage, and even death. Ants' fears are manifested in different ways and vary from person to person.

Ants' bite is often known to cause severe allergies. Some species of ants called Fire ants can kill large animals and can even kill humans. Films like Indian Jones have shown these ants. Biting ants may cause the throat to swell because the victim may be choking and suffocating. While this is normal, such news reports may cause a wave of panic among the people. The report of a 68-year-old South Carolina woman who suffered an anaphylactic shock after being bitten by ants while working in the garden is enough to cause great ant ants in the area.

Ants come close to their habitats in search of food. Fire ants can react directly to human cold; then crawl on the victims' legs to bite them. Biting red ants cause severe pain, and itching and may require immediate medical attention. The ants they know and black ants are attracted to wood and can cause property damage and land formation. These facts can cause Myrmecophobia in some people. Often, people who are not very fond of insects tend to dislike or be afraid of ants.

Fear of ants may have its roots in evolution; the first humans had to sleep and eat in an open area where ants often bit or bit their food. The human brain is thus programmed to detect the disgusting reaction of ants.

Ants in the tropics are often larger: their size helps them survive under hostile conditions. These ants feed on small and medium-sized animals. Documents, TV shows, or movies featuring a swarm of termites can trigger the fear of ants.

Like other Entomophobias, Myrmecophobia may occur as a result of a serious or traumatic event in the past. A child who has been bitten by ants may remember the pain, again and again, every time he is confronted with ants. Caregivers and parents may instill fear in the ants by unknowingly infecting ants with ants.

People suffering from Myrmecophobia suffer from a variety of physical and emotional symptoms:

1. Shivering, trembling, feeling of fear/sight of ants. Some phobias may lose consciousness for a while when they come in contact with ants. Uncontrolled crying, feeling like running away and hiding, or panicking full of other symptoms of Myrmecophobia.

2. Phobics may think of "deadly ants attacking and dragging themselves to their Queen" over and over again as seen in other movies/games.

3. They may avoid plowing or going out in the summer and spring when ants are rampant.

4 Some people are afraid that ants will pollute their food or invade their homes. This leads to compulsive behavior such as pressure to clean the house, locking doors and windows, or overreacting to the use of pesticides to prevent ants in their homes and premises.

While most cases of Myrmecophobia do not interfere with daily life, others can be so severe that phobic needs medical attention.

Often, ants' fears are compounded by other health problems; therefore a proper examination may be required to determine the condition. A qualified health care provider needs to determine the specific causes of phobia, especially to determine if a person is suffering from common Entomophobia or Myrmecophobia.

Once the diagnosis is made, the doctor may recommend a series of treatment/counseling sessions to help the person overcome the fear. Slow resistance is one of the most common ways to overcome the phobia. This involves a series of steps that start with a slight phobiac exposure in ants under safe conditions until they are fully able to control the anxiety they experience. Small doses of medication may be prescribed in the event that a person's Myrmecophobia disrupts daily life.

Lepidopterophobia

Although butterflies are widely regarded for their beauty, some people have a phobia (irrational fear and exaggeration) of butterflies called lepidopterophobia. Contact with a butterfly may cause panic or fear, and they may avoid places where they can see the butterfly.

Fear of butterflies or moths is called lepidopterophobia. The name is derived from Lepidoptera, a generic name for insects that includes butterflies and moths.

When a person has a phobia, he has so much fear that it can interfere with his daily life. Fear of butterflies is a form of anxiety disorder, which is classified as a specific phobia (type of animal). About 12.5% of adults in the United States have experienced some form of phobia at some point in their lives

With this phobia, some people are afraid of an insect, be it flying or flying or everything about it.

There are various symptoms of lepidopterophobia, and they are common in some phobias. The trigger can be a picture of a butterfly, the thought of a butterfly, or a realistic view of an insect.

A person with this condition can experience anxiety or panic immediately almost every time they encounter a cause. They may feel shortness of breath, tremors, sweating, and rapid heartbeat. They may shout and run away. Physical symptoms are caused by the release of adrenaline, a hormone that produces a fight-or-flight response.

Avoiding places where I can see butterflies may be another way of life for people with a phobia. They may avoid parks (especially during the seasonal season when there may be butterflies), zoos, or other facilities that may have butterflies.

For a person with this phobia, the fear lasts for at least six months, causing great stress, or greatly affecting their daily life.

Phobias can disrupt normal life and can lead to other problems of anxiety and depression. It is important to get the help you need if you or someone you know is living with phobia.

You can bring your concerns to your primary health care provider, who will ask you questions about your health. They will ask you questions that are specific to your symptoms and phobia. They may refer you to a licensed mental health professional who can help you deal with phobia so it will not interfere with your health.

A mental health professional will check your symptoms. They will use the criteria from the Fifth Diagnostic and Statistical Manual of Mental Disorders (DSM-5) to determine if there is a specific phobia or other problem.5

According to DSM-5, diagnostic methods for phobia include:

· The object of fear is creating a level of fear.

· The reaction almost always happens as soon as there is a cause for fear (like a butterfly).

· The reaction is not equal to any risk the object may be experiencing.

· Fear causes a person to avoid the cause of fear or to tolerate extreme reactions and stress.

· Fear or phobia limits daily life.

· Fear, anxiety, or avoidance lasts for six months or more.

· Disorders are not best described as symptoms of other mental disorders.

The cause of fear of butterflies and other phobias is unclear. Phobia can occur as a result of learning behaviors (such as looking at a parent with similar fears), genetics, or past experience that has worked to intimidate insects, flying insects, or insects.

Treatment options will depend on the severity of the phobia. This is something you will work on with your mental health professionals. Some helpful remedies are:

· Cognitive Behavioral therapy (CBT) is a form of psychotherapy (talk therapy) that challenges negative thoughts and behaviors.

· Exposure therapy: In this CBT form, you will work with your therapist to detoxify the butterflies. This can be done by visual aids, by exposure to real life, or by exposure to something that is not real.

· Relaxation and breathing techniques: This may help you to cope with the reaction of the butterflies

Equinophobia

Equinophobia or hippophobia is a mental fear of horses. Equinophobia is derived from the Greek word φόβος (phóbos), meaning "fear" and the Latin word Equus, meaning "horse". The term hippophobia is also derived from the Greek word phóbos and is derived from the Greek word for horse, ἵππος (híppos).

An example of phobia can be found in Freud's psychoanalytic research by Little Hans.

The following symptoms may be present when a person with equinophobia thinks about or near a horse physically: Feeling nervous, anxious (even if the horse is considered friendly and relaxed), shivering, panic, heartbeat, shortness of breath, the sudden increase in heart rate, nausea, crying. People with equinophobia may be afraid of other predators such as donkeys and mules

Negative experiences with horses during childhood can lead to this phobia. Equinophobia may be caused by a horse fall (A bad example is when Christopher Reeve, a superstar known as Superman, fell on a horse, broke his neck, and became paralyzed from the neck down for the rest of his life). In many cases, people begin to avoid horses and this gradually grows from fear to severe phobia.

Phobia may be caused by fear of the animal itself. The size and weight of a horse and its large teeth may frighten some people, especially children. The negative media coverage of horses and horses can add to one's fears.

Many treatment options are available for those who suffer from it. Behavioral therapy is one treatment for people who suffer from certain phobias. It focuses on the fear of man and the reason for his existence. It seeks to change and challenge the thought processes that cause human fear. Studies have shown that it is effective in treating people with equinophobia.

Convincing the patient that horses are not a natural threat to humans and that even humans have been horse hunters can help. During the Paleolithic period, wild horses formed an important source of human food. In many parts of Europe, the consumption of horse meat continued through the Middle Ages until modern times, despite the pope's ban on horse meat in 732.

Ichthyophobia

The word ichthyophobia comes from the Greek ἰχθῦς - ichthus, meaning "fish" and φόβος - Phobos, "fear". [3] Galeophobia comes from the Greek γαλεός - galeos, "little shark"

Fear of fish or ichthyophobia ranges from cultural factors such as fear of eating fish, fear of catching raw fish, or fear of dead fish, to irrational fear (some fear). Selachophobia, or galeophobia, is a special fear of sharks. Ichthyophobia is defined in Psychology: An International Perspective as a specific "unusual" phobia. Both symptoms and remedies for ichthyophobia are common in special phobias.

The American psychologist John B. Watson, a well-known term in ethics, cites an example, cited in many psychological textbooks, of the relative fear of goldfish infants and how to alleviate the fears of what is now called graduated exposure therapy.

Try another option. He approaches his four-year-old brother, who is not afraid of fish in a bowl, and catches fish. Watching a fearless child play with these harmless animals will not remove the baby's fears. Try to embarrass him, make him a scapegoat. Your efforts are just as futile. Let's try, however, this simple method. Place the child at meal time on one side of table ten or twelve feet long, then move the fish bowl to another large part of the table and cover it. As soon as the dish is placed in front of him remove the lid from the bowl. In the event of a disturbance, extend your table and place the container too far away, too far away from disturbance. Diet occurs normally, and digestion is not disrupted. Repeat the process the next day, but move the container slightly. In four or five days the container can be delivered directly to the food tray without causing minor inconvenience. Then take a small glass bowl, fill it with water and put the bowl back, and at the next meal bring it closer to him. And in three or four days a small glass bowl can be placed on a tray next to her milk. The old fear of being taken out of training, and intolerance has taken place, and this unconditional rule remains permanent.

In contrast, antidepressant therapy was successfully used to treat a man with a "life-threatening effect" of fish phobia in a 2007 series, Panic Room.

Historically, the Navajo people were described as Ichthyophobic, because of their hatred of fishing. However, this was later recognized as a cultural or mythical abomination for marine life, not for attitude. The Journal of the American Medical Association has published a research paper on the fear of eating fish among those who are concerned about pollution, such as mercury, accumulation in their diet.

Musophobia

Fear of rats and mice is one of the most common phobias. It is sometimes called musophobia (from the Greek μῦς "mouse") or Murophobia (a coin derived from the taxonomic adjective "murine" of the Muridae family that includes mice and mice, and the Latin Mure "Rat/mouse"), or like Suriphobia, from French Souris, "mouse".

Phobia, such as irrational fear and inequality, is different from rational concern about rats and mice contaminating food, which may occur at all times, places, and cultures where stored grain attracts rats, and then eats or contaminates food.

In many cases, the fear of rats is a social reaction, which is compounded by (and emerged) the shocking response (response to an unexpected motive) common to many animals, including humans, rather than actual disturbances. At the same time, as is common with some phobias, occasional panic attacks can cause serious anxiety that needs to be treated.

Fear of rats can be treated with any standard treatment for certain phobias. The most common treatment for fear of an animal is systemic allergies, and this can be done in a consultation room, or with an addiction. Some doctors use a combination of both methods to eliminate allergies during treatment. It can be helpful to encourage patients to experience a positive association with mice: the feared motivation is paired with positive rather than continuous and negative reinforcement.

It is commonly believed that elephants are afraid of rats. The earliest reference to this claim is probably by Pliny the Elder in his book Naturalis Historia, Volume VIII. As translated by Philemon Holland (1601), "Of all living beings, [elephants] cannot live with the mouse or the mouse." Many zoos and zoologists have shown that elephants can be put in a position to prevent them from responding. MythBusters conducted a study in which, indeed, many elephants tried to avoid the mouse, indicating that there may be some basis for this belief. Regardless, elephantine Murophobia remains the basis for a variety of humor and metaphors. The old board game Dou Shou Qi says that the Mouse killed the Elephant, and many legal systems say that the Mouse got into the Elephant's ears to get into his brain. This is considered a human myth.

Excessive fear of rats and mice has been described as common among women, with many books, cartoons, television programs, and films depicting women screaming and jumping on chairs or tables when they see a mouse. Apart from this manifestation, Murophobia has been observed in people of both sexes. However, women are twice as likely as men to suffer from certain phobias, such as musophobia.

In George Orwell's book Nineteen Eighty-Four, the main character Winston Smith is terrified of rats. Tying a cage of hungry mice to his face is a tactic used to lure his lover into a mental crime.

In the Seinfeld TV series, Frank Costanza has a profound fear of rats. In the episode 'Raincoats, Part 2', Frank threatens to move houses after George suggested that there might be rats in their house. Kramer also appears to be scared of rats in that same episode.

Indiana Jones and The Last Crusade, Dr. Jones, Sr. is described as "scared to death" because of rats.

The protagonist in the Doraemon series is afraid of rats because his robot ears have been bitten by rats due to Sewashi's erroneous order, as stated in the 1995 short film 2112: The Birth of Doraemon.

The human birth of Princess Zelda from The Legend of Zelda: Spirit Tracks will be frozen with fear when she is confronted by rats.

Madame Medusa, a major opponent of Disney's The Rescuers (1977), based on Margery Sharp's children's novels, suffers from musophobia and is disturbed when she encounters film characters, a pair of friendly mice while aiming to defend herself by jumping into a. in a chair and firing his shotgun. Surprisingly, the most feared crocodiles do not bother him at all.

Tin Top from Roary the Racing Car showed musophobia in the episode "Tin Top Gets scared".

Injun Joe is scared of rats and mice in the 1995 anime movie, Huck and Tom's Mississippi Adventure.

In the Donkey Kong Country 3 video game: Dixie Kong Double Problem! elephant riding Ellie is scared of rats and he has to throw a drum at them.

Bloodsport, as featured in the "Suicide Squad (film)" scary mice, is used many times as a result of humor. Lofty, a large blue anthropomorphic mobile crane from the Bob the Builder franchise, is known for its fear of rats. This fear was so great that he ran until he came to a courtyard in the distance. However, the next production completely removes this fear.

Ophidiophobia

Ophidiophobia (or ophiophobia) is a form of phobia, the irrational fear of snakes. It is sometimes called the common name, herpetophobia, fear of reptiles. The word comes from the Greek word "Ophis" (ὄφις), the serpent, and "phobia" (φοβία) meaning fear.

In The Handbook of the Emotions (1993), psychologist Arne Öhman learns to equate the unconditional motive with the neutral motive (snakes and spiders) associated with evolution with fear (snakes and spiders) comparing the evolution-unimaginable evolutionary response of random response, flowers, guns, and electronics stores) in human studies and found that ophidiophobia and arachnophobia require only one pair to develop a positive response while Mycophobia, anthophobia, phobias representation of polyhedra, guns, and locations of electrical outlets require a lot of pairing and ended up without further ado. condition while acute ophidiophobia and arachnophobia are permanent. Similarly, psychologists Susan Mineka, Richard Keir, and Veda Price found that rhesus macaques promoted in the laboratory did not indicate fear when they had to reach a toy snake to get a banana unless the macaque was shown a video of another macaque withdrawing due to fear. a toy (which produced a never-ending response to fear), while being shown the same video by another fear-mongering flower did not produce the same response.

Psychologist Paul Ekman quotes the following anecdote from Charles Darwin in his book The Expression of the Emotions in Man and Animals (1872) about Öhman's research: I placed my face next to a thick glass plate in front of the puff-adder Zoological Gardens, with a firm determination not to look back when the serpent strikes me; but, as soon as the blow hit, my decision went awry, and I jumped one or two yards back with incredible speed. My will and my thinking were incapable of resisting the thought of an accident that had never happened before.

Psychologist Randolph M. Nesse notes that although responses to panic attacks in the emergence of dangerous objects such as electrical outlets are possible, the situation is slow because these symptoms are not linked to fear, noting that despite the emphasis on the dangers of running and getting drunk. driving with a driving education, alone does not provide reliable protection from road accidents and that about a quarter of all deaths in 2014 people aged 15 to 24 in the United States were at risk of a head-on collision. In addition, Nesse, psychiatrist Isaac Marks, and evolutionist George C. Williams have noted that people with systematically defective responses to a variety of adaptive phobias (e.g. ophidiophobia, arachnophobia, basophobia) do not care. psychologically and may end up in fatal danger and have suggested that such deficient phobia should be described as "Hypophobia" because of the selfish genetic effects.

A 2001 study at the Karolinska Institute in Sweden suggested that mammals may have a negative reaction to snakes (and spiders), which were essential for survival as they allowed these threats to be detected more quickly. A 2009 report of a 40-year research program showed a strong fear of snakes in humans and a rapid analysis of snake images without hearing; these mediate a network of fears in the human brain that includes the amygdala. A 2013 study provided neurobiological evidence for primates (macaques) of natural selection to see snakes faster.

If you are someone who finds that ophidiophobia is affecting your health in ways you would not be able to deal with, you may want to look for behavioral psychotherapy or CBT. CBT is a commonly used form of treatment for certain phobias such as snake phobia. It includes several treatments to overcome the horrible reaction, each of which can be reproduced in your home. CBT treatments and ways you can repeat them are described below.

Exposure Therapy Exposure therapy is just how it sounds — that is, exposing yourself to a snake, but in a safe and controlled environment. You do not want to go out into the field for one. Starting small, with a toy snake or a picture of a snake, can help you work to present yourself as a real live snake, which you can find at your local zoo or pet store. The idea of exposure therapy is that after repeated exposure where you focus on keeping yourself calm and realizing that you are not being harmed, your brain will learn that responses to intense fear and anxiety are not needed in the presence of snakes.

Reorganization of the Mind Rethinking involves identifying negative and false beliefs and patterns of thinking that cause your fears of snakes. An example would be the idea that snakes have a small bodies, or that they like to kill people. Write about your fears of snakes, or take time to reflect on them and ask yourself about the reasons for your fears, and good ways to identify certain beliefs and thought patterns that increase your stress. Once you have identified them, you can talk to them directly by finding out if they are based on their intentions or not and replace them with real, straightforward beliefs and thought patterns that will go down rather than increase your level of fear the next time you meet a snake.

Relaxation Training Relaxation training aims to give you the skills and techniques you need to relax when faced with something you are afraid of. These techniques can include but are not limited to eye-tracking procedures, controlled breathing tests, calculation tests, and good assurance. You can spend time Google Google to get ideas, create your own unique strategies that will work better for you, or join a meditation group. Meditation is an activity that allows you to practice gaining both peaces of mind and body at will.

Even if snakes are not a big part of your life, overcoming your ophidiophobia will allow you to enjoy and enjoy a creature that has fascinated and terrified the world for centuries, without letting it scare you.

Ornithophobia

Ornithophobia is a rare and irrational fear of birds, as well as some form of phobia. The term may also refer to the strong dislike of birds. People with Ornithophobia often fear certain types of birds, for example, chickens, ducks, and/or birds of prey in grain-producing areas.

The origin of ornitho- means "of birds or of birds", from the Ancient Greek ὄρνις (órnis, "bird"). American physician Marshall Mathers (Eminem), says he suffers from a form of ornithophobia, especially fear of owls. England footballer David Beckham also suffers from anxiety, as well as Ataxophobia of fear of dirt and uncleanness. Actress Scarlett Johansson said she had ornithophobia. He said after working on the film, We Bought a Zoo, "I'm just scared of birds, something with wings and beaks and batting". Other nervous people included: Ingmar Bergman, Niall Horan Chris

Fehn, Lucille Ball, and Trae Young.

It is difficult to know how many people have a specific phobia, such as ornithophobia. We know that about 1 in 1000 adults worldwide and 1 in 500 young people experience some form of phobic at some point in their lives.

The number of people with ornithophobia may have increased in the 1960s after the release of Alfred Hitchcock's film, The Birds. In the film, herds of vicious birds (especially ravens and seagulls) attack the inhabitants of a small beach town. Edgar Allen Poe's poem, "The Raven," also depicts fearsome ravens. Ravens are often described as being ugly or scary. In fact, a raven is called a murderer.

Birds abound in nature, making it difficult to avoid them altogether. It is unhealthy or useless to stay indoors to prevent the birds from the meeting. If previous bird experience causes ornithophobia, experts can help you learn to think of birds differently and control your reaction. In time, you can go out and explore without fear of birds.

Ostraconophobia

Ostraconophobia, or fear of shellfish, is common. For many people, this simply means little food restrictions. In some cases, though, it may be life-threatening.

Shellfish phobias often, though not always, can be divided into a few common themes. Some people are deeply afraid of food poisoning, others overstep the bounds of food religion. In some cases, fear of texture or taste is more than the food itself. People who are allergic to shellfish often show strong fear when exposed to potentially shellfish food, but since this fear is associated with physical condition, it is not considered a phobia. However, some people are afraid to develop shellfish allergies, even though they have never had such allergies before.

Shellfish poisoning is a real threat, albeit a rare one. According to the National Institutes of Health (NIH), there are three main types of mussel toxins: paralytic, neurotoxic, and amnestic. Although predictability is generally good, all three types can cause serious illness. The toxins are stable in the heat, so cooking does not remove the threat.

If you have ever been exposed to shellfish poisoning, you may be understandably hesitant to risk eating shellfish again. Even if poisoning can happen to someone else, you may fear that in the future it will happen to you. However, it is easy to overlook healthy concerns.

According to the NIH, there is some truth in the case of adult females that shellfish should not be eaten during the months whose names do not contain R. Old toxic toxins are most active during the months of May to August, as well as during and after the red tide. The NIH also states that these toxins are mainly found in clams, mussels, and oysters, and are rarely found in scallops. Some mussels have a very low risk. Of course, adults, children, and those with pre-existing medical conditions should talk to their doctor before eating any foods that may be harmful.

Some religions place restrictions or restrictions on certain foods. In particular, the definitions of Jews and other Islamic dietary laws prohibit the eating of shellfish. For those who practice these religions, abhorrence of illicit food is not considered a distraction.

However, as noted above, it can be a challenge for those who have been raised in a religiously divided household but who are not yet actively serving God. Like religious phobias, food-related phobias may arise when religious people have previously tried to eat or cook in country restaurants or houses. Most people make this change easily, but if you have a problem, consider seeking the help of a mental health professional or spiritual counselor in your new favorite religion.

In accordance with our Dietary Guidelines Guide, shellfish allergies are the most common adult food in the United States. Unlike most allergies, mussel allergies usually occur when a person is older and lasts a lifetime. Shellfish products are used in an amazing system of applications, and allergies can be serious and life-threatening. Therefore, regular monitoring is medically necessary.

However, just as worrying about shellfish poisoning, it is easy to take it too far with a mussel allergy. If you have an allergy, discuss your condition carefully with your doctor. Learn what foods to avoid and what to ask for, and decide together whether to carry an Epi-Pen. If you have a pen, make sure you can use it and carry it with you at all times.

In many cases, shellfish phobias have little effect on daily life. It is entirely possible to enjoy a healthy, varied diet without eating shellfish. However, this phobia can be life-threatening. Whether you train to be a chef, cook in a local lounge, or are interested in expanding your cooking horizons, it may help to overcome your fears.

Minor cases of shellfish phobia can usually be overcome with progressive exposure. Try biting a shellfish on a loved one's plate or grab a shrimp or two as you fill your plate into a buffet. Give yourself plenty of time to practice and overcome any problems of taste or texture.

If your shellfish phobia is very severe, or if your work or hobbies require you to quickly overcome phobia, consider seeking professional help. Mental-behavioral therapy can often make a big difference in a very short time.

Vermiphobia

Vermiphobia, also known as Scoleciphobia and helminthophobia, is a serious or irrational hatred or fear of worms. It is a phobic disorder in which the presence of any stimulus associated with these animals triggers a profound mental and physical reaction.

Worms are usually unpleasant to most people but those with vermiphobia may be terrified of thinking about them and expecting their appearance. Similarly, fear of worms is based on or related to the parasitic nature of certain species of animals.

As with all phobias, fear of worms can cause a variety of physical symptoms. These include nausea, dizziness, tachycardia, difficulty breathing or hyperventilation, sweating, and muscle stiffness, among others. In addition, there are often behavioral symptoms, such as avoiding situations where a person may come in contact with a worm, for example. Therefore, a person with vermiphobia will avoid planting potato plants or going to the countryside.

It is also easy to identify changes in perspective; one may believe that these animals are infected. This is because the fear of worms is caused by the disgust and fear of being a potentially dangerous parasite host. The feeling of being a source of food for these animals really frightens people who are afraid of worms.

In addition, it may be related to the fear of death. This is because worms provoke carcasses. In this case, it may be related to the fear of death itself.

It is often associated with fear or rejection of unclean conditions, too, as associated with the spread of disease or germs. Therefore, those with vermiphobia are almost germophobic and avoid contact with as much spoiled food as possible.

Several common theories may explain the origin of animal phobias. In fact, this fear is a product of evolution, which means that avoiding certain animals was essential to the survival of humans throughout history. In the case of worms and the like, it has probably helped to prevent diseases by making the food that looks bad look disgusting. It probably also prevents death from poisoning, as some worms are deadly.

On the other hand, with regard to phobias, it is inevitable to talk about learning about fear through bad experiences. In general, animal phobias develop in childhood and are maintained over time. Therefore, people who have been exposed to a worm-eating animal may have vermiphobia. Many people with this type of phobia report having intestinal worms at some point in their childhood.

In addition to these causes, it may be that fear of worms runs in the family. In other words, children learn to respond in kind, especially to their parents. The chances of learning and accepting that fear are higher if one parent is afraid of worms.

Phobias with a tendency to nausea are very difficult to eradicate and can be greatly reduced with appropriate intervention. Contact a psychiatrist if your fears are seriously affecting your daily life so that they can direct the process.

The most widely used strategies for this are incorporated into behavioral psychotherapy, which includes systematic psychotherapy, relaxation techniques, and mind reorganization. The first is a method of exposure that involves addressing the various motives chosen by the patient. The order of the list depends on the intensity of the stress caused by these animals. Therefore, they will need to express themselves gradually.

As a complement, the patient will train relaxation techniques, with the goal of reducing anxiety symptoms with each level of exposure. On the other hand, the reorganization of the mind focuses on dispelling irrational ideas about worms and replacing them with other dynamic ideas.

In short, fear of worms creates discomfort in the person experiencing them. In fact, it can shorten their daily life. However, one can greatly reduce it with appropriate intervention, by analyzing its origins and perhaps eliminating it. In addition, it will provide the patient with resources to deal with anxiety experienced in other areas or in relation to other animals.

2 Natural Environment Type Fear

Natural environment phobias are external specific phobias of particular conditions in the *natural* environment. They are different from situational phobias which are more related to particular circumstances people find themselves in.

Aquaphobia

Aquaphobia (from the Latin aqua 'water', as well as the ancient Greek ph (phóbos) 'fear') is an irrational fear of water.

Aquaphobia is considered a specific phobia of the natural environment in the Diagnostic and Statistical Manual of Mental Disorders. A specific phobia is a serious fear of something that poses little or no risk

The correct Greek word for "fear of water" is hydrophobia, derived from ὕδωρ (hudōr), "water" and φόβος (Phobos), "fear". However, the term has long been used in English to refer to the symptoms of the latest stage of rabies, which is seen in people as difficulty swallowing, fear of being given a drink, and inability to quench thirst. Fear or abhorrence of water is often called aquaphobia

Epidemiological data from 22 low-, middle-, middle- and high-income countries revealed "fears of stagnant water or weather events" increased by 2.3%, across the country; in the US the prevalence was 4.3%. In an article on anxiety disorders, Lindal and Stefansson suggested that aquaphobia could affect as many people as 1.8% of Icelandic people, or about one in fifty people. In the United States, 46% of American adults are afraid of shallow water and 64% are afraid of deep open water.

Some phobias are a type of anxiety disorder in which a person may feel very anxious or nervous when exposed to something frightening. Some phobias are common mental disorders.

Psychologists show that aquaphobia manifests itself in humans through a combination of knowledgeable genes and genes. The five most common causes of aquaphobia: are a natural fear of drowning, experiencing a personal traumatic event, having an overprotected parent with aquaphobia, difficulty getting used to the water, and distrust of water.

In the case of a 37-year-old professor of journalism, he noted that his fears first manifested themselves as "severe pain, accompanied by tightness of his forehead," and a feeling of choking, panic attacks, and a decrease in his fluid intake.

Physical reactions include nausea, dizziness, numbness, shortness of breath, increased heart rate, sweating, and tremors.

In addition to the above signs and symptoms, other common signs and symptoms a person may experience when responding to a particular phobia may include:

Symptoms: trembling, fever or chills, pain or tightness in the chest, butterflies in the stomach, fainting, dry mouth, itching in the ears, confusion.

Psychological symptoms: feeling fear of losing control, fainting, fear, and death.

A few treatment options include Hypnosis and Systemic Disorders - 28-year-old woman, aquaphobia from childhood, hypnosis, and systematic abnormalities in an 8-week program of sessions, 2 months and 1 year. A 37-year-old man, 10 years of extreme aquaphobia (who could not even drink water), 6 times hypnotherapy, treatment was successful, no recurrence and followed for 6 months.

Thalassophobia

Thalassophobia (Greek: θάλασσα, Thalassa, "sea"; and φόβος, Phobos, "fear") is a constant and powerful fear of deep waters such as oceans, seas, lakes, or lakes. Although closely related, thalassophobia should not be confused with aquaphobia which is classified as fear of the water itself. Thalassophobia can include fear of being in deep water, fear of large ocean voids, ocean waves, aquatic creatures, and fear of being far from land.

The causes of thalassophobia are vague and are the subject of research by medical professionals as they can vary greatly between individuals. Researchers have suggested that fear of deep water is in part a human response, and it may be related to popular cultural influences that cause fear and depression. It is also believed that the basic psychology of phobia stems from the symbolic state of water. Specifically, the ocean floor is often connected to the depths of an unconscious person.

The severity of thalassophobia and its associated symptoms are fluid and complex. People with thalassophobia go through many episodes of emotional and physical pain caused by a variety of causes. Treatment may include a combination of therapies and anxiolytics and are most effective when administered to patients during childhood when thalassophobia is usually more severe.

The fear of excess water is thought to be a hallmark of evolution and ancestry that has been passed down from generation to generation. People choose to be confident about risk and adaptable based on a history of learning and flexibility. Nicholas Carleton's 2016 study states that the 'Unknown Fear' is an evolutionary process that has driven the survival of the human race from the beginning. Demonstrating fear in deep waters is certainly appropriate as the ancestors of humanity understood that their survival depended on localization and not on aquatic life. This became a basic fear that passed from one generation to the next in order to ensure the survival of the human race.

Martin Antony, Professor of Psychiatry at Ryerson University and author of The Anti-Anxiety Workbook, states: "[f] from an evolutionary point of view, it is logical that humans could develop a tendency to be fearful and avoid deep water because of everything. He goes on to comment on the genetic predisposition to fear, stating: "[w] e were actually 'programmed' by evolution to fear certain conditions (e.g., altitude, deep water, snakes) more easily than others (e.g., flowers, teddy bears)"

In Judeo-Christian belief systems, the sea is often portrayed as a place of disaster and punishment. This is evident from the first book of the Bible (Genesis), with its parallel account of the Ark of Noah. "The incarnation of writers: Deep Writers: Marine Creatures and Famous Cultures Sean Harrington and Jon Hackett believe that these stories are a dynamic force in the sea. Gothic literature and supernatural forces have drawn the ocean as a fertile field, and as a result, created an image. This is thought to be true in both ancient and modern societies. The 1975 blockbuster film Jaws is often referred to as a moving image that promotes the modern movement of thalassophobia. , electric eels or other dangerous sea creatures that attack swimmers in the sea create fear in viewers and are thought to have a profound effect. c sinking and its drowning passengers have been made a horrible reality with their movie versions. People who are very afraid of violent death or especially drowning are also more likely to develop thalassophobia. These cultural influences (both ancient and modern) are thought to have added to the growing fear of deep water bodies over time.

A traumatic event or a tragic past may also trigger deep-seated fear. Traumatic events of panic while swimming, or possibly drowning are also the leading causes of thalassophobia. In addition, looking at others, especially the numbers of parents and other influential adults, who were also afraid of deep water is considered the factor that contributes to the development of thalassophobia later in life. Scientists also believe that genes and living organisms play a key role in counteracting fears of seas, oceans, and lakes. Such genetic traits include having a family member with thalassophobia, a personal attitude such as emptiness, empathy, or anxiety, and even hearing shocking news about water hazards. Personal experiences and personal upbringing are all factors that may be the cause of thalassophobia.

Thalassophobia is often described as a major fear. Considering that humans are terrestrial mammals and that we rely on our own eyes to collect food, it is a matter of evolution in our lives that the deep sea opposes that area. Marc Carlin describes phobia as, "We all have this fear of the dark because we do not see and rely on our vision to protect us. If you close your eyes and do not see, now you have to rely on nerves that you do not normally rely on. " He goes on to explain that in addition to using the senses we usually use, it puts us at risk, causing fear and darkness.

Carl Jung, a Swiss psychiatrist, studied archetypes in a coma. Archetypes are hidden meanings in images and messages to the public. Joint fainting is unconscious social thinking that is present in everyone. Jung notes in his research that water is a popular archetype in the unconscious as a manifestation of the darkest thoughts and desires of man.

Harrington asserts that in Freudian terms, the human ego, or personal identity is not at all compatible with their absolute reality. It is thought that all the darkest and most oppressive human thoughts and desires manifest in the water cause the feeling of fear and apprehension. Harrington thinks that in the same way, how the ocean is seen, or what we have been able to find, may not be in perfect harmony with the unprecedented possibilities of the ocean, which leads to fear of what the ocean can catch, such as. like sea monsters. Contemplation and comparison of the human mind with the sea can be a sign of abnormality of the human mind and identity, leading to a person having thalassophobia.

Many patients develop or eliminate all of their thalassophobia symptoms with treatment; however, some may need a combination of treatment and medication to accurately treat their symptoms. Medications cannot cure phobias such as thalassophobia, however, they can help reduce symptoms of anxiety and fear. Selected serotonin reuptake inhibitors (commonly referred to as SSRIs) are a type of antidepressant medication that can be prescribed by a trained physician. Other common medications used to treat thalassophobia include beta-blockers (which help to block the flow of adrenaline that occurs when a person is anxious) and benzodiazepines (fast-acting anti-anxiety drugs). Benzodiazepines should be given only when other therapies or treatments have not worked as they are sedative and addictive.

Acrophobia

Acrophobia is an extreme or irrational fear or phobia of a higher place, especially when a person is not very high. It belongs to the category of certain phobias, so-called location, and movement disorders, which share both causes and treatment options alike.

Many people experience a certain natural fear when they are exposed to heights, known as the fear of falling. On the other hand, those who are less afraid of such exposure are said to have a higher head. The high altitude is beneficial for those who hike or hike in mountainous terrain and for other activities such as steeplejacks or wind turbine mechanics.

People with acrophobia may experience panic attacks at higher altitudes and are more prone to lower themselves safely. About 2-5% of the population has acrophobia, with more women being twice as likely as men. The word comes from the Greek: ἄκρον, ákron, meaning "peak, peak, edge".

"Vertigo" is often used (incorrectly) to describe the fear of heights, but it expresses it most accurately when one is not cool. It can be started by looking down from a height, by looking directly up at a high point or object, or even by looking at something (i.e. a car or a bird) passing by at high speeds, but this alone does not mean vertigo. . True vertigo can be triggered by almost any type of movement (e.g., standing, sitting, walking) or changing the way you look at things (e.g., slipping, walking up or down stairs, looking out of a car window or moving train). Vertigo is called vertigo height when the vertigo sensor is caused by height.

Elevated vertigo is caused by a conflict between vision, vestibular and somatosensory nerves. This occurs when the vestibular and somatosensory systems sense invisible body movements. Further research shows that this conflict leads to both movement disorders and anxiety.

Traditionally, acrophobia is called, like other phobias, in a condition or painful experience. Recent research casts doubt on this explanation. People with acrophobia are found to have no painful experiences. However, this may be due to a failure to remember the experience, as the memory wears off over time. To address reporting problems and memory, a large group study with 1000 participants was conducted from birth; the results showed that participants with less fear of heights had more injuries due to falls. Further research has suggested the possible explanation for acrophobia is that it comes from a collection of experiences that are not traumatic events that will never be forgotten but may have an impact on future behavior. Also, fear of heights can be experienced when infants learn to crawl. If they fell, they would learn concepts about position, posture, balance, and movement. Cognitive factors may contribute to the development of acrophobia. People tend to misinterpret visuo-vestibular abnormalities such as dizziness and nausea and associate them with the coming fall. A conditional traumatic event of a fall may not be needed at this stage.

Fear of falling, as well as fear of loud noises, is another common fear that is born congenital or "uncommon". A new theory of disunity is the fear of high places to adapt to a world where falls have become a major threat. If this fear is inherited, people may be able to remove it by repeatedly exposing it to higher ground in the habitat. In other words, acrophobia can be caused by a lack of exposure in the early stages. The level of fear varies and the word phobia is reserved for those at the end of the spectrum. Researchers have argued that fear of heights is a natural reaction of many mammals, including pets and humans. Experiments using visible cliffs have shown that newborn humans and toddlers, as well as other animals of all ages, are reluctant to enter the glass area by looking at a few meters of the fall below it. Although newborns at first experienced panic attacks when crawling on a cliff, most of them overcame fear with practice, exposure and strength and maintained a healthy level of alertness. Although natural vigilance at high altitudes may help to survive, extreme anxiety can interfere with daily activities, such as standing on a ladder or a chair or even climbing stairs. However, it is uncertain whether acrophobia is related to failure to reach a certain stage of development. In addition to associative accounts, the diathetic-stress model is also particularly popular with consideration of both consecutive learning and genetic factors such as personality traits (i.e., neuroticism).

Another factor could be the inefficiency of maintaining balance. In this case, both concerns are well supported, and secondly. The human balance system incorporates precise, vestibular and proximity visual indicators to calculate location and movement. As the height rises, visual indicators decrease and the balance becomes poorer even for ordinary people. However, many people react by switching to greater reliance on the proprietary and vestibular branches of the equation system.

Some people are known to rely more on physical symptoms than on others. People who rely heavily on physical symptoms for control of body movements are less physically stable. Acrophobic, however, continues to rely heavily on visual signals whether due to insufficient vestibular function or improper strategy. Locomotion at higher altitudes requires more than normal visual processing. The visual cortex becomes overloaded, leading to confusion. Some proponents of a different view of acrophobia warn that it may not be advisable to encourage Acrophobic to expose themselves to height without resolving vestibular problems first. Research is underway at several clinics. Recent research has found that participants experienced an increase in anxiety not only during peak but also when they had to move sideways at constant heights.

An integrated model of acrophobia development is most likely, where learning features, psychological factors (e.g., interpretation), cognitive features (e.g. visual dependence), and biological (e.g., genetic) factors combine to evoke fear or resilience.

Traditional medicine for phobias is still used today. Its basic theory states that phobic anxiety has a condition and is caused by conditional stimulation. By avoiding the condition of phobia, anxiety decreases. However, avoidance behavior is reinforced by negative reinforcement. Wolpe developed a method called systematic desensitization to help participants avoid "avoidance". However, other studies have shown that therapists play a significant role in the treatment of acrophobia. Therapies such as enhanced exercise and self-medication were also developed.

There have been a number of studies on the use of virtual reality therapy for acrophobia. Botella and colleagues and Schneider were the first to use VR in therapy. Specifically, Schneider has used distorted telescopes to "transform" the truth. Later, in the mid-1990s, VR became a computer and was widely available to therapists. Cheap VR equipment uses a standard PC with a head-mounted display (HMD). In contrast, VRET uses an advanced computer automatic virtual environment (CAVE). VR has several advantages over Vivo treatment: (1) the therapist can better control the condition by managing the motives, in terms of quality, durability, duration, and quantity; (2) VR can help participants avoid public embarrassment and protect their privacy; (3) the medical office may be properly maintained; (4) VR encourages more people to seek treatment; (5) VR saves time and money as participants do not have to leave the consulting room.

Many types of medications are used to treat phobias such as panic attacks, which include traditional anti-anxiety drugs such as benzodiazepines, and new options such as antidepressants and beta-blockers. Other sympathetic therapies show a temporary improvement in symptoms. The success of long-term treatment was difficult.

About 2-5% of most people have acrophobia, which is twice as common in women as in men.

A related, mild form of fear caused by appearance or anxiety is called visual height intolerance (vHI). Up to one-third of people may experience some degree of intolerance of apparent height. Pure VHI tends to have less impact on people compared to acrophobia, depending on the severity of the symptom load, public health, and overall quality of life. However, only a handful of people with significant height intolerance seek professional help.

In Alfred Hitchcock's Vertigo film, John "Scottie" Ferguson, starring James Stewart, must resign from the police force after an incident that left him with acrophobia and vertigo. The word "vertigo" is mentioned only once, while the word "acrophobia" is mentioned several times. At the beginning of the film, Ferguson faints as he climbs the ladder.

There are many references throughout the film to the fear of rising and falling.

Basophobia (or basophobia)

Fear of falling (FOF), also called basophobia (or Basiphobia), is a natural and common fear of most people and mammals, with varying degrees of limitation. It is different from acrophobia (fear of heights), although the two fears are closely related. Fear of falling includes anxiety associated with hearing and the potential dangers of falling, as opposed to the height itself. Those with a slight fear of falling may be said to have a high head. Basophobia is sometimes associated with astasia-abasia, fear of walking / standing upright.

Studies by psychologists Eleanor J. Gibson and Richard D. Walk have further explained the nature of this fear. One of their most popular subjects is the "visual cliff". Below is their description of the fall:

... A board placed over a large sheet of heavy glass supported by a foot or more above the floor. On one side of the board, a sheet of patterned material is placed bent under the glass, giving the glass its appearance and durability. On the other hand, a sheet of the same material is laid on the floor; this side of the board thus becomes a visible cliff.

Thirty-six infants were screened in their tests, ranging from six to fourteen months. Gibson and Walk found that when placed on a board, 27 children crawled on the shallow side when called by their mother; only three came out of the "edge" of the cliff. Many newborns crawled from their mothers' calling from the depths, while others cried because they could not reach their mothers without crossing a clear gorge. Some would pat the glass in the end, but even with this guarantee, they would not roll over the glass. These results, although unable to prove that this fear is normal, indicate that many human infants have developed a deeper understanding and are able to make a connection between the depths and the risks associated with falls.

In May 1998, Behavior Research and Therapy published a long-term study by psychologists Richie Poulton, Simon Davies, Ross G. Menzies, John D. Langley, and Phil A. Silva of studies taken from -Dunedin Multidisciplinary Health and Development Study for the injured. in the fall between the ages of 5 and 9, compared with children without similar injuries, and found that at 18 years, acrophobia was present in only 2 percent of the known cases of trauma but was present in 7 percent of people who had no fatal falls (sample) the same finding that normal basophobia was 7 times more common in 18-year-old subjects known to be traumatic as children than subjects who did not). Psychiatrists Isaac Marks and Randolph M. Nesse and evolutionary biologist George C. Williams noted that people with systematically defective responses to a variety of adaptive phobias (e.g. basophobia, ophidiophobia, arachnophobia) are mentally retarded and they may end up in fatal danger and have suggested that such a lack of fear should be described as "Hypophobia" because of the selfish genetic effects.

For a long time, the fear of falling was believed to be the result of mental trauma from the fall, also called "post-fall syndrome". The disease was first reported in 1982 by Murphy and Isaacs, [8] who noted that after a fall, nomadic people experienced severe anxiety and mobility. Fear of falling has been identified as one of the main symptoms of the disease. Since then, the FOF has been recognized as a specific health problem among the elderly. However, FOF was usually found in older people who had never fallen.

The prevalence of FOF appears to increase with age and is higher for women. Age is always important in the analysis of multiple order declines. The results of various studies have reported sex as a significant risk factor for fear of decline. Other risk factors for fear of falls in the elderly include dizziness, moderate to severe health problems, depression, and problems with navigation and balance.

Research into non-human theories supports the notion that falling is a natural fear. Gibson and Walk conducted similar experiments on chicks, tortoises, mice, kids, lambs, kids, and puppies. The results were similar to those of newborns, although each animal behaved slightly differently according to the characteristics of its species.

Chicks are tested within 24 hours of hatching. He suggested that deep understanding grows faster in chickens, as the chicks did not make the "mistake" of getting off the "deep" side of the cliff. Kids and lambs are also tested as soon as they become independent. During the test, no goat or sheep ever got into the deep side glass. When placed there, the animals displayed normal behavior by going to a defensive position, with their forelegs stiff and their hind legs limp. In this state of motion, the animals were pushed forward across the glass until their heads and vertebrae crossed the solid edge on the other side of the cliff; Then the goats and lambs were relieved and moved forward on their faces. Based on the results of the animals tested, the risk and fear of falling on the animals are very young.

Factors influencing the fear of falling
Post control

The postural control system has two functions: to ensure that the balance is maintained by strengthening the body against gravity and to adjust the shape and form of the elements that act as a reference framework for seeing and acting in relation to the outside world. Postural control is based on multiple sensory processing and motor responses that appear spontaneous and occur spontaneously. Studies have shown that people who are afraid of rising or falling have poor postural control, especially when there are no strong visual symptoms. These people rely heavily on vision to control their posture and balance. When faced with high or unstable soils, the vestibular system in these individuals feels unstable and attempts to correct it by amplifying the postural sway to re-activate the visual balance (postural sway refers to the constant movement and adjustment of the central position. Gravity within the support base.). This often fails, however, resulting in a feeling of increased instability and anxiety, which is often interpreted as fear.

Elevated vertigo

Closely related to postural control vertigo sensation: a warning signal created by the loss of postural control when the distance between the viewer and the vertical material becomes too large and is caused by a malfunction of the vestibular system in the inner ear. In short, a sense of movement when a person is really standing. Symptoms of vertigo include dizziness, nausea, vomiting, shortness of breath, and inability to walk or stand. Some people rely more heavily on visual cues to control posture than others. Vestibular nerves can occur when abnormal information is obtained from the nerve channels (this happens even in those with normal vestibular function), and feelings of vertigo can lead to people with postural control problems.

The discomfort of space and movement

Studies have shown that people with acrophobia and/or severe fear of falls have a higher score of SMD, or discomfort in space and movement. These are physical symptoms caused by visual or kinesthetic information that is not sufficient for the normal posture. Space tension and movement occur when conflicting information is obtained between visual, kinesthetic, and vestibular channels. Evidence supports the claim that patients with anxiety and SMD rely more on visual perceptions of postural changes.

Falling in dreams

According to Sigmund Freud's Interpretation of Dreams, dreams fall under the category of "normal dreams", meaning "dreams almost everyone has the same dream and we are accustomed to having the same meaning for everyone". In a recent study, "Ordinary Dreams of University of Canada Students", common dreams are investigated by the use of TDQ. The results confirmed that normal dreams are consistent with time, region, and gender, and a few themes can be considered almost universal: falls (73.8 percent increase), flying or flying (48.3%), and swimming (34.3%). In 1967, Saul and Curtis published a paper entitled "Dream Form and Strength of Impulse in Dreams of Falling and Other Dreams of Descent". According to Saul and Curtis, dreams of falling can have a variety of meanings, such as a feeling of drowsiness, a depiction of the true danger of falling asleep in bed, a recurring pattern of painful experiences, or feelings of falling in one's parents' arms during childhood. , birth and birth, desire for prominence or commitment, or life experience such as flying. They cite another author, Gutheil (1951), who proposes a range of definitions that may be derived from the common sense of (psychological) loss of equality. These include irritability, loss of self-control, withdrawal, decreased acceptable behavior, or loss of consciousness. Research conducted in recent years on the dream patterns of a group of 685 high school students in Milan has concluded that, in dreams, fear is often associated with falls, while happiness is linked to flight, and surprise by direct stops and movements (ascending, descending, stairs) content.

In the Alfred Hitchcock film Vertigo, the hero, played by James Stewart, has to resign from the police force after a long-running incident with acrophobia and vertigo. At the beginning of the film, he faints as he climbs the ladder. There are many references throughout the film to the fear of rising and falling.

Astraphobia

Astraphobia, also known as astrapophobia, brontophobia, keraunophobia, or Tonitrophobia, is a rare fear of thunder and lightning or an unnecessary fear of the weather and/or one, a form of phobia. It is a treatable phobia that can develop in both humans and animals. The word astraphobia is composed of the Greek words ἀστραπή (astrape; lightning).

A person with astraphobia will feel anxious during thunderstorms even when they understand that the threat to them is minimal. Other symptoms are those associated with many frightening things, such as tremors, crying, sweating, panic attacks, nausea, nausea, panic attacks, ringing in the ears, and rapid heartbeat. However, there is a different reaction to astraphobia. For example, reassurance from others is often needed, and symptoms are worse when you are alone. Many people with astraphobia will seek extra shelter from the storm. They may hide under a bed, under a cover, in a room, in a basement, or any other place where they feel safe. Efforts are often made to silence the thunder; one can close his ears or close the windows.

A common sign that someone has astraphobia is a very high interest in weather forecasting. A person with astraphobia may be aware of the news of incoming storms. They may watch the weather on television every rainy season and may also monitor online thunderstorms. This can be so bad that one may not go outside without checking the weather first. This can also cause anxiety and in severe cases, agoraphobia, and fear of leaving home.

In 2007, scientists identified astraphobia as the third most common location in the US. It can happen to people of any age. It happens to many children, and it should not be immediately seen as a phobia because naturally, children experience a lot of fear as they grow up. Their fear of thunder and lightning cannot be considered a fully developed phobia unless it persists for more than six months. In this case, the child's phobia should be addressed, as it may be a major problem in adulthood.

To reduce the child's fears during thunderstorms, the child may be distracted by games and activities. A brave way to treat a storm as a hobby.

The most widely used and possibly the most effective way to treat astraphobia is exposure to thunderstorms and ultimately building up the immune system. Other therapies include cognitive behavioral therapy. (CBT) and dialectical behavior therapy (DBT). The patient will often be instructed to repeat phrases in order to remain calm during a storm. Excessive breathing exercises can strengthen this effort.

Dogs may show great concern during thunderstorms; between 15 and 30 percent may be affected. Studies confirm high levels of cortisol - a stress-related hormone - affect dogs during and after a thunderstorm. Remedies include anti-depressant therapies to combat allergies, anti-anxiety medications, and a pleasing pheromone for dogs, a synthetic hormone analog released by nursing mothers.

Studies have also shown that cats can be very sensitive to thunderstorms. Although common, cats are known to hide under a table or behind a bed during thunderstorms.

Usually, when an animal is anxious during a thunderstorm or other similar, harmless event (e.g. fireworks display), we are advised to simply continue behaving normally, instead of trying to comfort the animals.

Lilapsophobia

The basic Greek word is λαῖλα | ψ -απος laíla | ps -apos which is why the name should actually be * Lailapophobia - like myrmecophobia from mýrmē | x -ēkos. Greek words ending in ψ (ps) and ξ (ks) will usually be -pos / -kos (respectively) in inclined cases, usually given as a birthmark. This law is also found in Latin, cf. pax, pac | is, and appears in the claim form pacem where all Romance languages have taken their names as "peace". Historically the law is "forgotten" - another result of the deceptive neologism "lilapsophobia".

How I got into the picture instead of the ai is still to be resolved. Hypothesis: As the Greek word lailaps may indicate the American use of the term * lilaps [laílæps] - in the US where hurricanes are common - the final version of "hypercorrect" became a written method.

Lilapsophobia is a rare fear of storms or hurricanes. Lilapsophobia is considered to be the most severe form of astraphobia, which is the fear of thunder and lightning. Survivors of these storms are advised to seek professional advice, especially to find out if a person has post-traumatic stress disorder. This fear can be caused by reading stories about hurricanes or hurricanes through the media, such as television, the Internet, radio, or newspaper, even though they occur far from home.

If a person hears that someone in the family has a phobia, then that person is more likely to get it

Lilapsophobes spend a lot of time watching the weather or checking the weather online to monitor future storms. When a storm hits, patients may either look for warnings of the elements or hide behind them, such as under a bed or in a windowless room. In the worst cases, patients flee the storm as soon as it starts to rain, usually in a basement or storm shelter. Patients with a weather radio or cell phone can watch the radar and warnings while using it while in hiding.

Like many other phobias, lilapsophobia can usually be treated with psychotherapy, but if it is caused by post-traumatic stress disorder, then alternative therapies may be highly recommended.

Like astraphobia, Lilapsophobia is a common fear in children, although it is very rare. Because children learn to distinguish between a dream and a reality, broadcasting a major storm on television or a parental conversation may cause the fear that the storm is coming with great force or storm.

Because fear is part of the normal development of a child, this phobia is not diagnosed unless it persists for more than six months. Parents must overcome a child's fears by telling him how rare hurricanes are affecting his hometown.

Gerascophobia

The word gerascophobia comes from the Greek γηράσκω, gerasko, "I'm getting old". Some authors refer to it as gerontophobia, although this may refer to the fear of older people due to memento mori.

Gerascophobia is a rare or chronic fear of aging or old age (senescence). Gerascophobia is a clinical phobia that is often classified under specific phobias or fear of a single panic trigger. Gerascophobia may be based on anxiety about being left without resources and the inability to care for themselves due to age-related disability.

Because of the high risk of death, sufferers often feel that aging is the first sign that their immune system is weakening, making them more vulnerable and more susceptible to disease.

Some sufferers want to have plastic surgery to look younger, while others who are more concerned about their own are afraid of the internal, natural damage caused by aging.

3 Situational type fear

A situational phobia is a type of phobic disorder in which the irrational fear of a particular condition triggers a strong physical and emotional response. Unlike rational fear associated with the danger of real life, phobia creates extreme and irrational fears that disrupt a person's daily life. People with status phobias may even know that their fears are irrational, but a strong physical reaction to this condition is real and may include symptoms such as panic, fear, tremors, hyperventilating, and avoiding triggers. Common phobias include fear of closed spaces, open spaces, heights, flight, dentists, and needles.

Claustrophobia

Claustrophobia is a fear of confined spaces. It can be caused by many situations or motives, including elevators, especially when crowded, windowless rooms, and hotel rooms with closed doors and shut windows. Even bedrooms with locks on the outside, small cars, and tight-fitting clothing can cause reactions in those with claustrophobia. It is generally considered to be an anxiety disorder, which often leads to panic attacks. The onset of claustrophobia has been attributed to a number of factors, including a reduction in amygdala size and classical conditioning.

Some studies show that anywhere from 5-10% of the world's population is affected by severe claustrophobia, but only a small percentage of these people receive some form of treatment for the disease.

The word claustrophobia comes from the Latin claustrum "a shut-in place".

Claustrophobia is classified as a disorder of the mind and heart, particularly anxiety disorders. Symptoms usually appear in childhood or adolescence. Claustrophobia is generally thought to have one important characteristic: fear of drowning. At least in one place, if not a few, in the following: small rooms, MRI or CAT scans, cars, buses, planes, trains, tunnels, underwater caves, cellars, elevators, and caves.

Closure or the thought of being trapped in a confined space may cause fear of not being able to breathe properly and shortness of breath. It is not always the small area that causes these feelings, but the fear of the possibility of what might happen while in that place. When anxiety levels start to reach a certain level of PPO, a person may begin to experience: sweating and/or chills, rapid heartbeat and high blood pressure, dizziness, fainting, lightheadedness, and chills due to fear, dry mouth, high fever, tremors or tremors. and feeling of "butterflies" in the stomach, nausea, headache, numbness, feeling of choking, chest pain and difficulty breathing, craving to use the toilet, confusion or confusion, and fear. injury or illness

Fear of confined spaces is an irrational fear. Most claustrophobic people who find themselves in a room without windows know that they are not in danger, yet these people will be frightened, perhaps frightened to the point of not being able to function, and many do not know why.

The amygdala is one of the smallest structures in the brain, but it is also one of the most powerful. The amygdala is needed to stop panic attacks or to build a fight-or-flight response. The fight-or-flight response is made when motivation is associated with a traumatic situation. Cheng believes that the roots of phobia are in this anti-flight response.

In producing a fight-or-flight response, the amygdala acts as follows: The anterior nuclei of the amygdala are associated with fear of each other. Nuclei send nuclei to other nuclei, affecting respiratory rate, physical arousal, adrenaline release, blood pressure, heart rate, behavioral nervous response, and immune responses, which may include colds. This reaction creates an 'automatic failure' in the panic attack.

A study by Fumi Hayano found that the right amygdala was small in patients suffering from panic disorder. The reduction in size occurred in a structure known as the Corticommedial nuclear group of which the nucleus of the CE is a component. This causes confusion, which in turn causes abnormal reactions that trigger the opposition in those with panic attacks. For people with Claustrophobic, this translates as panic or overreacting to a situation where a person finds themselves physically locked up.

Claustrophobia results when the brain comes to links confinement with risk. It usually occurs as a result of traumatic childhood experiences, although the onset may come at any time in a person's life. Such experiences can be repeated many times, or only once, in order to be permanently visualized. The majority of claustrophobic participants in a study conducted by Lars-Göran Öst reported that their fears were "acquired through conditioning experience." In many cases, claustrophobia seems to be the result of past experiences.

A few examples of common experiences that can lead to the onset of claustrophobia in children (or adults) are as follows: A child (or, more commonly, an adult) is locked in a dark room and cannot find a door or door. Light-switch., The child is locked in a box, The child is locked in a room, falls into a deep pool, and cannot swim, the child is separated from his parents in the crowd and is lost. The child puts his head between the phone bars and is unable to get out. The child crawls into the hole and gets stuck, or is unable to find a way back. A child is left in his parent's car, truck, or van. The child is in a crowded place with no windows (classroom, basement, etc.) and meets other people, or is placed there as a form of punishment.

The word "past tense," according to one writer, can refer to the time of birth. In John A. Speyrer's book "Claustrophobia and the Fear of Death and Dying", the reader is led to conclude that the highest incidence of claustrophobia is due to trauma at birth, which he says is "one of the worst things we can experience in our lifetime." helpless when a baby has claustrophobia.

Magnetic resonance imaging (MRI) can cause claustrophobia. An MRI scan involves sleeping for some time on a small tube. In a study that included claustrophobia and MRI, it was reported that 13% of patients had panic attacks during the procedure. This process is associated not only with the onset of 'pre-claustrophobia', but also with the onset of the condition in some people. Panic attacks experienced during the process can stop a person from correcting the situation, thus furthering the fear. S.J. Rachman cites a case in point, quoting from the experience of 21 miners. The miners were trapped underground for 14 days, during which six miners died of suffocation. After their rescue, ten miners studied for ten years. All but one were deeply affected by the experience, and the six phobias developed "shutting down or limiting situations". The only miner who did not have visible signs was the one acting as a leader.

Another factor that can trigger the onset of claustrophobia is "acquired knowledge." As Aureau Walding points out in the "Causes of Claustrophobia", many people, especially children, learn who and what to fear by looking at their parents or peers. This approach works not only for the teacher's awareness but also for the victims. Vicarious classical conditioning also includes when one sees another person directly exposed to a particularly unpleasant situation.

There is research suggesting that claustrophobia is not entirely a planned or studied phobia. It is not really a congenital fear, but it is more likely a so-called prepared phobia. As Erin Gersley points out in "Phobias: Causes and

Treatments", people have a genetic predisposition to fear harm. Claustrophobia may fall under this category due to "widespread distribution ... its onset is early and appears to be relatively easy to detect, with its subtleties." Acquiring claustrophobia may be part of an evolutionary lifestyle, fear of being caught and/or. congestion was once essential to the survival of the human race and could not be easily revived at any time. The hostile circumstances in the past would make this kind of pre-planned fear necessary, so the human mind developed the ability to "effectively prepare fear for certain stages of dangerous motives".

Rachman gives the argument for this idea in his article: "Phobias". He agrees with the statement that phobias often affect objects that pose a direct threat to human survival, and that many of these conditions are quickly detected due to "inherited legitimacy". This brings a phobia that is prepared, unborn, but widely and easily read. As Rachman explains in the article: "The main characteristics of modified phobias are that they are very accessible, selective, stable, biologically important, and almost [mindless]. 'Choice' and 'biological significance' means that they are only related to things that threaten health, safety, or personal life in danger. 'Ignorance' implies that this fear is acquired through ignorance. Both factors point to the idea that claustrophobia is a prearranged phobia that has been programmed into the human mind.

Claustrophobia is a fear of being confined to a small area. It is often considered an anxiety disorder and often leads to more severe anxiety attacks. It is also sometimes confused with Cleithrophobia (fear of confinement).

Diagnosis of claustrophobia often comes from consultation about other conditions related to anxiety. Certain conditions must be met in order to be diagnosed with certain phobias. This process includes:

· persistent or extreme fear caused by the presence or expectation of a particular situation

· a response to concern when encouragement is shown; can cause panic attacks in adults or, in children, rash, nausea, crying, etc.

· acknowledging older patients that their fears are caused by an expected threat or danger

· engage in activities to avoid a horrible thing or situation, or a tendency to deal with a situation but with sadness or anxiety

· A person's escape from an object or situation disrupts daily life and relationships

· Phobia persists, usually for 6 months or more

· Symptoms may not be associated with other sub-cognitive disorders, such as Obsessive-compulsive disorder (OCD) or post-traumatic stress disorder (PTSD)

This method was developed in 1979 by translating files of patients diagnosed with claustrophobia and reading various scientific articles on the diagnosis. When the first scale was made, it was tested and molded by a few experts in the field. Today, there are 20 questions that determine the level of anxiety and the desire to avoid certain situations. Numerous studies have proven this scale to be effective in diagnosing claustrophobia.

The questionnaire system was developed by Rachman and Taylor, two experts in the field, in 1993. This method is effective in distinguishing symptoms caused by fear of congestion. In 2001, it was adjusted from 36 to 24 items by one team of local experts. This study was also proven to be very effective in a variety of subjects.

Kenophobia

Kenophobia is a major fear of empty spaces or spaces. A conditional phobia, in which a person is subjected to an unreasonable reaction to a situation that does not pose a real threat. a word meaning "fear." A person with kenophobia may avoid being in a vacuum, such as an empty space or a large area.

When a person with kenophobia encounters an old phobia, they may have deep feelings of depression. This can cause symptoms such as shortness of breath, sweating, tremors, and dizziness.

There is no cause for kenophobia. Certain phobias may develop over time as a result of studied history, past knowledge, or biological features.

Kenophobia is a state phobia. It is not necessary for a person to be in an empty place to feel the symptoms of kenophobia. Symptoms can also occur by thinking or talking about empty spaces.

There are similarities between kenophobia and agoraphobia. However, they are not the same problem.

Kenophobia is the fear of empty spaces and voids, such as an open field or an empty room.

In contrast, agoraphobia is a fear of being in situations or places that one cannot escape. This usually refers to busy public places such as shopping malls or public transportation. However, a person with agoraphobia may fear unfamiliar areas.

The exact causes of certain phobias are unknown. However, there are a number of possible influences on the development of phobias, such as learned behavior or trauma.

Examples of possible causes of kenophobia include:

· **Behavior learned from childhood**: If you grow up close to a parent or caregiver who is experiencing anxiety in certain situations and avoids empty spaces, you may be able to overcome this fear and avoid the behavior.

· **Coping with anxiety:** You may experience anxiety when you are in an empty area, but you may also start to panic by showing signs of anxiety. This exacerbates the condition and can lead to an irrational phobia.

· **Genetics:** There is some research that suggests that genes may transmit phobias. If a parent has kenophobia, you may have developed this condition. This is to avoid the situation so never find evidence that contradicts the belief that the situation could be dangerous for you.

Although the exact cause of certain phobias such as kenophobia is unknown, studies indicate that it is possible to obtain phobias from a parent or other close relative.

It is also possible to accept the absurd fears of a parent or caregiver. If you grow up around a person who actively avoids empty spaces and shows signs of anxiety when faced with such situations, you may learn to respond in a similar way.

Some phobias like kenophobia can affect anyone of any age. Anxiety disorders are the most common mental illness in the US, affecting about 40 million adults. This includes 19 million adults who experience some form of phobia.

Anxiety disorders also affect children, with approximately 25.1% of children between the ages of 13 and 18 experiencing some form of anxiety disorder. If a young child cannot express his phobia when he is in an empty place, he may show this fear by crying, limping, clinging to a parent or loved one, or being angry.

Only about 10-25% of people with specific phobias will receive treatment. If you do not want treatment for your phobia, it can lead to problems.

This can make your phobia worse, especially if you avoid empty spaces. Avoidance can actually make your brain realize that there is a real threat, which can make your phobia even stronger the next time you can avoid the situation.

If your phobia persists, there is a chance that you could pass it on to someone else as a learned behavior. For example, if you live or spend a lot of time with a young child, he or she may see your response in blank spaces and may have similar concerns.

Symptoms of phobias such as kenophobia can vary from person to person, and they can get worse over time if you avoid empty spaces.

Nyctophobia

Fear of the dark is a common fear or phobia among children and, to a degree, adults. Fear of the dark does not always trouble the darkness itself; it may also be fear of possible or imagined dangers obscured by darkness. A certain level of fear of the dark is natural, especially as a child grows up. Most viewers report that fear of darkness is rarely seen before 2 years of age. When the fear of darkness reaches a level hard enough to be considered pathological, it is sometimes called scotophobia (from σκότος - "darkness"), or lygophobia (from λυγή - "evening").

Some researchers, starting with Sigmund Freud, view the fear of darkness as a manifestation of a disturbing anxiety disorder.

Another theory was introduced in the 1960s when scientists experimented with searching for memory molecules. In another experiment, mice, usually nocturnal animals, were placed in a state of dreaded darkness, and a substance called "Scotophobin" was said to be released from the rat brain; this was said to cause the recollection of this fear. These findings were then dismissed.

Nyctophobia is a phobia that is characterized by severe nightmares. It is caused by a brain paralysis of what is going to happen, or what may happen if you are in a nightclub. It can also be started temporarily if the mind is not focused or afraid of recent events or ideas, or intellectual engagement is threatening (examples may include indulging in horrible content, seeing obscene acts, linking a dark place with previous events. Or mind-boggling ideas). In general, since people are not naturally at night by nature, they are usually more alert or vigilant at night than during the day, as darkness is a very different place. Nyctophobia produces more than normal natural symptoms, such as shortness of breath, sweating, nausea, dry mouth, sickness, tremors, palpitations, inability to speak or think clearly, or feeling alienated from reality and death. Nyctophobia can be very dangerous physically and mentally if these symptoms are not resolved. There are many treatments that help treat Nyctophobia.

Nyctophobia can be linked to nocturnal creatures, whether real or imagined. For example, a person who experiences Sanguivoriphobia, fear of vampires, may also have Nyctophobia due to contact with vampires. Or a person with Chiroptophobia, or who is afraid of bats, may also have Nyctophobia due to meeting there at night or in dark places.

Exposure therapy can be very effective when you put a person in the dark. In this way, the therapist can help with relaxation techniques such as meditation. Another form of treatment is Cognitive Behavioral Therapy. Physicians can help guide patients through daily and nightly behavioral procedures to reduce the symptoms associated with Nyctophobia. In severe cases, anti-depressants and anti-anxiety medications may work for those who are experiencing symptoms that may be uncontrollable if treatment can reduce the symptoms of Nyctophobia.

Despite its full nature, there has been a lack of etiological research on the subject. Nyctophobia is commonly seen in children but, according to the article by J. According to Adrian Williams, "Indirect Hypnotic Therapy of Nyctophobia: A Case Report", many clinics with pediatric patients have a good chance of having adults with nyctophobia. The same article states that "phobia has been known to severely affect older patients and ... is disabling".

The word nyctophobia comes from the Greek words νυκτός, Nyktos, genitive νύξ, Nyx, "night".

Scotophobia

Although not clinically recognized Scotophobia has acquired a tendency in social circles, it is often described as an obscure version of Nyctophobia, referred to simply as darkness or dark places. Those suffering from Scotophobia may be afraid of dark underground chambers, tunnels, forests, rooms, or other dimly lit spaces.

Other names for this place are Achluophobia (from the Greek ἀχλύς, Akhlus, meaning "mist" or "darkness", and φόβος, phobos, meaning "fear", and Lygophobia (from the Greek λυγή, Lygos, meaning "dusk".

Phasmophobia

Fear of ghosts in many human cultures is based on the belief that some ghosts can be cruel to humans and dangerous (among all the other possible attitudes, including bullying, fairness, indifference, etc.). It has to do with the fear of the dark.

Persistent fear of ghosts is sometimes called phasmophobia, a form of phobia. It is derived from the Greek word "phasma" meaning "state" and "phobos" meaning "fear". It is often brought on by childhood experiences and causes patients to suffer from panic attacks.

Fear of ghosts, their vengeance, and evil is a common basis for plots in ghost genres and ghost films. In cartoons and comics, Casper's attempts to make friends are interrupted by people, animals, and even inanimate objects who scurry off, screaming and running away when they see him. It can be said that the characters Shaggy and Scooby from TV and the movie Franchise Scooby-Doo suffered from phasmophobia, with the added humor that the ghosts they encountered were usually ghostly criminals, especially eating human phasmophobia as a cover for their crimes. jobs.

4 Blood-injection-injury type phobias

A blood-injection-injury (BII) type of phobia is a type of phobia that is characterized by excessive fear, unreasonable reaction to a blood transfusion, injury, or injection, or anticipation of an injection, injury, or blood exposure. Blood-like stimuli (paint, sauce) may also trigger a reaction. This is a common phobia with an estimated 3-4% increase in population, although it has been found to occur more frequently in small and educated groups. The prevalence of needle fear that does not meet the BII phobia process is high. The correct BII name has not yet been created.

When exposed to phobic factors, those with phobia often experience a two-stage response: an initial increase in heart rate and blood pressure, followed by rapid bradycardia (decreased heart rate) and hypotension (decreased blood pressure). This slows down the supply of brain blood, and will often lead to a seizure response. In a person with BII phobia, the manifestation of these symptoms or similar symptoms of a blood reaction, injection, or injury usually begins before ten years. Many with a phobia will take steps to avoid exposure to grades. This can lead to health problems for people with phobia due to hospital avoidance, doctor appointments, blood tests, vaccinations, or injections needed for those with diabetes and multiple sclerosis (MS). Because of the constant avoidance of phobic causes, the personal and professional lives of the BII may be limited. Some may feel that their phobia prevents them from joining a health care provider, or from pregnancy. Phobia can also affect the health of those who do not; BII-phobia, for example, may have difficulty providing help to someone in an emergency where blood is present.

The causes of BII phobia should not be fully understood. There is ample evidence to suggest that phobia has its genetic basis, although many people with phobias also cite a traumatic event as the cause of their fears. The unconscious reaction associated with a phobia may have emerged as a dynamic evolutionary process.

Applied tension (AT), a method by which people take turns and relax their muscles while exposing themselves to a phobic trigger, is widely known as an effective treatment for BII phobia. Although AT is generally a recommended treatment modality, active relaxation techniques (AR) and exposure-cognitive-behavioral therapy (CBT) have been found to be effective in reducing the phobiac response in some cases. Other techniques can be used to temporarily alleviate symptoms associated with a phobiac reaction, such as coughing to increase blood flow to the cranial. Critical symptoms associated with the activation episode are usually fully resolved within minutes of system removal.

BII phobia has some similarities with other phobic disorders: in particular, dental phobia (often considered a minor type of BII phobia) and hemophobia. In all of these phobias, the response to biphasic exhaustion is a common reaction to the trigger.

In many parts of particular phobias, affected people experience growing anxiety when exposed to a phobic trigger. While BII-phobics experience a similar reaction at first when exposed, most end up responding to biphasic, or two phases, a seizure response. In the first stage, phobias often experience anxiety disorders characterized by high heart rate and high blood pressure, as in many other phobias. This is a result of increasing the activity of the sympathetic nervous system. However, with BII phobia, the second stage usually follows closely, in which the shy person experiences a massive immersion in the heartbeat and blood pressure known as the vasovagal response. The stimulation of the vagus nerve, which is part of the parasympathetic nervous system, is responsible for promoting reduced heart rate and lowering blood pressure. These physiological changes limit blood flow to the brain and may promote pre-syncope (lightheadedness, fainting spells) and syncope (fainting): included in this condition as vasovagal coma. In this second stage, fainting is rare in other phobias.

The depleted response pattern is not seen in all people with BII phobia, but it is found in many. Up to 80% of those with BII phobia report syncope or pre-syncope as a symptom when exposed to a trigger.

Other symptoms that may change when they are triggered by phobic triggers include chest tightness, dizziness, nausea, shock, vertigo, diaphoresis (profuse sweating), nausea, and in rare cases asystole (cardiac arrest) and death. Increased release of stress hormones (especially cortisol and corticotrophin) is common.

Neurological responses to phobic causes include activation of the bilateral occipito-parietal cortex and thalamus. It was also suggested that exposing a person with BII-phobia to the trigger would lead to a decrease in function in the brain's medial prefrontal cortex (MPFC). The reduced function of MPFC is linked to the ineffective ability to control emotional responses. This reduction of emotional control may contribute to the inability to control the symptoms of anxiety that occur when exposed to the phobic trigger.

Complications

The lives of people with BII phobia can be at risk due to this condition due to the avoidance of phobic triggers. Since modern health care is highly dependent on injections, it can be difficult for shy people to get the care they need, as conditions include injections, vaccinations, blood transfusions, etc. they are usually avoided. Avoidance behaviors can be particularly dangerous for a person if he or she is diabetic and in need of insulin injections or is experiencing other illnesses or conditions that require injectable treatment, such as MS. There may be improper discontinuation of injection therapy by people with a phobia, which may lead to adverse events or reduce the effectiveness of the treatment.

Physical injury may also persist during a coma in response to a phobic trigger.

Comorbidity and other health conditions. High levels of comorbidity and BII phobia are indicated by the following: other long-term effects, marijuana abuse, clinical depression, panic disorder, Obsessive-compulsive disorder (OCD), agoraphobia (AG), social anxiety disorder (AG). SAD)

For people with diabetes: cardiovascular disease, and heart disease, In most people's lives, BII phobia is more likely to affect the health of more people than the general population with phobia. A person with a phobia may, for example, be unable to respond appropriately and/or provide assistance in an emergency where another person is injured or injured.

Avoiding vaccines due to BII phobia may also appear to be dangerous to public health, as reduced levels of vaccination in humans often increase the risk of outbreaks of infectious diseases.

Considering that BII phobics will usually avoid conditions involving exposure to blood or needles, these individuals may avoid blood donation. Public health benefits can come from helping them overcome their phobia, as giving has become a viable option. BII phobia can affect the personal and professional decisions of those with the condition. Women with BII-phobicity, for example, may choose not to conceive, as they fear injections, vaccinations, and labor-related pain associated with childbirth.

Those with a phobia may also be unable to pursue a career in health-related careers, such as nursing, which may require repeated exposure to traumatic material. People with Phobic can find their ability to finish medical school with a severe disability.

Related disorder

Dental phobia

Dental fear is often regarded as a minor form of BII phobia, as dental phobia often fears the invading dentist's traits (those that usually involve blood and injections). Some people with dental phobia, however, have a much more intense fear of relaxation or oral contraceptives during dental surgery.

Like most people with BII phobia, most dental phobias will try to avoid their causes. This can lead to refusal to seek dental care, which can contribute to tooth decay and poor oral health. People with dental phobia show symptoms similar to those with BII phobia when exposed to a phobic trigger, which includes syncope and pre-syncope.

BII phobia is closely related to hemophobia (fear of blood), although both are not the same. Although BII-phobics problems often extend beyond the fear of blood on the nerves of pain, broken needles inside the body or needle-to-bone contact, homophobic are often particularly concerned with exposure to blood. However, in both phobias, humans experience similar symptoms when exposed to phobic factors.

The cause of BII phobia is not yet fully understood. Various studies indicate the underlying cause of genetic predisposition, which genes put a person at greater risk for developing certain phobias. Influential genes have not yet been identified.

BII phobia has a strong family reunion - if present in the family, most members may have a phobia. This combination is stronger for BII phobia than any other known phobic problem: more than 60% of those with phobia have first-degree relatives also BII-phobias. It is believed that this proves the genetic support for phobia. One study estimated the true prevalence of phobia at 59%.

In addition, most phobias say that their fears are caused by natural factors. For example, a specific type of traumatic event involving blood, injury, or injection puts them in a state of panic for those specific causes. Some report being in a situation where they see someone else reacting to a stimulus with a constant pattern of fear.

It has been suggested that demonstrating the vasovagal response to blood transfusions was beneficial for evolution and that this phobia is the result of the evolution of ancestors. A coma may serve as a stabilizing influence, allowing the ancients to play dead in a bloodbath, perhaps helping them to avoid enemy attention. It has also been suggested that a decrease in blood pressure associated with seeing blood - such as when a person sees blood on his wound - occurs to reduce blood loss.

People often seek treatment for BII phobia in an effort to reduce the symptoms that arise when they are exposed to the phobic trigger. Therapists may use a combination of physical and psychological interventions, such as cognitive-behavioral therapy and applied tension (AT), to help suppress a person's response to fear.

Early research on ways to combat vasovagal convulsions found that exercise on certain legs and that person who is irritated by a hypothetical condition can increase blood pressure, thereby increasing blood flow to the brain and preventing fainting when exposed to a phobic trigger. A recent experimental study used muscle tension as a means of preventing seizures when a person with a fear of injury is exposed to visual stimuli. Lars-Göran Öst expanded on this study, enabling BII enthusiasts to participate in muscle compression while being exposed to blood pressure. Those trained in this procedure showed significant improvement in symptoms during five five-hour treatment sessions.

AT treatment usually involves a person being instructed to grasp the arm, leg, and chest muscles 10 to 15 times as they are systematically exposed to the causes of blood-like or needle-like triggers. This program is designed to increase heart rate and blood pressure, and counteract vasovagal reactions.

The tension method used remains popular - it is the most common treatment for BII phobia, and has been found to be very effective in most BII phobias. However, exposure-only cognitive-behavioral therapy (CBT) may be effective, as there may be an Applied relaxation (AR) approach.

CBT is a technique that promotes the elimination of fear in the form of gradual exposure, over and over again to the things that are feared. BII-phobics may be given pictures of needles or blood, asked to illustrate needles or scenes with blood, or to talk about their phobic causes. This progresses in a systematic way to the point where one has to deal directly with the phobic motive: being given a needle, seeing blood drawn, etc. As exposure continues, the phobic response is expected to diminish, and symptoms diminish.

While AT is focused on the physical response to phobia, which is aimed at raising blood pressure and directly preventing fainting, AR is more focused on helping a person avoid phobia-related anxiety. The phobic will learn continuous relaxation techniques to help lower itself when exposed to a trigger.

Temporary relief of symptoms

Drinking water before a thrilling experience such as donating blood has been shown to help prevent seizures. Water will increase the activity of the sympathetic nervous system, increase blood pressure and fight vasovagal reactions.

Some physical guidance also has the potential to temporarily increase blood pressure, reducing pre-syncope symptoms such as bright light by improving blood flow to the brain. This includes a person with phobic jumping over his legs, making strong fists with both hands, or attractive muscles of the trunk or arms. Coughing, which may similarly increase cranial blood flow, may also be helpful as a precautionary measure to avoid pre-syncope and syncope.

Symptoms of a phobic reaction can usually be fully revealed within a few minutes by removing the phobic trigger. BII phobia is one of the most common forms of phobia - estimated to affect about 3-4% of the general population.

The onset of a phobia usually occurs in middle age, before ten years. There are more reports of cases of phobia in young people and those with lower levels of education. Some studies suggest that women also experience phobia more often, yet the results are mixed about the related prevalence of phobia between the sexes.

Trypanophobia

Fear of needles, known in medical literature as needle phobia, is a major fear of medical procedures involving injections or hypodermic needles. This can lead to avoiding health care, which includes doubts about the policy.

It is sometimes referred to as aichmophobia, although the term may refer to a common fear of sharp objects.

This condition was officially recognized in 1994 in DSM-IV (Diagnostic and Statistical Manual of Mental Disorders, fourth edition) as a specific phobia of blood-injection-injury type phobia (BII phobia). Phobic-level responses to injections cause patients to avoid injections, blood tests, and in more severe cases, all medical care.

It is estimated that at least 10% of American adults are afraid of needles, and it is possible that the actual number is large, as the worst cases are never recorded due to the patient's tendency to avoid all treatment. The diagnostic value of BII phobias is robust, estimated at 3-4% of the general population, and this includes blood-related phobias.

The prevalence of needle fear has increased, as two studies show an increase in children from 25% in 1995 to 65% in 2012 (for those born after 1999). University of Augusta professor Amy Baxter says the increase is due to an increase in promotional imagery at 5 years of age, old enough to remember and young enough to contribute to the formation of phobia.

According to Drs. James G. Hamilton, the author of the first paper on needle phobia, probably has a genetic need for evolution, as thousands of years ago people carefully avoided stabbing and other wounds. incidents of mutilated meat can have a greater chance of survival.

The evolutionary discussion of the evolution of needle phobia in Hamilton's review article touches on the vasovagal form of needle phobia, which is a less common form of blood-injection-injury type phobia. This type of needle phobia is particularly noticeable with a two-stage vasovagal response. First, there is a brief heart rate and blood pressure. This is followed by a rapid decrease in both heart rate and blood pressure, sometimes leading to seizures. Loss of consciousness is sometimes accompanied by convulsions and many rapid changes in many different hormone levels.

Other medical journal articles have discussed additional features of this potential link between vasovagal syncope and the evolutionary significance of blood-injected phobias.

The theory of evolutionary psychology explains the combination of vasovagal syncope that some forms of fainting are non-verbal cues formed in response to an increase in violence between groups during paleolithic times. An unconscious military person indicates that they are not a threat. This may explain the connection between fainting and triggers such as bleeding and injury.

Although needle phobia is simply defined as the extreme fear of medical shooting/injections, it occurs in a variety of forms.

Vasovagal

Although many specialized phobias come from humans themselves, the most common type of needle phobia, affecting 50% of victims, is the inherited vasovagal reflex. About 80% of needle-prone people report that a relative between the first qualifications shows a similar disorder.

People suffering from vasovagal and needle phobia are afraid to see, think, or feel the needles or things like a needle. The physiological changes associated with this type of phobia include numbness, sweating, dizziness, nausea, dizziness, tinnitus, panic attacks, initially high blood pressure, and heart rate followed by a decrease in both during the injection. The main symptom of vasovagal fear is vasovagal syncope or fainting due to decreased blood pressure.

Most people who suffer from fainting during needle procedures do not report a conscious fear of the needle procedure itself, but greater fear of vasovagal syncope reaction. People are very afraid of the negative effects of low blood pressure caused by needle vision.

A study in the medical journal Circulation concluded that in many patients with this condition (as well as patients with a wide range of blood pressure/panic injuries), the first episode of vasovagal syncope during injection surgery may be a major cause of needle phobia. rather than any basic fear of needles. These findings reverse the commonly held beliefs about pattern-and effects of need phobics with vasovagal syncope.

Although many phobias are dangerous to some degree, needle phobia is one of the few things that actually kills. In cases of severe phobia, a decrease in blood pressure caused by the vasovagal shock reflex may result in death. In Hamilton's 1995 review article on needle phobia, he was able to document the deaths of 23 people as a direct result of vasovagal trauma during needle surgery.

The best treatment for this type of needle phobia has historically been the desensitization or continuous exposure of a patient to a gradual stimulus, which allows them to be less sensitive to the stimulus that triggers the phobic response. In recent years, the so-called "applied tension" method has become increasingly accepted as a more effective way of maintaining blood pressure to avoid unpleasantly, and sometimes dangerous, vasovagal reactions.

Associative

Joint fear of needles is the second most common type, affecting 30% of touch needles. This type is a form of phobia where a traumatic event such as a very painful medical procedure or seeing a family member or friend experience this, causes the patient to associate all the procedures involving needles with the original negative information.

This type of needle fear causes major psychological symptoms, such as unexplained anxiety, insomnia, preoccupation with the future, and panic attacks. Effective treatment includes psychiatric treatment, hypnosis, and/or anti-anxiety medications.

Resistance

Strong fear of needles occurs when the underlying fear involves not only needles or injections but also control or prevention. It usually results from increased [quoted] pressure or misalignment of previous needle procedures (e.g., forced physical or emotional restraint).

This type of needle phobia affects about 20% of those who suffer. Symptoms include fighting, high heart rate associated with high blood pressure, resistance to violence, avoidance, and flight. Recommended treatment for psychotherapy, may include teaching the patient self-injection techniques or finding a trusted healthcare provider.

Hyperalgesic

Fear of hyperalgesic needles is another unrelated form of fear of a real needle. Patients with this form have hypersensitivity inherited as a painful, or hyperalgesia. For them, the pain of the injection is excruciating and many do not understand how anyone can tolerate such procedures.

This type of fear needle affects about 10 percent of people who have a fear needle. Symptoms include excessive anxiety, as well as high blood pressure, and a rapid heartbeat when the needle enters or seconds before. Recommended therapies include some form of anesthesia, which may be a common or general condition.

Vicarious

While witnessing procedures involving needles may be embarrassing for a shy person to experience the symptoms of a needle attack without injecting. Caused by seeing a phobic injection may show common symptoms of vasovagal syncope and fainting or falls are common. Although the cause of this is unknown, it may be due to the phobiac thinking of the procedure themselves. Recent neuroscience studies show that feeling a pin punching and watching someone else's hand being pierced by a pin activates the part of the brain.

Comorbidity and causes

Fear of needles, especially in your most severe forms, is often accompanied by other phobias and mental illnesses; for example, iatrophobia, or unreasonable fear of physicians, is more common in patients with needles.

A patient with a need phobic does not need to be in a doctor's office to deal with the panic attack or anxiety caused by need phobia. There are many factors that cause global warming. Some of these are blood, injuries, needle or screen needles, paper pins, syringes, examination rooms, white lab coats, dentists, nurses, the stench that accompanies offices and hospitals, and physical appearances like a normal patient's health care provider, or even a study of fear.

Treatment, reduction, and other methods

Medical literature raises the number of treatments that have been shown to be effective in certain cases of needle phobia, but it provides very little guidance in predicting which treatment may be effective in any particular condition. The following are some of the treatments that have been shown to work in some cases.

• Ethyl chloride spray (and other freezers). It is easily controlled but only provides superficial pain control.

• Jet injections. The jet injection works by introducing substances into the body with a high-pressure gas jet instead of a needle. Although these eliminate the needle, some people report that they cause a lot of pain. Also, they are only useful in a very limited number of cases involving needles; for example, insulin and injections.

• Iontophoresis. Iontophoresis draws nerves to the skin through electrical activity. It provides active sensors but is generally not available to consumers in the commercial market and some see it as useless to use it.

• EMLA. EMLA is a topical anesthetic that is a eutectic mixture of lidocaine and prilocaine. It is a prescription cream in the United States and is available without a prescription in other countries. Although it does not act as iontophoresis, as EMLA does not go as deep as iontophoresis-driven anesthetics, EMLA offers a simpler application than iontophoresis. EMLA goes much deeper than conventional anesthesia, and it works well for most people.

• Ametop. Ametop gel appears to be more effective than EMLA in relieving pain during venepuncture release.

• Lidocaine / tetracaine patch. A warming compound containing the eutectic compounds lidocaine and tetracaine is available in several countries and is specifically approved by government agencies for use in needle procedures. This clip is sold under the trade name Synera in the United States and Rapydan in the European Union. Each bag is packed in an airtight bag. It starts to heat up a bit when the patch is taken out of the pocket and exposed to the air. The episode requires 20 to 30 minutes to achieve the perfect anesthetic effect. Synera Episode was approved by the United States Food and Drug Administration on 23 June 2005.

• Behavioral therapy. The effectiveness of this varies greatly depending on the individual and the severity of the condition. There is controversy about the efficacy of behavioral therapy for certain phobias, although some data are available to support the effectiveness of methods such as exposure therapy. Any treatment that allows for relaxation methods may be prevented with the treatment of fear needles as this method promotes lower blood pressure which only increases the vasovagal reflex. In response to this, moderate exposure modes may include part of dealing with dependence on stress used as a means of preventing problems associated with a vasovagal reaction in particular blood, injury, or type of stimulus injection.

• Nitrous oxide (laughing gas). This will provide sedation and reduce the patient's anxiety, as well as some mild analgesic effects.

• Normal sense of smell. This will eliminate all the pain and all the memory of any needle procedure. However, it is often regarded as the ultimate solution. It is not covered by insurance in most cases, and most doctors will not order it. It can be dangerous and expensive and may require hospitalization.

• Benzodiazepines, such as diazepam (Valium), lorazepam (Ativan), alprazolam (Xanax), or clonazepam (Klonopin), can help reduce the need for anxiety phobics, according to Dr. James Hamilton. . These drugs have an effect within 5 to 15 minutes from ingestion. A larger oral volume may be required.

• Strengthening the abdominal muscles can help prevent fainting.

• Swearing can reduce perceived pain.

• Disorders can reduce perceived pain, for example pretending to cough, doing a visual activity, watching a video, listening to music, or playing a video game.

• Some medicines and vaccines, such as a flu shot, can be given through the nose.

Hemophobia

Blood phobia (also known as hemophobia or hematophobia in American English and hemophobia or haematophobia in British English) is a very irrational fear of blood, a form of fear. Severe conditions of this fear can cause an abnormal immune response to many other frightening substances, especially vasovagal syncope (fainting). A similar reaction can also occur with trypanophobia and traumatophobia. For this reason, these phobias are classified as a blood-injection-injury phobia by DSM-IV. Some earlier texts refer to this category as "blood-injury-illness phobia."

Blood phobia is often the result of direct or indirect trauma in childhood. Although some have suggested that it might be genetically related, twin studies suggest that learning about social events and traumatic events, not genetics, is even more important. Blood-injection-injury phobia (BII) affects about 4% of the population in the United States.

The inclusion of BII within the category of specific or simple phobias in classification systems reflects the perception that fear plays a key role in disruption. In line with this hypothesis, blood injury phobia appears to share a common etiology with other phobias. Kendler, Neale, Kessler, Heath, and Eaves (1992) have argued the data comparing monozygotic and dizygotic twins to the common genetic trait in all phobias (agoraphobia, social) phobia, as well as certain phobias), puts a person first in certain phobias.

Inherited risk recognition is common in all phobias in line with the notion that a high level of anxiety causes a person to develop anxiety disorders. Signal anxiety provides a heart-wrenching wake-up call that allows for instantaneous action or flight response. In the case of certain events that make it work, setting the stage is one way in which the motives can evoke anxiety. It is believed that these changes are controlled by the vagus nerve, which affects the functioning of the chest and abdomen.

Therefore, a traumatic experience may trigger a panic-stricken injury. Researchers typically identify approximately 60 percent of people who report a blood injury phobia as the first person to experience rehabilitation. However, an examination of the available summaries of each case casts doubt on the conclusion that positioning episodes are as common as they have been reported. For example, Thyer et al. (1985) produced a conditioning episode in which "a patient receives an injection at the age of 13 and fainted", and another person when "at the age of six heard his elementary school teacher give a talk on the circulatory system. Syncope point."

The standard of care is similar to other phobias — psychotherapy-behavioral therapy, allergies, and perhaps medications to help with anxiety and discomfort. In recent years, a method known as applied tension, applying muscle tension in an effort to increase blood pressure, has gained favor as a common treatment for blood phobia associated with low blood pressure and fainting.

Because fear of blood is so common, it is often exploited in popular culture. Horror movies and Halloween festivities consume our natural appetite for blood, which often includes large amounts of counterfeit blood.

Traumatophobia

According to the DSM-IV category of psychiatric disorders, the traumatic phobia is a specific blood phobia/ injection/injury. It is a rare, pathological fear of injury.

Another name for the injury phobia is traumatophobia, from the Greek τραῦμα (trauma), "wound, pain" and φόβος (phobos), "fear". Associated with BII (Blood-Injury-Injection) Phobia. Patients show unreasonable or excessive anxiety and a desire to avoid certain horrible situations, to the point of avoiding life-saving medical procedures. According to one study, it is more common in women.

What makes injury phobia different is that it is when a person is exposed to blood, injured, or injected, that they begin to feel extreme feelings of fear, such as shortness of breath; excessive sweating; dry mouth; feeling sick; earthquake; heartbeat; inability to speak or think clearly; fear of death, insanity, or loss of self-control; a sense of separation from the truth; or attacks of full anxiety. Significantly, dental phobia is different from traumatophobia.

The therapies available are usually behavioral and psychological therapies, which are very common behaviors. Another way to treat behavioral traumatophobia is to expose the client to a stimulus, this time exposure to blood, injury, and injections, and then repeat the procedure until the client's response and/or treatment are reduced. Hypnotherapy is also an option.

5 Other Phobias

Phonophobia

Phonophobia, also called ligyrophobia or sonophobia, is the fear or dislike of loud noises (eg explosives) —a form of fear. It is a very rare phobia that is often a sign of hyperacusis. Sonophobia can refer to a patient's hypersensitivity to hearing and may be part of a migraine diagnosis. It is sometimes called acousticophobia.

The word phonophobia comes from the Greek φωνή - phōnē, "voice" or "sound" and φόβος - Phobos, "fear".

Ligyrophobics may frighten devices that may suddenly cause loud noises, such as computer speakers or fire alarms. When using a device such as a home theater system, computer, television, or CD player, they may wish to have the volume reduced all the time before doing anything that could cause the speakers to emit a sound, so that there is a production command. audio is provided, and the user can raise the volume of the speakers at a free listening level. They may avoid parades and carnivals because of the loud music like drums. As festive occasions are accompanied by the music of more than 120 decibels, many shy people experience agoraphobia. Some ligyrophobics also avoid any incidents where the explosives should be closed.

Another example is watching someone blow a balloon over its normal capacity. This is often doubtful, and it is a disturbing thing for a person with ligyrophobia to see it, as they expect a loud noise when the balloon comes out. When balloons explode, two types of respiratory reactions and panic attacks. The sufferer is anxious to escape the source of the loud noise and may have a headache. It may also be related to, caused by, or confused with, hyperacusis, excessive sensitivity to high-pitched sounds. Honophobia has also been suggested to refer to a more severe form of misophonia.

Extreme noise, especially when unexpected, can be unpleasant or confusing to anyone. If you have phonophobia, your fear of loud noise may be frustrating, causing you to panic and feel very anxious.

Fear of loud noise is called phonophobia, sonophobia, or ligyrophobia. This condition is not caused by hearing loss, or any form of hearing loss.

Phonophobia is a specific phobia. Some phobias are extreme, irrational fears of situations or things that do not authorize a great response.

Like all phobias, phonophobia is a treatable anxiety disorder. It is considered a great fear of loud noise.

A person with this condition may be experiencing severe depression with a loud noise that he knows is coming, as well as an unexpected loud noise.

Loud noises can be pleasant and uncomfortable. Normally a person enjoys a never-ending car alarm or an alarming ambulance alarm. Some loud noises, such as those made by fireworks, can be easily tolerated as they are associated with exciting events. These are things that most people can relate to.

However, if you have phonophobia, you will get a very strong reaction to any type of loud noise, regardless of the combination or cause.

People with this condition experience intense stress and anxiety as they wait for a loud noise. They also have an extreme reaction to loud noises, if any.

Phonophobia is different from other uncomfortable situations to sound like a symptom. These include:

· **Hyperacusis.** This condition is not a phobia. Instead, the hearing problem that makes the sounds louder than you really are. Hyperacusis has many causes, including brain damage, Lyme disease, and post-traumatic stress disorder (PTSD).

· **Misophonia.** This condition is emotional in nature, but not a phobia. People with misophonia have a strong, emotional reaction, such as hatred or panic, to a certain sound, such as a dripping tap or a snoring person. Sound does not have to be high to produce this effect.

Symptoms of phonophobia can make it difficult to enjoy daily activities and daily life. A person with this condition may have these symptoms in anticipation of loud noise, during, or after. Includes anxiety, fear, sweating, shortness of breath, rapid heartbeat or increased heart rate, chest pain, dizziness, lightheadedness, nausea, fainting, etc.

conclusion

If you have decided that it is time to seek professional help for your fears, take the time to prepare for your first appointment. To take full advantage of your appointment, and to help your doctor determine if you have any fears or phobias, create three lists:

1. Symptoms: Make a list of physical and psychological symptoms, including your bullet, how you deal with your fears, and things that make your anxiety worse or worse.

2. Personal health: Make a list of any stressful things that happen in your life, including relationship issues or problems at work. Listing new situations that seem positive, including promotional or emerging romance, is also important, as good news can cause anxiety, too.

3. Medicines and Ingredients: Make a list of all the medicines and ingredients you use regularly, such as vitamins and herbal teas. These things can affect your mood and interfere with treatment.

People with a certain phobia may realize that their fears are irrational, but knowing this does not mean that their fears are not real and are often harmful. Some phobias are common, and often focus on the natural fears of most people (even those who do not have a phobia diagnosis) and understand. It is important to remember that effective treatment options are available that can help alleviate these fears and the symptoms that cause them.

IV

Agoraphobia

The term "agoraphobia" was coined in German in 1871 by German pioneer psychologist Carl Friedrich Otto Westphal, 1833-1890, in his article "Die Agoraphobie, a neuropathische Erscheinung." Archives for Psychiatry and Nervenkrankheiten, Berlin, 1871–72; 3: 138-161. It is derived from the Greek ἀγορά, agorā́, meaning "meeting place" or "market place" and -φοβία, -phobía, meaning "fear".

Agoraphobia is a mental and behavioral disorder, especially anxiety disorder characterized by symptoms of anxiety in situations where a person sees their environment as unsafe and has no easy way out. These situations may include open spaces, public transportation, shopping centers, or simply being outside their home. Being in these situations can lead to panic attacks. Affected people will try to avoid these situations. In extreme cases, people may not be able to get out of their homes at all.

Agoraphobia is believed to be caused by a combination of genetic and environmental factors. This condition is more common in families, and stressful or traumatic events such as the death of a parent or assault may be the cause. In DSM-5 agoraphobia is classified as a phobia with specific phobias and social phobia. Other conditions that may produce similar symptoms include anxiety disorders, post-traumatic stress disorder, and major depressive disorder. Diagnosis of agoraphobia has been shown to be associated with depression, substance abuse, and suicidal ideation.

Without treatment, it is rare for agoraphobia to resolve. Treatment usually consists of a type of counseling called cognitive-behavioral therapy (CBT). CBT results in the resolution of about half of the population. In some cases, those with a diagnosis of agoraphobia have reported taking benzodiazepines and the addition of antipsychotics. Agoraphobia affects about 1.7% of adults. Women are affected about twice as often as men. This condition usually begins in adulthood and progresses to aging. It is rare for children.

Agoraphobia is a condition in which people become anxious in unfamiliar areas or where they realize they have no control over it. Causes of these concerns may include open spaces, crowds (public concern), or walking (even short distances). Agoraphobia is common, but not always, associated with the fear of public embarrassment, as agoraphobic fears the onset of panic attacks and the appearance of frustration in society. They often avoid these areas and live in a comfortable environment, usually their home.

Agoraphobia is also described as "fear, sometimes terrifying, by those who have suffered from one or more fears". In these cases, the patient is terrified of an area because he or she has had panic attacks in the same area in the past. Fearing the onset of another frightening attack, the patient fears or even avoids the scene. Some refuse to leave their homes even in medical emergencies because the fear of being outside their comfort zone is too great.

A person with this condition can sometimes travel long distances to avoid areas where they have been panicked. Agoraphobia, as described in this way, is actually a symptom that experts evaluate when diagnosing a panic disorder. Some syndromes such as obsessive-compulsive disorder or post-traumatic stress disorder can cause agoraphobia. In fact, any irrational fear that might keep a person from going out could cause disease.

People with agoraphobia may experience temporary anxiety disorders when other family members move away from temporary residences, such as a parent or spouse, or when they are left alone at home. Such temporary circumstances may cause increased anxiety or panic or a feeling of isolation from family or friends.

People with agoraphobia are sometimes afraid to wait outside for too long; that symptom can be called "macrophobia".

Agoraphobia patients may experience sudden panic attacks when visiting places where they fear they are uncontrollable, may find it difficult to get help or may feel embarrassed. During a panic attack, epinephrine is released in large amounts, triggering a natural fight-or-flight response. A panic attack usually starts suddenly, develops within a maximum of 10 to 15 minutes, and rarely lasts longer than 30 minutes. Symptoms of panic attacks include palpitations, rapid heartbeat, sweating, tremors, nausea, vomiting, dizziness, sore throat, and difficulty breathing. Many patients report fear of death, fear of losing control of their emotions, or fear of losing control of their behavior.

Agoraphobia is believed to be caused by a combination of genetic and environmental factors. This condition is more common in families, and stressful or traumatic events such as the death of a parent or assault may be the cause.

Research has revealed a link between agoraphobia and the difficulty of locating. People without agoraphobia are able to maintain balance by integrating information from their vestibular system, their visual system, and their sense of perception. An unequal number of agoraphobics have a weak vestibular function and are therefore highly dependent on visual or auditory signals. They may be confused when the visual cues are few (such as in open areas) or confusing (such as in crowds). Similarly, they may be confused by sloping or unfamiliar areas. In a randomized controlled trial, agoraphobics showed a negative analysis of audiovisual data change compared to subjects without agoraphobia.

Chronic use of sedatives and sleeping pills such as benzodiazepines has been linked to the onset of agoraphobia. In 10 patients who had experienced agoraphobia during benzodiazepine dependence, symptoms decreased during the first year of relief. Similarly, alcohol abuse disorders are associated with or without agoraphobia; this association may be due to the long-term effects of alcohol-induced chemical reactions on brain chemistry. Smoking has been linked to the development and emergence of agoraphobia, often with panic disorder; it is not clear how smoking causes anxiety - fear with or without the symptoms of agoraphobia, but the direct effects of nicotine dependence or the effects of secondhand smoke have been suggested as potential causes. Self-medication or a combination of substances may explain the link between smoking and agoraphobia and panic attacks.

Attachment theory

Some experts have described agoraphobia as a lack of attachment, that is, a temporary loss of ability to tolerate the separation of space from a protected base. Recent research has also linked local perceptions of agoraphobia.

Attachment theory focuses on relationships and relationships (especially long-term) between people, including those between parent and child and between loving partners.

British psychologist John Bowlby was the first inventor of the adhesive. He described adherence as "a lasting psychological connection between people." Bowlby was interested in understanding the anxiety and stress children experience when they are separated from their primary caregivers.

Some of the first ethical considerations suggested that the attachment was learned behavior. These theories suggested that adherence was simply the result of a child's eating relationship with a caregiver. Because the caregiver feeds the baby and feeds it, the baby attaches itself.

Bowlby noted that the feed did not reduce anxiety about separation. When children become frightened, they want to get closer to their primary caregiver in order to receive both comfort and care.

Adherence is an emotional bond with another person. Bowlby believed that early bonds formed by children and their caregivers had a profound and lasting effect on life. He suggested that adherence helps to keep the baby close to the mother, thus improving the baby's chances of survival.

Bowlby viewed attachment as a product of evolutionary processes. While the ethical theory of attachment suggests that attachment is a learned process, Bowlby and others suggest that children are born with a natural instinct to build links with caregivers.

Throughout history, children who keep close to the attached value are more likely to find comfort and protection, so they are more likely to survive into adulthood. Through the natural selection process, a promotional program designed to control attachment emerged.

So what determines successful attachment? Behavioralists suggest that it was food that led to the formation of this attachment behavior, but Bowlby and others showed that nutrition and reaction were the main factors for adherence.

In his study of the 1970s, psychologist Mary Ainsworth greatly expanded Bowlby's early work. His tragic study of the "strange state of affairs" revealed the profound effects of moral restraint. In this study, the researchers looked at children between the ages of 12 and 18 when they reacted to a situation where they were left alone for a while and then reunited with their mother.

Based on the researchers' responses, Ainsworth described three major types of attachments: secure attachments, non-slip attachments - unsecured, and unstable attachments to avoid. Later, researchers Main and Solomon (1986) added a fourth style of attachment called a non-invasive attachment based on their research.

Many studies since then have supported Ainsworth adhesive styles and have shown that adhesive styles also contribute to later life behaviors.

Harry Harlow's notorious studies of motherhood and isolation during the 1950s and 1960's also examined early bonds. In a series of experiments, Harlow demonstrated how such bonds emerge and the powerful influence they have on behavior and performance.

In one version of his study, newborn rhesus monkeys were isolated from their mothers and raised by their mothers. Newborn monkeys were placed in cages with two mother monkeys. One of the wire monkeys carried a bottle of a baby monkey on which he could find food, and the other monkey with the wire was covered with a soft terry cloth.

Although newborn monkeys would go to the mother of the telephone for food, they would spend a lot of time with the mother of the soft cloth. When frightened, the baby monkeys would turn to their mother-in-law for comfort and security.

Stages of attachment

Researchers Rudolph Schaffer and Peggy Emerson analyzed the number of attachment relationships infants performed in a long-term study with 60 children. These babies were monitored every four weeks for the first year of life, and then again at 18 months.

Based on their observations, Schaffer and Emerson developed four different stages of attachment, including:

Pre-attachment Stage

From birth to 3 months, infants do not show any attachment to a particular caregiver. The baby's symptoms, such as crying and arguing, naturally attract the caregiver's attention and the baby's direct response encourages the caregiver to stay close.

Impartial Attachment

Between 6 weeks and 7 months, infants begin to express a preference for primary and secondary caregivers. Infants develop confidence that the caregiver will respond to their needs. Although they still accept the care of others, infants begin to distinguish between ordinary and unfamiliar people, responding well to the primary caregiver.

Discriminate Attachment

At this point, from about 7 to 11 years of age, infants demonstrate strong adherence to one-person preferences. They will protest when they are separated from the first number attached (anxiety separately), and begin to show concern for strangers (anxiety of a stranger).

Various Attachments

At about 9 months of age, children begin to build strong emotional bonds with other caregivers beyond the initial figure attached. This usually includes a stepparent, older siblings, and a grandparent.

Factors Affecting Attachment

While this process may seem straightforward, there are some factors that can influence how and when an attachment occurs, including:

• **The opportunity for attachment**: Children who do not have foster carers, such as those raised in orphanages, may not be able to develop the confidence needed to build a relationship.

• **quality caregiving:** When caregivers respond quickly and consistently, children learn that they can depend on the people responsible for their care, which is an important foundation for intimacy. This is an important aspect.

Attachment styles
There are four attachment patterns, which include:
• **Ambivalent attachment:** These children get very stressed when the parent leaves. The ambivalent attachment style is considered uncommon, affecting an average of 7% to 15% of U.S. children. Because of the poor availability of parents, these children are unable to rely on their primary caregivers to be there when they need them.

• **Avoidant attachment:** Avoidable children often avoid parents or caregivers, not showing a choice between a caregiver and a complete stranger. This attachment style may be the result of abusive or careless caregivers. Children who are disciplined for reliance on the caregiver will learn to avoid seeking help in the future.

• **Disorganized attachment:** These children show a confusing mix of behavior, which seems confused, confused, or confused. They may avoid or even oppose the parent. The lack of a clear attachment pattern may be associated with the caregiver's consistent behavior. In such cases, parents can be a source of comfort and fear, which in turn leads to disorderly conduct.

• **Secure attachment:** Children who can rely on their caregivers show stress when they are separated and happy when reunited. Although the child may be upset, he feels confident that the caregiver will return. When frightened, children who are securely attached are free to seek reassurance from caregivers. This is the most common paste style.

The Lasting Impact of Original Attachment
Studies suggest that failure to make safe attachments early in life can adversely affect childhood and overall well-being.

Children diagnosed with the oppositional defiant disorder (ODD), conduct disorder (CD), or post-traumatic stress disorder (PTSD) often show adherence problems, which may be due to premature abuse, neglect, or trauma. Children born after the age of 6 may have a higher risk of attachment problems.

Although the attachment styles shown in adulthood are not the same as those seen in childhood, premature attachment can have a serious impact on later relationships. Adults who were securely attached to childhood tend to have better self-esteem, strong romantic relationships, and the ability to express themselves to others.

Spatial theory
In social science, perceived clinical bias is present in the study of agoraphobia. Branches of social science, especially geography, are increasingly interested in what might be considered a local phenomenon. One such approach links the development of agoraphobia with modern. Factors considered to be part of modern agoraphobia are traffic congestion and urbanization. This has helped to improve the expansion of the public space and the narrowing of the private space, thus creating in the minds of people prone to agoraphobia a turbulent, unbroken gap between the two.

Evolutionary psychology
The theory of evolutionary psychology that agoraphobia is rarely uncommon without panic attacks may be due to a different approach from agoraphobia and panic attacks. Basic agoraphobia without panic attacks may be a form of self-described fear when it is beneficial for evolution to avoid exposed, large, open areas without covering or hiding. Agoraphobia with a panic attack may be the second avoidance response to a panic attack, due to fear in situations where a panic attack has occurred.

Diagnosis
Many people who introduce themselves to mental health professionals develop agoraphobia after the onset of panic disorder. Agoraphobia is best understood as a negative consequence of a recurring panic attack and subsequent anxiety and anxiety about these attacks that lead to avoiding situations where panic attacks may occur. Early treatment of panic disorder can usually prevent agoraphobia. Agoraphobia is usually diagnosed when symptoms are worse than panic disorder, but also do not meet the criteria for other anxiety disorders such as depression. In rare cases where agoraphobics do not meet the procedure used to diagnose panic disorder, a formal diagnosis of agoraphobia without a history of panic disorder is used (primary agoraphobia).

Planned intolerance can provide lasting relief for most patients with panic disorder and agoraphobia. Disappearance to avoid residual agoraphobic and sub-clinical, and not just panic attacks, should be the goal of exposure treatment. Most patients are more likely to deal with exposure if they are in the company of a trusted confidant. Patients should remain in this condition until the anxiety subsides because if they leave the condition, the phobiac response will not decrease and may increase.

Exposure-related exposure to in vivo, is a behavioral therapy approach, which exposes patients to dreaded situations or objects. This treatment was most effective with an effect size ranging from d = 0.78 to d = 1.34, and these results were shown to increase over time, proving that the treatment was longer active (up to 12 months after treatment).

Psychological interventions combined with drug therapy were more effective than treatments involving CBT or medication. Further studies have shown that there is no significant effect between using the CBT group against each CBT.

Psychological restructuring has been shown to be effective in the treatment of agoraphobia. This treatment involves training the participant in a dianoetic discussion, with the goal of transforming absurd, contradictory, beliefs into positive and beneficial ones.

Relaxation techniques are often useful skills for agoraphobic development, as they can be used to stop or prevent symptoms of anxiety and panic.

Videoconferencing Psychotherapy (VCP)

Videoconferencing psychotherapy (VCP) is a short-term method used to treat various disorders at a distance. Similar to conventional face-to-face interventions, VCP can be used to administer CBT. The use of VCP has been shown to be equally effective as a face-to-face intervention in the treatment of panic disorder and agoraphobia (PDA) and to encourage the client to continue treatment.

Medications

The most commonly used antidepressant drugs in the treatment of dementia are selective serotonin reuptake inhibitors. Benzodiazepines, a monoamine oxidase inhibitor, and tricyclic antidepressants are sometimes prescribed for the treatment of agoraphobia. Antidepressants are important because some have anxiolytic effects. Antidepressants should be used in combination with exposure to self-medication or psychotherapy. The combination of medications and behavioral therapy is sometimes the most effective treatment for agoraphobia.

Benzodiazepines and other anxiolytic drugs such as alprazolam and clonazepam are used to treat anxiety and can help control the symptoms of panic attacks.

A different Medicine

Eye movement desensitization and reprocessing (EMDR) has been evaluated as a treatment for agoraphobia, with side effects. Therefore, EMDR is only recommended in cases where psychological methods have proven ineffective or in cases where agoraphobia has developed following trauma.

Many people with anxiety disorders benefit from joining a self-help or support group (telephone conference support groups or online support groups are a special help for people who are completely homeless). Sharing problems and successes with others, as well as sharing various self-help tools, are common tasks for these groups. In particular, stress management strategies with a variety of meditation techniques and visualization techniques can help people with anxiety problems to calm down and may improve treatment outcomes, as it may work for others, which may interfere with the normal absorption. anxiety disorders. Also, preliminary evidence suggests that aerobic exercise may have a cooling effect. Since caffeine, certain illicit drugs, and even cold-blooded medicines over the counter can increase the symptoms of anxiety disorders, they should be avoided.

Agoraphobia occurs twice as often in women as in men. Panic disorder with or without agoraphobia affects approximately 5.1% of Americans, and approximately 1/3 of this number of people with panic disorder have co-morbid agoraphobia. It is rare to have agoraphobia without panic attacks, with only 0.17% of people with agoraphobia showing no panic disorder.

Panic Attack

Panic attacks are sudden episodes of severe anxiety and discomfort that may include heart palpitations, sweating, chest pain or chest discomfort, shortness of breath, tremors, dizziness, numbness, confusion, or feeling of impending disaster or loss of self-control. Typically, symptoms reach a peak within the first ten minutes and last for about 30 minutes, but the duration can vary from seconds to hours. Although it can be frightening and very stressful, the panic attack itself is not harmful to the body.

The key features of a panic attack remain unchanged, although the DSM-IV complex term to describe different types of panic attacks (i.e., arrests/assumptions, conditional expectations, and unexpected/unmistakable) is replaced by unexpected and unexpected words. Anxiety attacks serve as a marker and a predictable feature of diagnostic difficulty, course, and comorbidity across a wide range of disorders, including but not limited to anxiety disorders. Therefore, panic attacks can be listed as an explanation that applies to all DSM-5 disorders.

Panic attacks may be due to a number of disorders including panic disorder, social anxiety disorder, post-traumatic stress disorder, substance abuse disorders, depression, and medical problems. They may be activated or may occur unexpectedly. Smoking, caffeine, and depression increase the risk of panic attacks. Prior to diagnosis, conditions that show similar symptoms should be excluded, such as hyperthyroidism, hyperparathyroidism, heart disease, lung disease, substance abuse, and dysautonomia.

Treatment of panic attacks should be focused on the underlying cause. For those who regularly suffer, counsel or medication may be used. Respiratory training and muscle relaxation techniques can also help. Affected people are at greater risk of suicide.

About 5 percent of the world's population suffers from anxiety over one year or another. They are more common in women than men. They usually begin in adolescence or later. Children and adults are less likely to be affected. People with panic attacks often report fear of death or heart attack, lightheadedness or other visual disturbances, fainting or nausea, numbness all over the body, shortness of breath and excessive breathing, or loss of body control. Some people also find vision in the tunnel, mainly due to the blood flow that leaves the head to the most sensitive parts of the body for protection. These feelings may trigger a strong desire to escape or to escape from where the attack started (the result of a "fight or flight response", in which the hormone that triggers this response is released in critical amounts). This response replenishes the body with hormones, particularly epinephrine (adrenaline), which help to protect against injury. The most common symptoms include tremors, dyspnea (shortness of breath), heart palpitations, chest pain (or chest tightness), fever, chills, hot flashes (especially on the face or neck), sweating, and nausea, dizziness (or mild vertigo).), lightheadedness, heavy headaches, hyperactivity, paresthesias (feeling itchy), feeling choked or tingling, difficulty moving, isolation, and/or imperfections. These physical symptoms are interpreted by an alarm in people who are prone to panic attacks. This causes increased anxiety and creates a loop of positive feedback.

Shortness of breath and chest pain are the most common symptoms. Many people who suffer from a panic attack say that they have a bad heart attack and thus seek treatment in the emergency room. Because chest pain and shortness of breath are significant symptoms of cardiovascular disease, including chronic angina and myocardial infarction (heart attack), the diagnosis of exclusion (rule out in some cases) should be made before diagnosing panic attacks. It is very important to do this for people with mental health and unknown heart health. This can be done using an electrocardiogram and a mental health check.

Anorexia nervosa is a disorder characterized by certain types of anxiety and their sudden, episodic nature. They often experience a combination of anxiety disorders and other psychological traits, although panic attacks usually do not indicate a mental disorder.

There are long-term, biological, environmental, and social causes for fear. In 1993, Fava et al. proposed a staged approach to understanding the root of the problem. The first stage of disease development involves risk factors, such as genetics, personality traits, and social ills. Panic disorder usually occurs in later life, although it may appear at any age. It happens more often to women and more often to people who are overweight. Various twin studies in which one twin with anxiety has reported a higher incidence of another twin with a diagnosis of anxiety disorder.

Biological causes may include compulsive disorder, postural orthostatic tachycardia syndrome, post-traumatic stress disorder, hypoglycemia, hyperthyroidism, Wilson's disease, mitral valve prolapse, pheochromocytoma, and internal ear disorders ((labyrinthitis). Norepinephrine system dysfunction in the locus coeruleus, the brain stem area, has been linked to panic attacks.

Panic attacks may occur due to temporary stress. Significant personal loss, including emotional attachment to a partner, life changes, and significant changes in life may trigger a panic attack. A person with anxiety, excessive need for reassurance, hypochondriacal fear, alertness to the world, and increased stress have been associated with panic attacks. For children, social change can also be a factor.

People often experience panic attacks as a direct result of exposure to an object/condition with a phobia. Panic can also be tied to a situation where certain situations are associated with panic attacks because of previous attacks in that situation. People may also have a mental or behavioral tendency to develop fear attacks in certain situations.

Other ongoing causes include avoiding situations or areas that cause panic, anxious/negative self-expression (thinking "what-if"), erroneous beliefs ("these symptoms are dangerous and/or dangerous"), and seized emotions.

Hyperventilation syndrome can occur when a person breathes in the chest, which can lead to excessive breathing (excessive carbon dioxide associated with the amount of oxygen in a person's blood). Hyperventilation syndrome can cause respiratory alkalosis and hypocapnia. The disease usually involves prominent respiratory infections as well. This triggers a set of symptoms, including rapid heartbeat, dizziness, and lightheadedness, which may trigger a panic attack.

Panic can be caused by things. A marked cessation or reduction in the dose of a substance such as a drug (drug withdrawal), for example, antidepressant (antidepressant discontinuation syndrome), may cause panic attacks. According to The Harvard Mental Health Letter, "the most commonly reported effects of marijuana use are anxiety and fear. Smoking cigarettes is another factor that has been linked to panic attacks.

A common feature of current psychological approaches to dementia is that no real risk exists, and human anxiety is unjustified.

People who have been repeatedly attacked, persisted, or felt very anxious about relapse are said to have panic disorder. Panic disorder is significantly different from other types of anxiety disorders in that panic attacks are often sudden and uncontrollable. However, the fears experienced by those with panic disorder can also be linked to or exacerbated by certain areas or situations, making daily life difficult.

Symptoms of panic attacks may be performed by laboratory tests in a variety of ways. Among them, for research purposes, by providing bolus injection of neuropeptide cholecystokinin-tetrapeptide (CCK-4). Different types of panic attacks have been tested.

Neurotransmitter imbalance

Many neurotransmitters are affected when the body is under a lot of stress and anxiety associated with panic attacks. Others include serotonin, GABA (gamma-aminobutyric acid), dopamine, norepinephrine, and glutamate. Further research into how these neurotransmitters interact with each other during panic attacks is necessary to make any firm conclusions.

Increased serotonin levels in certain brain pathways appear to be associated with reduced anxiety. Further evidence suggesting that serotonin plays a role in anxiety is that people taking SSRIs often experience a decrease in anxiety when their brain has too much serotonin available to use.

The main neurotransmitter that blocks the central nervous system (CNS) is GABA. Many methods that use GABA tend to reduce anxiety quickly.

The role of Dopamine in anxiety is not well understood. Some antipsychotic drugs that affect dopamine production have been shown to cure anxiety. However, this may be due to dopamine's tendency to increase mood and self-esteem, which in turn reduces indirect anxiety.

Many physical symptoms of anxiety, such as rapid heartbeat and tremors, are controlled by norepinephrine. Drugs that counteract the effect of norepinephrine may be effective in reducing the physical symptoms of panic attacks. However, some drugs that increase 'back' norepinephrine levels such as tricyclics and SNRIs are effective in treating long-term anxiety attacks, possibly by suppressing the norepinephrine spikes associated with panic attacks.

Because glutamate is a major neurotransmitter involved in the central nervous system (CNS), it can be found in almost every neural pathway in the body. Glutamate is probably involved in rehabilitation, which is the process by which certain fears are built up, and extinction, which is the elimination of these fears.

Pathophysiology

Symptoms of a panic attacks may make a person feel like their body is failing. Symptoms can be understood as follows. First, there is the sudden onset of irritability with minimal irritability. This leads to the release of adrenaline (epinephrine) which triggers an anti-or-flight response as the body prepares for strenuous physical activity. This leads to an increase in heart rate (tachycardia), shortness of breath (hyperventilation) which can be seen as shortness of breath (dyspnea), and sweating. Because hard work rarely occurs, hot air leads to a decrease in carbon dioxide levels in the lungs and then in the blood. This leads to a change in blood pH (respiratory alkalosis or hypocapnia), resulting in metabolic acidosis compensation that activates the chemosensing mechanisms that translate this pH conversion into spontaneous and respiratory responses.

In addition, this hypocapnia and the release of adrenaline during panic attacks cause vasoconstriction that leads to slow blood flow to the head causing dizziness and lightheadedness. A panic attack can cause blood sugar to be expelled from the brain and into large muscles. Neuroimaging promotes higher activity in the amygdala, thalamus, hypothalamus, and brainstem regions including the periaqueductal gray, parabrachial nucleus, and Locus coeruleus. In particular, the amygdala has been suggested to play a significant role. The combination of increased activity in the amygdala (fear center) and brainstem and decreased blood flow and blood sugar in the brain can lead to a decrease in activity in the prefrontal cortex (PFC) of the brain. There is evidence that having an anxiety disorder increases the risk of coronary heart disease (CVD). Those who are affected have a decrease in heart rate variability.

Cardiovascular disease

People diagnosed with panic disorder have twice the risk of coronary heart disease. Certain responses to depression have also been shown to increase the risk and those who are diagnosed with both depression and anxiety are almost three times more likely to be at risk.

Panic disorder is often successfully treated through a variety of interventions, including psychotherapy and medication. Psychiatric-behavioral therapy has a very long-lasting effect, followed by selected serotonin reuptake inhibitors. The 2009 review found positive results from treatment and treatment and a much better result when both were combined.

Lifestyle changes

Caffeine can cause or increase anxiety. Anxiety may develop temporarily during withdrawal from caffeine and various other drugs.

Extended and organized aerobic exercise such as running has been shown to have a positive effect on fighting anxiety. There is evidence to suggest that this effect is associated with the release of endorphins from the body and the subsequent reduction of the stress hormone cortisol.

There is still a chance that the symptoms of panic attacks will start or worsen due to the increased respiratory rate that occurs during aerobic exercise. This increase in respiratory rate can lead to hyperventilation and hyperventilation syndrome, which mimics the symptoms of a heart attack, thus causing panic attacks. The benefits of including an exercise regimen have shown the best results when walking properly.

Muscle relaxation techniques are helpful for some people. These can be read using recordings, videos, or books. Although muscle relaxation appears to be less effective than psycho-behavioral therapy in controlled trials, most people still experience at least temporary relief from muscle relaxation.

Respiratory tests

In many cases, hyperventilation is involved, increasing the effects of panic attacks. Breathing exercises help balance oxygen and CO2 levels in the blood

David D. Burns recommends breathing exercises for those with anxiety. One such respiratory exercise is 5-2-5. Using the abdomen (or diaphragm) - not the chest - breathe (feel the abdomen come out, as opposed to the growing chest) for 5 seconds. As the high point of smell is reached, hold your breath for 2 seconds. Then exhale slowly, over 5 seconds. Repeat this cycle twice and breathe 5 'normal' cycles (1 cycle = 1 inhale + 1 exhale). The point is to focus on breathing and release the heartbeat. Normal diaphragmatic breathing may be achieved by extending the air you exhale by counting or whispering.

Although breathing in a paper bag was a common recommendation for short-term treatment of symptoms of severe hepatitis, it has been criticized as being lower than moderate breathing, which may exacerbate panic attacks and possibly lower oxygen demand. Although the paper bag system increases the required carbon dioxide and thus reduces symptoms, it can significantly lower the levels of oxygen in the blood.

Capnometry, which provides air-cooled CO2 levels, can help regulate respiration.

According to the American Psychological Association, "many experts agree that a combination of psychological and behavioral therapies is the best treatment for panic disorder. Medication may be appropriate in some cases." The first part of treatment is primarily knowledgeable; most people are greatly helped by simply understanding what panic disorder is and how many others suffer from it. Many people with panic disorder worry that their panic attack means they are "crazy" or that panic may be causing a heart attack. The reorganization of the mind helps people to formulate those thoughts in a more realistic, positive way. Avoidance behavior is one of the most important factors in preventing people with common anxiety from working in a healthy way. Exposure therapy, which includes repeated coping with long-term stressors and physical emotions, helps to weaken anxiety response to these external and internal causes and strengthens practical ways to look for symptoms of panic.

At a deeper level in psychoanalytic methods, especially relational theory, panic attacks are often associated with dissociation (psychology), paranoid-schizoid and stress levels, as well as confused anxiety. They are often found to be associated with borderline personality problems and child sexual abuse. Paranoid anxiety may reach the level of anxiety disorder persecution.

Meditation may also be helpful in treating nervous disorders. There was a meta-analysis of comorbidity for panic disorders and agoraphobia. It has used exposure therapy to treat patients over a period of time. Hundreds of patients were used in these studies and all met the DSM-IV procedure for both of these problems. The result was that thirty-two percent of patients experienced a panic attack after treatment. They concluded that the use of exposure therapy is long-term for a client living with dementia and agoraphobia.

The effectiveness of group therapy in addition to standardized individual treatment for people with panic disorder or non-agoraphobia appears to be similar.

Alternative treatment options for panic attacks usually include benzodiazepines and antidepressants. Benzodiazepines are given slowly due to possible side effects, such as dependence, fatigue, slurred speech, and memory loss. Anti-depressant medications for panic attacks include selective serotonin reuptake inhibitors (SSRIs), serotonin noradrenaline reuptake inhibitors (SNRIs), tricyclic antidepressants (TCAs), and MAO inhibitors (MAOIs). SSRIs are generally the first drug used to treat panic attacks. Selected serotonin reuptake inhibitors (SSRIs) and tricyclic antidepressants appear to have a short-term effect.

SSRIs carry a relatively low risk as they are not associated with excessive tolerance or dependence, and are difficult to overuse. TCAs are similar to SSRIs in many of their benefits but come with common side effects such as weight gain and mental disorders. And it is easy to overdo it. MAOIs are generally recommended for patients who have not responded to other forms of treatment.

Although the use of drugs to treat panic attacks may be a great success, it is generally recommended that people have other forms of treatment, such as psychiatric-behavioral therapy. Drug treatment is usually used throughout the duration of symptoms of panic attacks and is discontinued after the patient has had no symptoms for at least six months. It is usually safer to withdraw these medications gradually during treatment. [22] Although drug treatment seems promising to children and adolescents, they are at greater risk of suicide while taking these drugs and their well-being should be monitored closely.

About a third do not respond well to treatment. These people continue to experience anxiety and other symptoms of panic disorder after receiving treatment.

Most people who are treated for panic attacks begin to experience mild symptoms. This panic attack is not very widespread, with less than four physical symptoms found.

It is not uncommon for them to have only one or two symptoms at a time, such as tremors in their legs, shortness of breath, or intense heat waves rising through their bodies, unlike the heat caused by estrogen deficiency. Some symptoms, such as leg tremors, are quite different from any normal sensation of panic disorder. Some of the symptoms listed may occur in people who may or may not have panic disorder. Panic disorder does not require four or more symptoms to occur at the same time. Unnecessary panic and a steady heartbeat are enough to indicate a panic attack.

Mysophobia

The word mysophobia comes from the Greek words μύσος (musos), "filth" and φόβος (phobos), "fear." It is normal and wise to be concerned about such matters as food pollution, exposure to body fluids, and hygiene. However, if you have mysophobia, these common anxiety disorders become more severe and disrupt daily life. Mysophobia, also known as verminophobia, germophobia, germaphobia, bacillophobia, and bacteriophobia, is a pathological fear of infection and infection. The term was coined by William A. Hammond in 1879 when he described a case of obsessive-compulsive disorder (OCD) characterized by repeated hand washing. Mysophobia has long been associated with compulsory hand washing. Words directly related to fear of uncleanness and abnormalities include molysmophobia or molysomophobia, rhypophobia, and rupophobia, while the terms bacillophobia and bacteriophobia refer to fear of germs and viruses in general.

Phobia is often associated with obsessive-compulsive disorder (OCD), but people without OCD can have it. Phobia is believed to be commonplace and can affect people from all walks of life.

This article discusses symptoms, diagnoses, causes, and treatment of mysophobia, and lists some of the things you can do to deal with this type of phobia.

Because people with mysophobia are afraid of infections that can be carried by others, this condition can make people avoid social situations. You may avoid expected gatherings such as work parties, holiday parties, and meetings. If you participate, you may find yourself avoiding physical contact and washing your hands often.

Over time, these behaviors can lead to divorce. Your friends and relatives may not understand, and they may view you as a hostile or confused person. You can develop a social phobia when you start to be afraid to connect with others.

Mysophobia is thought to be related to obsessive-compulsive disorder (OCD). OCD obsessions is repeated, persistent, with unwanted desires or images that cause depression or anxiety. This tendency can be overwhelming if you try to think or do something else.

Obsessions often have themes, such as:
· Fear of infection
· The need for order and balance
· Angry or scary thoughts about hurting yourself or others
· Unwanted thoughts, including anger, or sexual or religious issues

One of the most common symptoms of mysophobia is hand washing, which is also a common symptom of OCD. However, the motive for washing hands is different.

Mysophobia can cause great stress and disruption to your health, but it is important to remember that effective treatment is available. Talking to your doctor is a good place to start, but you can also practice coping strategies on your own that will help relieve stress and anxiety.

Enochlophobia

Enochlophobia is a phobia (irrational fear) of crowds that negatively affects your daily life. Although enochlophobia is not a real mental health problem, this condition causes symptoms similar to other types of anxiety disorders.

Most people are not comfortable in large groups of people. However, if this is true of you, it does not mean that you have enochlophobia. Phobia is an irrational, persistent fear of something that causes a person to avoid the situation as much as possible, or to become very depressed when the situation is unavoidable.

People with enochlophobia may avoid traveling by train, bus, or plane because of overcrowded conditions. They may also avoid going to major cities, events such as concerts or parks, or going out to a restaurant, a theater, or a mall.

Enochlophobia can cause symptoms when you are in a crowd, or even when you are thinking of being in a crowd. Symptoms of the body, which are associated with other types of anxiety disorders, include Sweating, Shivering, Nausea, Chest pain, Shortness of breath, Heart palpitations, Fever or chills, Dizziness, Feeling of impending disaster, Fainting, etc.

The exact cause of enochlophobia is unknown, but this condition may be affected by chemical imbalances of neurotransmitters (such as dopamine and serotonin) in the brain. Phobias can also develop into traumatic experiences in your life or by hearing about the bad things other people do.

Genetics and certain cultural beliefs may play a role in your risk of developing enochlophobia. If you are a depressed person, your attitude may cause you to have enochlophobia.

Mental health conditions are diagnosed using the Diagnostic and Statistical Manual of Mental Disorders, Program Five (DSM-5). Enochlophobia is not included in the DSM-5. However, similar to certain phobias, the DSM-5 describes it as persistent, unreasonable fear of a job, person, object, or situation.

Some phobias are detected using the following methods:

· Extreme, or irrational fear related to being, or thinking, in a particular situation

· Anxiety that has persisted, usually for at least six months

· Fear against the real threat of being in the crowd

· Immediate response to anxiety when expressed in crowds

· Get out of your way to avoid crowds, or tolerate crowded crowds

A variety of treatments are available for enochlophobia, which includes psychotherapy, relaxation / mental training, and sometimes medication.

Psychotherapy, or speech therapy, is an effective treatment for enochlophobia. Another common psychiatric treatment used to treat phobias is psychotherapy (CBT). This type of treatment focuses on identifying patterns of thinking that trigger your irrational fears. Your doctor will teach you how to challenge your thoughts and reduce your symptoms when dealing with your fears.

CBT may include treatment for exposure. This treatment helps you to deal with your fear of crowds in small steps. You might start by thinking about being in a crowd, or looking at pictures of a crowd while using coping techniques to alleviate your anxiety. Eventually, with the help of your therapist, you will work your way up until you become a crowd of people.

Relaxation and mindfulness techniques can help reduce symptoms of anxiety. These can include deep breathing, visualization, guided images, and thought training.

Medication is usually not the first step in treating phobias. However, if your fear of crowds prevents you from engaging in vital day-to-day activities, you may need to seek medical attention.

Benzodiazepines such as Klonopin (clonazepam), Xanax (alprazolam), Valium (diazepam), and Ativan (lorazepam) are the most common types of drugs used to treat phobias. These medicines are taken when you feel your symptoms, or just before you are diagnosed with a condition that causes your symptoms. These drugs are short-lived.

Benzodiazepines should be used with caution. They often cause drowsiness and dysfunction, and people who take them should not drive or do other dangerous activities for a few hours thereafter.

Also, benzodiazepines can cause drug tolerance (when the drugs no longer work as they do), dependence, and the problem of drug use. It may be difficult to stop them even if you have a few days to pick them up, and you may experience unpleasant withdrawal symptoms if you suddenly stop.

In some cases, your doctor may prescribe additional medications that treat anxiety disorders that affect the neurotransmitters in your brain, such as selected serotonin reuptake inhibitors (SSRIs). Common SSRIs are Prozac (fluoxetine), Zoloft (sertraline), Lexapro (escitalopram), Celexa (citalopram), and Paxil (paroxetine).

Enochlophobia is an irrational fear of crowds that can impair your ability to perform everyday activities such as public transportation, running a graveyard, or socializing with friends. This condition causes symptoms of anxiety, such as rapid heartbeat, sweating, and dizziness. A mental health professional such as a psychiatrist can work with you to help you deal with, or overcome, your fears using psychotherapy, coping strategies, and, in some cases, medication.

It may be embarrassing to admit that your fear of crowds can prevent you from seeing your loved ones or completing your daily activities. But help and support are available for you. Consider joining a visible support group if you are not comfortable with crowds and talk to your healthcare provider or doctor about treatment options.

Autophobia

Autophobia, also called monophobia, isolophobia, or eremophobia, is a specific phobia of isolation; the worst fear of self-esteem, or the fear of being alone or isolated. Those with this condition do not need to be physically isolated, but simply believe that they are ignored or unloved. Contrary to what can be defined by the literal reading of a word, autophobia does not define "fear" and is not a fear of cars (despite various cultures abbreviating the car as "auto"). It is often initiated and associated with other anxiety disorders.

Autophobia can be associated with or associated with other phobias, such as agoraphobia, and is generally considered part of the agoraphobic group, meaning it has many of the same characteristics as certain anxiety disorders and hyperventilation disorders. Of particular concern to people with phobias in the agoraphobic collection is their ability to get help in an emergency. This often causes them to fear exposure, mob violence, isolation, or imprisonment.

Autophobia should not be confused with agoraphobia (fear of being in public or being caught in a crowd), self-loathing, or social anxiety, although it may be related to them. It is a distinct phobia that is often accompanied by other anxiety disorders and phobias.

Symptoms of autophobia vary depending on the case. However, there are other symptoms that a crowd of sufferers has. Excessive anxiety and anxiety when you are alone or thinking about situations where you may be alone are one of the most common symptoms of autophobic behavior. People with Down syndrome also believe that a catastrophe is imminent whenever they are left alone. For this reason, autophobes travel long distances to avoid isolation. However, people with this condition often do not need to be alone to feel abandoned. Autophobes will usually be in a crowded place or group of people and feel completely isolated.

There is also some association with the diagnosis of autophobia in people with borderline personality disorders.

Below is a list of other symptoms sometimes associated with autophobia:

· **Psychological symptoms:**

o Fear of fainting

o Disability to focus on anything other than disease

o Fear of losing your mind

o Failure to think clearly

· **Emotional symptoms:**

o Future stress and places where you may be alone

o Fear of being alone

· **Physical symptoms:**

o Bright head, dizziness

o Sweating

o Shivering

o Nausea

o Cold and hot

o Feelings of numbness or stinging

o Dry mouth

o Increased heart rate

o Stability when alone

o Shaking hands and legs

Autophobia can be found in social anxiety. When people with this phobia are left alone, they will often experience liver attacks, which is a common reaction of those with social anxiety. This condition can also be caused by depression because when people become overly resentful, they begin to find certain tasks and tasks that are almost impossible to eradicate. This usually happens when autophobia is exposed to the opportunity to enter a public place where there are many people or just a place that they are uncomfortable or unfamiliar with. This phobia may also be closely related to agoraphobia, leading to lower self-esteem and uncertainty about their ability to complete certain tasks that need to be performed alone. People with this phobia often think of a more serious condition. For example, they may panic and think that they are going to die.

Another experience doctors believe is that leads people to develop this phobia of abandoned children, usually their parents, at a very young age. This onset creates an environment in which children can become emotionally involved as they grow older. This turns into autophobia because they now fear that all the important people in their life will leave them or abandon them. Therefore, this particular phobia can be attributed to the behaviors and experiences these people have experienced while growing up. However, being rejected does not mean that you are left alone physically, this includes financial or emotional separation. Having a difficult, life-changing experience, especially causes more trauma that makes this phobia worse. People with very high anxiety and in this case "very strong," are at greater risk for this phobia.

Although this phobia is usually developed at an early age, it can develop later in life. People sometimes develop this fear of losing a loved one or the end of an important relationship. Autophobia can also be defined as the fear of not being with someone. Traumatic events in a person's life can create this fear of not being around anyone, but this will often lead to fears of confinement.

Autophobia is closely related to monophobia, isolophobia, and eremophobia. However, it differs slightly in the definition. According to the Merriam-Webster Medical Dictionary, eremophobia is a frightening fear of isolation. In contrast, The Practitioner's Medical Dictionary defines autophobia as a morbid dread of being alone or in private.

Autophobia is a type of anxiety that can cause a young child to experience extreme danger or fear when they are alone. There is no specific treatment for autophobia as it affects each person differently. Most people with this condition are treated with psychotherapy when the time for solitude increases slightly. There are no complete studies yet to support any medication used as a treatment. If the anxiety is severe, medication has been used to help the patient continue treatment.

It is not uncommon for affected people to become aware that they have these concerns and to dismiss the idea of seeking help. Like drug abuse, autophobia is psychological and physical and requires help from a medical professional. Medications can be used to stabilize symptoms and prevent further drug abuse. Group and individual treatments are used to help relieve symptoms and treat the phobia.

In mild cases of autophobia, treatment can sometimes be very simple. Therapists recommend many different remedies to make patients feel isolated even when that is the case, such as listening to music while performing tasks alone or turning on the television when you are at home, even if it is loud. Using noise to disturb the peace of isolated situations can often be very helpful to people with autophobia.

However, it is important to remember that just because a person may feel lonely does not always mean that they have autophobia. Many people feel lonely and lonely at times; this is not a rare occurrence. It is only when the fear of loneliness begins to interfere with one's daily life that the idea of being independent becomes a reality.

In the article entitled "Psychogenic Hyperventilation and Death Anxiety" by Herbert R. Lazarus, M.D., and John J. Kostan, Jr., M.S.W., autophobia or monophobia is referred to as being closely related to death anxiety, or a sense of intimacy. destruction. The patient may feel so overwhelmed by autophobia that they may become hyperventilate and feel that they may die of it. It is also noted that patients with hyperventilation and death anxiety may develop or develop autophobia because they are so afraid of death, serious injury, or find themselves in a very serious condition, so much so that they fear death alone. With the exception of someone who will help them if they need it, anxiety caused by autophobia may also occur with other disorders or phobias included in the agoraphobic group.

Ways to help yourself manage agoraphobia

The key to overcoming agoraphobia is to learn to control the symptoms of anxiety and gradually enter into a state of fear.

Seek guidance from your doctor or therapist, but general suggestions for self-help include:

• Breath deeply - inhaling (breathing very fast and not deep) will only make the symptoms worse. Hold your breath carefully. Focus on expanding your abdomen, not your chest, with all the scent.

• Use relaxation techniques - learning to relax may include techniques such as meditation, deep muscle relaxation or regular exercise. You may need to check to find a way to relax or ways that work best for you.

• Find out about your condition - overcoming agoraphobia involves understanding how anxiety affects the mind and body.

• Change your lifestyle - it may help to reduce or avoid caffeine, alcohol, and certain medications. Regular exercise burns stress chemicals and is known to reduce anxiety levels. Consult your physician for more information and advice.

• Gradually increase exposure - this includes dealing with the feared area in a controlled manner. This will help you to see that nothing bad will happen. Usually, you choose the most threatening place first, go with a trusted friend or provider as support, and use a few breathing and other coping strategies you have learned to control your anxiety. With regular practice, fear of the place or situation will subside. This process is also known as systematic desensitization. It is important to have the guidance of mental health professional.

V

Social Anxiety Disorder (SAD)

Social Anxiety Disorder (SAD), also known as social phobia, is a disorder characterized by feelings of fear and anxiety in social situations, resulting in severe depression and the ability to work at least in certain aspects of daily life. This fear may be triggered by a thought or actual observation from others. People with social anxiety are afraid of negative reviews from other people.

Physical symptoms often include excessive shyness, excessive sweating, tremors, palpitations, and nausea. Stuttering may be present, as well as rapid speech. Panic attacks may occur under intense fear and discomfort. Some victims may use alcohol or other drugs to alleviate fear and ban recreational activities. It is common for those with social phobia to receive treatment in this way, especially if they have not been diagnosed, treated, or both; this can lead to alcoholism, eating disorders, or other forms of drug abuse. SAD is sometimes referred to as a missed opportunity when "people make big life decisions to deal with their illness". According to ICD-10 guidelines, the main diagnostic criteria for social phobia are fear of focusing on care, or fear of behaving in a way that will be embarrassing or embarrassing, avoidance, and symptoms of anxiety. Standard measurement scales can be used to assess community anxiety disorders and to measure anxiety severity.

The first line of social anxiety treatment is cognitive-behavioral therapy (CBT). Medications such as SSRIs are effective in social activities, especially paroxetine. CBT is effective in treating the disease, whether it is delivered individually or in a group setting. Psychological and behavioral components seek to change patterns of thought and the body's response to stressful situations. The attention given to the problem of public concern has grown significantly since 1999 with the approval and marketing of their therapeutic drugs. Prescribed drugs include several classes of antidepressants: selective serotonin reuptake inhibitors (SSRIs), serotonin-norepinephrine reuptake inhibitors (SNRIs), and monoamine oxidase inhibitors (MAOIs). Other commonly used drugs include beta-blockers and benzodiazepines.

Written explanations of shame can be traced back to the days of Hippocrates about 400 B.C. Hippocrates described a person as "one who with shame, suspicion, and fear; who loves darkness as life and cannot tolerate light or live in bright places; his hat is still in his eyes, he will not see or be seen. by his goodwill. He never comes with her for fear that she may be abused, humiliated, shot herself in demonstrations or speeches, or sick; he thinks everyone is watching him."

The first mention of the term "social phobia" (phobie des situations sociales) was made in the early 1900s. Psychologists used the term "social neurosis" to describe patients who were very shy in the 1930s. After Joseph Wolpe's great work on systematic resistance, research into phobias and their treatment grew. The notion that social phobia differs from other phobias came from British psychiatrist Isaac Marks in the 1960s. This was approved by the American Psychiatric Association and officially included in the third edition of the Diagnostic and Statistical Manual of Mental Disorders. The definition of phobia was revised in 1989 to allow for interaction and avoidance of human interference and introduced a common social phobia. Social phobia was largely ignored before 1985.

Following the call to action by psychiatrist Michael Liebowitz and psychiatrist Richard Heimberg, there was an increase in attention and research on the disease. DSM-IV gave social phobia another name for "social Anxiety

Disorder". Research on the psychology and social sciences of everyday social anxiety continued. Cognitive-behavioral models and therapies are designed for social anxiety disorders. In the 1990s, paroxetine became the first prescription drug in the US to treat anxiety disorders, and others followed.

Version 10 of the International Classification of Diseases (ICD-10) classifies social anxiety as a mental and behavioral disorder.

Psychological factors or Cognitive aspects

In cognitive models of social disorder, those with social phobias are afraid of how they will present themselves to others. They may feel overwhelmed, overworked, or have high self-esteem. From the point of view of social psychology of self-presentation, the person involved tries to build a positive attitude towards others but believes that they are unable to do so. Many times, before a social situation can cause concern, they may deliberately review what might go wrong and how they can deal with each unexpected case. After the event, they may be tempted to do something unsatisfactory. As a result, they will see anything that may have been considered unusual. These thoughts may extend to weeks or more. Psychiatry is a significant symptom and is studied in CBT (psycho-behavioral therapy). Thoughts tend to be self-destructive and inaccurate. Those with social phobia often translate into neutral or vague conversations with negative attitudes and many studies suggest that people who are socially distressed remember worse memories than those that are less depressed.

An example of this would be a work in progress introducing colleagues. During the presentation, someone may stutter words, at which point he may worry that other people are being too careful and may think that their opinions about him as a presenter are corrupt. This perception of perception promotes additional anxiety which includes stuttering, sweating, and, possibly, panic attacks.

Behavioral factors

Social Anxiety Disorder is an ongoing fear of one or more situations in which a person is exposed to possible tests by others and fears that they may do something or act in a humiliating or embarrassing way. It transcends common "shame" as it leads to extreme social avoidance and serious social or work corruption. Dreaded activities can include almost any form of social networking, especially small groups, dating, parties, talking to strangers, restaurants, chat rooms, etc.

Those with social problems are afraid of being judged by others in the community. In particular, people with social anxiety are afraid in front of people in authority and feel uncomfortable during physical examinations. People with this condition may behave in a certain way or say something and maybe be embarrassed or embarrassed afterward. As a result, they often choose to isolate themselves from society to avoid such situations. They may also feel uncomfortable meeting strangers and acting away when they have large groups of people. In some cases, they can show evidence of this disorder by avoiding eye contact, or blinking when someone speaks to them.

According to psychologist B. F. Skinner, fear is controlled by escape and avoidance habits. For example, a student may leave the room when he is speaking in front of the class (escape) and avoid making oral submissions due to previous anxiety attacks (avoid). Extreme behavioral avoidance may include almost pathology or compulsive lying to maintain your image and avoid judging in front of others. Minor avoidance actions are manifested when a person avoids eye contact and crosses their arms to hide visible vibrations. Fight-or-flight response and configuration for such events.

Physiological aspects

Physiological effects, similar to those in other anxiety disorders, exist in social phobias. In adults, it may cause tears and sweating, nausea, shortness of breath, tremors, and heart palpitations in response to a fight or flight. Disruption of mobility (when a person is so anxious about the way he walks that he loses balance) can be seen, especially when passing a group of people. Blushing is often expressed by people with social phobia. These physical symptoms only intensify the anxiety in front of others. A 2006 study found that the amygdala, part of the limbic system, is extremely active when patients are exposed to a threatening face or to traumatic events. They found that patients with severe social phobia showed a correlation with increased response to their amygdalae. People with SAD may avoid looking at other people, even those around them, to a greater extent than their peers, perhaps reducing the risk of eye contact, which can be interpreted as an invisible signal of openness in social interaction.

Social factors

People with SAD avoid conditions that most people consider "normal". They may have difficulty understanding how others can handle these situations so easily. People with SAD avoid all or most social situations and hide from others, which can affect their personal relationships. Social phobia can completely remove people from social situations because of the irrational fear of these situations. People with SAD may become socially addicted, sleep-deprived, and feel happy when they avoid social interactions. SAD can also lead to low self-esteem, negative thoughts, severe depression, criticism, and poor social skills. People with SAD experience anxiety in a variety of social situations, from important, meaningful interactions, to less important day-to-day activities. These people may feel very insecure about job interviews, dates, dealing with authority, or at work.

SAD shows a high level of exposure to other mental illnesses. In fact, a population-based study found that 66 percent of those with SAD had one or more mental health problems. SAD often occurs in conjunction with low self-esteem and very common clinical depression, possibly due to a lack of personal relationships and long periods of isolation associated with social avoidance. Clinical depression is 1.49 to 3.5 times more likely to occur in those with SAD. Studies have also shown that the presence of certain social fears (e.g., avoidance of small groups, avoidance of a party) is more likely to cause symptoms of depression associated with other social fears, and thus should be carefully researched during clinical trials. among patients with SAD.

Anxiety disorders outside of SAD are also very common in patients with SAD, especially generalized anxiety disorders. An avoidant personality disorder is closely related to SAD, with disease rates ranging from 25% to 89%.

In an effort to alleviate their anxiety and reduce stress, people with social phobia may use alcohol or other drugs, which can lead to substance abuse disorders. It is estimated that one in five patients with anxiety disorders also have alcohol problems.

However, other studies show that SAD is not related, to or protects against alcohol-related problems. Those with both alcohol use disorders and social anxiety disorders are more likely to avoid group-based treatment and re-start compared to people who do not have this combination.

Research into the causes of social anxiety and social phobia is broad, covering many theories from neuroscience to sociology. Scientists have not yet identified the causes. Research suggests that genes may also play a role in integration with environmental factors. Social phobia is not caused by another mental disorder or drug use. Often, social anxiety starts somewhere in one's life. This will increase over time as one struggles to recover. Finally, social ills can develop into symptoms of social anxiety or phobia. The use of inactive social media can cause social anxiety for some people.

It has been shown that there is a two- to three-fold increase in the risk of social phobia if the first relative also has the disorder. This may be due to genetics and/or to children experiencing social stigma and avoidance through observational learning or parenting psychological education. A study of identical twins raised (by adoption) in different families showed that, when one twin had a social concern, the other was between 30 percent and 50 percent above average in developing the disease. To some extent, this "inheritance" may not be clear - for example, research has found that if a parent has any type of anxiety disorder or clinical depression, then the child may have an anxiety disorder or social phobia. Studies suggest that parents of those with social anxiety disorder are more likely to isolate themselves from people (Bruch and Heimberg, 1994; Caster et al., 1999), and shame on adoptive parents is closely related to embarrassment in adopted children (Daniels and Plomin, 1985).

Growing up with overprotective and hypercritical parents has also been linked to community anxiety disorder. Adolescents rated as unprotected (ambivalent-ambivalent) and their mothers as children were twice as likely to develop anxiety disorders as puberty, including social phobia.

A list of related studies investigated 'behavioral restrictions' in newborns - the first symptoms of a restricted and irrational or frightening environment. Studies have shown that about 10-15 percent of people show this attitude, which appears to be due in part to genetics. Some continue to manifest this trait in youth and adulthood and appear to have potential social problems.

Social experiences

Previous negative social experiences can be a cause for fear of social cohesion, perhaps, especially for people at the top of "empathy". For about half of those diagnosed with social anxiety, some traumatic or embarrassing social event, appear to be associated with the onset or spread of the disease; this type of event appears to be particularly related to a particular social phobia, for example, with regard to public speaking (Rememberg et al., 1995). As well as direct experience, watching or hearing about negative social events of others (e.g. faux pas performed by someone), or verbal warnings of social problems and dangers, can also make the development of social anxiety a major concern. Disruption of public concern may be the result of long-term consequences of non-access, exploitation, rejection, or neglect. Shy teenagers or avoidable adults have highlighted unpleasant experiences with peers or child abuse or bullying. In one study, popularity was found to be negatively related to social anxiety, and children who were ignored by their peers reported higher social anxiety and fear of negative assessment than other categories of children. Children who are socially shy seem to be less likely to respond to peer pressure, and children who are distressed or even paralyzed may find themselves isolated.

Cultural influences

Cultural factors associated with a social anxiety disorder include public attitudes toward shyness and avoidance, affecting the ability to build relationships or access to work or education, and shyness. One study found that the effects of parenthood vary from culture to culture: American children appear to be more likely to develop social anxiety disorder if their parents emphasize the importance of others' opinions and use stigma as a disciplinary measure (Leung et al., 1994), but this organization has not found children. Chinese / Chinese-American. In China, studies have shown that shy children are more accepted than their peers and are more likely to be considered leaders and to be considered competent, unlike those found in Western countries. Statistical variables can also play a role.

Problems in developing social skills, or 'social stigma', may be the cause of some social disruption, the inability or lack of confidence to communicate with the community, and the response and acceptance of others. These courses are mixed, however, some subjects do not find major problems in social skills while others have problems. What seems clear is that social activists see their social skills as inferior. It is possible that the increasing demand for complex social skills in building relationships or activities, as well as emphasizing assertiveness and competitiveness, exacerbates social anxiety problems, at least among the 'middle classes. Personal or media emphasis on 'normal' or 'attractive' personal traits has also been argued as fueling perfection and feelings of inadequacy or self-doubt about the improper evaluation of others. The need for public acceptance or standing in public has been articulated in other research lines related to community concerns.

Remedies

Although alcohol initially relieves social phobia, excessive alcohol abuse can impair the symptoms of social phobia and cause panic attacks to increase or worsen during alcoholism and especially during alcoholism. This effect is not limited to alcohol but can also occur with long-term use of drugs that have the same effect on alcohol as benzodiazepines which are sometimes prescribed as antiretrovirals. Benzodiazepines have anti-anxiety properties and may be helpful in the temporary treatment of major anxiety. Like anticonvulsants, they are usually mild and well-tolerated, although there is a risk of addiction. Benzodiazepines are usually administered orally to treat anxiety; However, sometimes lorazepam or diazepam may be given intravenously to treat anxiety.

The World Council of Anxiety does not recommend benzodiazepines for the long-term treatment of anxiety due to a list of problems associated with long-term use including tolerance, mental retardation, mental and memory impairment, physical dependence, and benzodiazepine withdrawal syndrome when discontinued. benzodiazepines. Despite the increasing focus on the use of antidepressants and other agents in the treatment of anxiety, benzodiazepines have remained a mainstay of anxiolytic pharmacotherapy due to its strong efficacy, rapid onset of therapeutic effect, and profile of adverse side effects in general. The therapeutic patterns of psychotropic drugs appear to be stable over the past decade, and benzodiazepines are the most widely used drug for panic disorder.

Many people who are addicted to alcohol or who have been given benzodiazepines when told that they have a choice between ongoing mental illness or quitting and recovering from their symptoms decide to abstain from alcohol or their benzodiazepines. Symptoms may worsen temporarily, however, during alcohol withdrawal or benzodiazepine withdrawal.

Psychological factors

Research has shown the role of 'basic' or 'unconditional beliefs' (e.g., "I cannot") and 'conditional' beliefs around the area (e.g., "If I show myself, I will be rejected"). They are thought to have developed on the basis of personality and bad knowledge and are made to work when a person feels threatened. Recent research has also highlighted those conditional beliefs may be playful (e.g., "If people see that I'm worried, they'll think I'm weak").

The second aspect is secrecy, which includes the concealment of an individual's true identity or beliefs. One line of work focuses on the key role of anxiety in the present. The resulting stressful situations seem to interfere with community functioning and the ability to focus on interaction, which in turn creates many social problems, and reinforces the wrong schema. Another highlight was high concentration and anxiety about the symptoms of anxiety themselves and how they might be seen by others. The same model emphasizes the development of distorted personal representation and over-consideration of the opportunities and consequences of negative assessment, as well as the levels of performance of others. Such models of mental behavior consider the role of biased memories of the past and the processes of thunder after an event, as well as horrible expectations before it.

The study also highlighted the role of covert avoidance and defensive traits, and showed that efforts to avoid dreaded testing or the use of 'safety behaviors' (Clark & Wells, 1995) can make public communication more difficult and worsen over time. . This work has contributed to the development of Cognitive Behavioral Therapy for social anxiety disorder, which has been shown to be effective.

There are many studies investigating the neural foundations of social anxiety disorder. Although specific neural mechanisms are not yet available, there is evidence related to public concern for imbalances in other neurochemicals and dysfunction in other areas of the brain.

Neurotransmitters

Sociology is closely related to dopaminergic neurotransmission. In a 2011 study, a direct relationship was found between the volunteers' social status and the binding of dopamine D2 / 3 receptors in the striatum. Other studies show that the binding of dopamine D2 receptors in the striatum of people with social anxiety is lower than in controls. Other studies show abnormalities in dopamine transporter density in the striatum of those with social anxiety. However, some researchers have not been able to replicate previously found evidence of dopamine abnormalities in social anxiety disorder. Studies have shown a wide range of social concerns in Parkinson's disease and heart disease. In a recent study, social phobia was detected in 50% of patients with Parkinson's disease. Some researchers have found symptoms of social phobia in patients treated with dopamine antagonists such as haloperidol, which underscore the role of dopamine neurotransmission in social anxiety disorder.

Other evidence suggests that social anxiety disorder may involve reduced binding of the serotonin receptor. Recent research reports that it has increased serotonin binding activity in psychotropic-naive patients with generalized social anxiety disorder. Although there is little evidence of abnormalities in serotonin neurotransmission, the limited efficacy of drugs that affect serotonin levels may indicate the role of this mechanism. Paroxetine, sertraline, and fluvoxamine are three FRI-approved SSRIs to treat community anxiety disorders. Some researchers believe that SSRIs reduce the activity of the amygdala. There is also a growing focus on other candidate transmitters, e.g. norepinephrine and glutamate, which may be extremely effective in social anxiety, and the inhibitory transmitter GABA, which may not function properly in the thalamus.

Areas of the brain

The amygdala is part of the limbic system associated with the fear of understanding and emotional learning. People with social anxiety disorder have been diagnosed with a hypersensitive amygdala; for example in relation to indicators of social threats (e.g. negatively thought-out tests by another person), angry or hostile faces, and when waiting to give a speech. Recent studies have shown that another area of the brain, the anterior cingulate cortex, which is already known to be involved in physical pain experiences, also appears to be involved in 'social pain' experiences, for example, to detect group discharge. . Recent research has also highlighted the powerful role of the prefrontal cortex, especially its dorsolateral component, in maintaining the cognitive bias involved in SAD. A 2007 meta-analysis also found that people with social anxiety had hyperactivation in the amygdala and insula areas that are often associated with fear and negative emotional processing.

ICD-10 defines social phobia as the fear of being judged by other people that leads to the avoidance of social conditions. Symptoms of anxiety may present as complaints of dizziness, trembling of the hand, nausea, or urgency of micturition. Symptoms may extend to panic attacks.

Standardized measurement measures such as the Social Phobia Inventory, SPAI-B, Liebowitz Social Anxiety Scale, and the Social Interaction Anxiety Scale can be used to assess social anxiety disorders and to measure anxiety severity.

DSM-5 defines Social Anxiety Disorder as marking, or severe, fear or anxiety of social situations in which a person may be tested individually.

Diagnostic criteria for DSM-5 with diagnostic features:

1. A noted fear or concern about one or more social situations in which a person is exposed to a potential test by others. Examples include social media (e.g., having a conversation, meeting strangers), being seen (e.g., eating or drinking), and acting in front of others (e.g., giving a speech). Note: For children, anxiety should occur in peer settings and not just when interacting with adults.

2. The person fears that he or she will act in a way or show signs of anxiety that will be negatively assessed (i.e., humiliating or embarrassing: will lead to rejection or annoyance to others). When confronted with such a situation, a person fears that he or she will be mistreated. A person is worried that they will be considered anxious, weak, insane, stupid, boring, intimidating, dirty, or unpopular. A person is afraid that he or she will act or appear in a certain way or show signs of anxiety, such as trembling, trembling, sweating, stumbling over someone's words, or staring, which will be looked down upon by others.

3. Social conditions almost always cause fear or anxiety. Therefore, a person who has only occasional anxiety in a public setting will not be diagnosed with a social anxiety disorder. Note: In children, fear or anxiety may be expressed through crying, irritability, coldness, tightness, dizziness, or difficulty speaking in social situations.

4. Social conditions are avoided or tolerated with great fear or anxiety. Otherwise, situations are tolerated by intense fear or anxiety.

5. Fear or anxiety is not equated with the real threat posed by social and social status. Fear or anxiety is considered to be contrary to the real risk of negative testing or to the results of such negative tests. Sometimes, anxiety may not be judged as extreme, because it is related to real danger (e.g., bullying or harassment by others). However, people with social anxiety disorder often overdose on the negative effects of social conditions, so the clinic determines that it is out of proportion.

6. Fear, anxiety, or avoidance persists, usually lasting 6 months or more. This time limit helps to distinguish common social disturbances and fears, especially between children and the community. However, the duration requirement should be used as a general guideline, permitted with a certain degree of flexibility.

7. Fear, anxiety, or avoidance causes significant clinical stress or deterioration in social, work, or other important areas of work. Fear, anxiety, and avoidance should significantly disrupt a person's normal routine, performance or education, or social activities or relationships, or should cause significant clinical stress or deterioration in the community, workplace, or other important areas of work. For example, a person who is afraid to speak in public will not be diagnosed with a social anxiety disorder if this function is not regularly met at work or in-class work, and if that person is not very depressed about it. However, if one avoids, or is passed, the job or education that one really needs because of the symptoms of social anxiety is met.

8. Fear, anxiety, or avoidance is not the result of the physical effects of something (e.g., addiction, medication) or any other health condition.

9. Fear, anxiety, or avoidance is not best explained by the symptoms of other mental disorders, such as mental disorders, physical disorders, or autism spectrum disorders.

10. If another health condition (e.g., Parkinson's disease, obesity, damage due to burns or injuries) is present, fear, anxiety, or avoidance is clearly unrelated or exacerbated.

When fear is limited to speaking or playing in public it is only a function of public concern disorder.

A different diagnosis

The DSM-IV procedure stated that a person cannot get a diagnosis of social anxiety disorder if their symptoms are better calculated by one of the autism spectrum disorders such as autism and Asperger syndrome.

Because of its close association with scattered symptoms, treating people with social phobia can help to understand basic communication and other mental disorders. Social anxiety disorders are often associated with bipolar disorder and attention deficit hyperactivity disorder (ADHD) and some believe they have a serious cyclothymic-anxious-sensitive disposition. The association between ADHD and social phobia is very high, especially if SCT symptoms are present.

Prevention of anxiety disorder is one of the main focuses of the study. The use of CBT and related methods may reduce the number of children with community anxiety disorder after the completion of prevention programs.

Psychotherapies

First-line treatment for community anxiety disorder is psychotherapy (CBT) with drugs such as serotonin reuptake inhibitors (SSRIs) selected for use only for those who have no interest in treatment. Self-help based on CBT principles is second-line treatment.

There is some emerging evidence of the use of Acceptance and commitment therapy (ACT) in the treatment of social anxiety disorders. The ACT is considered to be a traditional CBT sprout and emphasizes the acceptance of unpleasant symptoms rather than the ones you are struggling with, as well as adaptation - the ability to adapt to changing circumstances, to change one's perception of things, and to balance competing desires. ACT may be useful as a second-line treatment for this condition in cases where CBT is ineffective or rejected.

Some studies have suggested that community skills training (SST) can help with community anxiety. Examples of community-based SST skills for community anxiety issues include: initiating conversations, establishing friendships, communicating with members of the preferred sex, and building speech and advocacy skills. However, it is unclear whether strategies and specific community skills training is required, other than support for normal social functioning and exposure to social conditions.

Given the evidence that social anxiety disorders may predict the subsequent growth of other mental illnesses such as depression, early diagnosis and treatment are essential. Social anxiety disorders are still less recognized in primary care, and patients often present for treatment only after the onset of problems such as clinical depression or substance abuse disorders.

Selected serotonin reuptake inhibitors (SSRIs), a class of antidepressants, are the first-line treatment for generalized social phobia but second-line treatment. Compared with older types of drugs, there is less risk of tolerance and dependence on SSRI-related medications.

Paroxetine and paroxetine CR, Sertraline, Escitalopram, Venlafaxine XR, and Fluvoxamine CR (Luvox CR) are all approved for SAD, and all work on it, especially paroxetine. All SSRIs are effective in some public concerns other than placebo-equivalent fluoxetine in all clinical trials. Paroxetine has been able to change personality and greatly increase conversion.

In a 1995 double-blind placebo-controlled study, SSRI paroxetine was shown to have a clinically significant effect on 55% of patients with generalized social anxiety disorder, compared with 23.9% of those taking a placebo. An October 2004 study found similar results. Patients were treated with fluoxetine, psychotherapy, or placebo. The first four sets saw improvement in 50.8 percent to 54.2 percent of patients. Of those assigned to receive a placebo, 31.7% received a 1 or 2 rating on the Clinical Global Impression-Improvement scale. Those who sought both treatment and medication did not see any improvement. In double-blind, placebo-controlled trials some SSRIs such as fluvoxamine, escitalopram, and sertraline showed a decrease in symptoms of social anxiety, including anxiety, allergic reactions, and hostility. Citalopram also seems to work well.

Common side effects are common in the first few weeks when the body becomes accustomed to the drug. Symptoms may include headache, nausea, insomnia, and changes in sexual behavior. The safety of treatment during pregnancy has not yet been established. By the end of 2004 much media attention was given to the proposed link between the use of SSRIs and suicide [a term that includes suicidal ideation and suicide and suicide attempts]. For this reason, [although the source of the evidence between SSRI use and actual suicide has not been shown] the use of SSRIs in depressive pediatric cases has now been identified by the Food and Drug Administration as authorizing a warning to parents of children with SSRIs prescribed by a family physician. Recent research shows no increase in suicide rates. These tests, however, represent those who are diagnosed with depression, not those with social anxiety disorders.

In addition, studies show that more social patients treated with antidepressants develop hypomania than non-phobic controls. Hypomania can be seen as a drug that causes a new problem.

Other prescription drugs are also used if other methods do not work. Prior to the introduction of SSRIs, monoamine oxidase inhibitors (MAOIs) such as phenelzine were commonly used to treat community anxiety. Evidence continues to show that MAOIs are effective in treating and controlling social anxiety disorders and are still in use, but often as a last resort, due to dietary concerns, possible adverse drug interactions, and the recommendation for multiple doses daily. A new form of the drug, reversible inhibitors of monoamine oxidase subtype A (RIMAs) as the drug moclobemide, binds backward to the MAO-A enzyme, significantly reducing the risk of hypertension with tyramine intake. However, RIMAs have been found to be less effective in the public health problem than MAOIs that are not reversible like phenelzine.

Benzodiazepines are one of the SSRIs. Recommended use of these medications is for short-term relief, meaning over a period of more than a year, of severe anxiety, or disability. Although benzodiazepines are still restricted to long-term daily use in some countries, there are concerns about the development of drug tolerance, dependence, and substance abuse. It has been suggested that benzodiazepines be considered only for people who fail to respond to other medications. Benzodiazepines increase the action of GABA, a major neurotransmitter that blocks the brain; results usually begin within minutes or hours. In most patients, tolerance increases rapidly in the sedative effects of benzodiazepines, but not in the anxiolytic effects. Prolonged use of a benzodiazepine may cause physical dependence, and sudden discontinuation of the drug should be avoided due to the high risk of withdrawal symptoms (including tremors, insomnia, and in rare cases, fainting). The gradual decrease in the dose of clonazepam (reduction of 0.25 mg every 2 weeks), however, is well tolerated in patients with social anxiety disorders. Benzodiazepines are not recommended as monotherapy in patients with severe depression in addition to social anxiety and should be avoided in patients with a history of drug use.

Certain anticonvulsant drugs such as gabapentin are effective in treating anxiety and may be an alternative to benzodiazepines.

Serotonin-norepinephrine reuptake inhibitors (SNRIs) such as venlafaxine have shown similar efficacy in SSRIs. In Japan, Milnacipran is used in the treatment of Taijin fufufu, a Japanese variant of social anxiety disorder. The rare antidepressants mirtazapine and bupropion have been studied to treat general anxiety disorder, and they provide mixed results.

Some people with a form of social phobia called performance phobia have been helped by beta-blockers, which are widely used to control high blood pressure. They are taken in low doses, regulate the physical manifestation of anxiety, and can be taken before social work.

The novel treatment method has been developed recently as a result of translation research. It has been shown that the acute dosing combination of d-cycloserine (DCS) and exposure treatment facilitates the effects of social phobia exposure treatment. DCS is an old antibiotic used to treat tuberculosis and has no side effects per second. However, it acts as an agonist in the glutamatergic N-methyl-D-aspartate (NMDA) receptor, which is important for learning and remembering.

Kava-kava has also attracted attention as a possible treatment, although there are concerns about safety. Social anxiety disorder is known to occur at a young age in most cases. Fifty percent of sufferers are older by 11 years, and 80% by 20 years of age. and other psychological conflicts.

When frequency estimates were based on the evaluation of clinical samples of psychiatric disorders, social anxiety disorder was considered to be a relatively uncommon disorder. The opposite was found to be true; community anxiety was common, but many were afraid to seek psychological help, leading to a misunderstanding of the problem.

The National Comorbidity Survey of more than 8,000 American writers in 1994 revealed a frequency of 12 months and a lifetime of 7.9 percent and 13.3 percent, respectively; this makes it the third most commonly post-traumatic stress disorder with alcohol use, as well as the most common anxiety disorders. According to US epidemiological data from the National Institute of Mental Health, social phobia affects 15 million American adults in any given year. Rates vary between 2 percent and 7 percent of U.S. adults

The initial rate of social phobia is 10 to 13 years. Starting after 25 years is not uncommon and is preceded by panic attacks or major depression. Social anxiety disorders occur more often in women than in men. The prevalence of social phobia seems to be growing among white, married, and educated people. As a group, those with a common social phobia are less likely to graduate from high school and are more likely to rely on government financial support or to have lower incomes. A 2018 study shows that young people in England, Scotland, and Wales have a 0.4 percent, 1.8 percent, and 0.6 percent prevalence, respectively. In Canada, the prevalence of reported social anxiety among Nova Scotians 14-year-olds was 4.2 percent in June 2004 with women (4.6 percent) reporting more than men (3.8 percent). In Australia, social phobia is the 8th and 5th leading illness of men and women between the ages of 15 and 24 from 2018. Because of the difficulty in separating social phobia from social skills or shyness, some subjects have a greater distance. spread. The table also shows the highest increase in Sweden.

It is also called anthropophobia, meaning "fear of man", from the Greeks: άνθρωπος, ánthropos, "man" and φόβος, phóbos, "fear". Other names include interpersonal relation phobia. A form of Japanese culture is known as taijin kyofusho.

Anthropophobia

Anthropophobia is fear of people. It is not an official clinical diagnosis. Many experts consider this condition to be a form of phobia. People with anthropophobia feel very nervous or anxious when they think of being with other people. Unlike other social anxiety disorders, anthropophobia is a fear of the people themselves, not social conditions.

Anthropophobia is not a clinical disorder in the Diagnostic and Statistical Manual of Mental Disorders (DSM-5), but many people consider it a certain fear.

Like other phobias, anthropophobia involves intense anxiety that is not equal to the real threat. Most people with certain phobias know that fear is absurd. But they have difficulty controlling the symptoms or thoughts that are disturbing, and frightening.

Anthropophobia may be part of social anxiety, but the two names are not exactly the same. People with a social problems feel very stressed in social situations, such as going on a date or talking to a waiter. People with anthropophobia feel afraid of people, regardless of the situation.

Social phobia (sociophobia) is the original term for social anxiety disorder. A person with a social anxiety disorder may not feel anxious when he is in a crowd where no one knows him. But a person with anthropophobia feels anxious in any crowd. Their fears are directed at the people, not at the social settings.

Anthropophobia and other phobias are more common in adolescents and women. About 1 in 5 teens develops some type of phobia at some point. About 1 in 10 adults has some form of phobia in their life.

Anthropophobia does not always have a clear cause. You may be more likely to develop anthropophobia if you have experienced or experienced it: Betrayal from loved ones, Family history of anxiety disorders, Hormonal imbalances, and problems with the adrenal glands (glands that produce stress hormones).

Many people with anthropophobia experience "anxiety disorders." Expected anxiety is fear, anxiety, or fear of an upcoming event. With anthropophobia, people may be extremely anxious before being among other people. They may worry about: Judging others, Looking., Looking into the eyes.

This anxiety often causes physical symptoms. People may have Shortness of breath or shortness of breath (dyspnea), Flaky skin, Nausea or vomiting, rapid heartbeat or heartbeat, Sweating, Shivering, or tremors.

Anthropophobia does not have specific clinical diagnostic guidelines. However, your healthcare provider may detect the symptoms of anthropophobia by asking:

· Do the same social conditions always cause fear or anxiety?

· Does avoiding people interfere with your daily activities?

· Has the anxiety lasted six months or more?

Sometimes, fear of people is a symptom of another diagnosis, such as a disorder of social anxiety. Anthropophobia may also be closely related to genetic taijin. Taijin kyofusho is the stress or fear of relationships between people, especially the fear of offending others. Cultural-specific diagnoses are found in Korea and Japan.

There is no cure for anthropophobia. But, for most people, the symptoms get better with treatment. For some, fear of man diminishes enough to no longer interfere with daily life.

There is no specific treatment for anthropophobia. Some treatments for certain phobias can help:

• **Exposure therapy** is usually the first treatment for certain fears. Up to 90% of people who regularly use exposure to symptoms experience symptoms of weight loss. Exposure to therapy involves the gradual introduction of certain fears into your life. You may imagine yourself sharing with others. Later, you may get used to being around small groups of people.

• **Cognitive Behavioral therapy (CBT)** involves talking to a therapist about symptoms. You learn to recognize the wrong thoughts and replace them with the wrong ones. CBT may not be as effective as a treatment for exposure in people with severe phobia symptoms.

• **Hypnotherapy** involves directed relaxation and concentration. The provider directs you to a state of concentration so that you are temporarily unaware of your surroundings. Hypnotherapy often increases the effectiveness of phobia treatment.

• **Medication** may be helpful in anxiety disorders or other forms of anxiety. For example, you could take diazepam (Valium®) or alprazolam (Xanax®) before certain events to avoid panic attacks (severe, sudden anxiety that causes physical symptoms). Medication is not for everyone, so talk to your healthcare provider before starting a new medication.

People with anthropophobia can also learn relaxation techniques. Practicing these techniques can help you to reduce anxiety, especially if you are exposed to your fears. You can:

• Exercise, such as making 20 jugs when you feel anxious.
• Reflect or use targeted photo techniques to control pressure.
• Practice breathing techniques.

There is no guaranteed way to prevent anthropophobia. If you are struggling with anxious thoughts or behaviors, healthy habits can help reduce the severity of your symptoms. You can:

• Avoid dehydration by drinking plenty of water and reducing alcohol and caffeine.
• Eat whole grains, lean proteins, healthy fats, fruits, and vegetables.
• Exercise regularly.
• Sleep for at least seven to eight hours a night.
• Talk to your loved ones regularly to reduce the risk of social isolation.

With proper treatment, many people find that the symptoms of anthropophobia improve. Without treatment, anthropophobia can increase your risk:

• Emotional disorders, such as anxiety or depression.
• Social withdrawal or isolation.
• Drug abuse, including alcohol or drugs.

You may want to ask your healthcare provider:

• What may be the cause of anthropophobia?
• What are some ways I can practice at home to overcome the fear of man?
• How can I prevent the symptoms from getting worse?
• Will the fear of man ever disappear?

Anthropophobia is fear of people. It is not the same as a social anxiety disorder. Instead of fearing social situations, people with anthropophobia fear people directly. Anthropophobia can also cause physical symptoms, such as rapid heartbeat, sweating, or nausea. If fear of people interferes with your daily life, talk to your healthcare provider. Treatment may include medical treatment, medication, or home remedies.

Scopophobia

Scopophobia, scoptophobia, or ophthalmophobia is an anxiety disorder characterized by a frightening fear of being seen in public or being stared at by others.

Similar phobias include erythrophobia, fear of embarrassment, and fear of epilepsy, which can lead to such attacks. Scopophobia is also often associated with schizophrenia and other mental illnesses. Often, scopophobia will lead to common symptoms and other anxiety disorders. Scopophobia is considered a social phobia and a specific phobia.

The word scopophobia comes from the Greek word σκοπέω skopeō, "look to, examine", and φόβος Phobos, "fear". Ophthalmophobia comes from the Greek word ὀφθαλμός ophthalmos, "eye".

People with scopophobia often show symptoms in social situations where attention is brought to them like public speaking. There are other factors that cause public concern. Other examples include Introduction to young people, ridicule and/or criticism, easy embarrassment, and even answering a cell phone in public.

Often scopophobia will lead to common symptoms and other anxiety disorders. Symptoms of scopophobia include nausea, panic attacks, panic attacks, rapid heartbeat, shortness of breath, nausea, dry mouth, tremors, anxiety, and avoidance. Other symptoms associated with scopophobia may include hyperventilation, muscle spasms, dizziness, uncontrollable tremors or tremors, excessive eye-watering, and redness of the eyes.

Although scopophobia is a problem in itself, many people with scopophobia also experience other anxiety disorders. Scopophobia is associated with other irrational fears and phobias. Certain phobias and syndromes such as scopophobia include erythrophobia, panic attacks (especially found in teens), and fear of epilepsy, which may trigger such attacks. Scopophobia is also often associated with schizophrenia and other mental illnesses. It is not considered a symptom of other illnesses, but rather a psychological disorder that can be treated independently.

Sociologist Erving Goffman has suggested that just looking at the street is one of the most significant symptoms of a mental illness in the community. Many patients with scopophobia develop habits of voyeurism or exhibitionism. Another related, but very different disease, scopophilia, is an obsession with pornography.

Scopophobia differs from phobias in that the fear of being viewed as a social phobia and a specific phobia, because it is a specific phenomenon that occurs in the public sphere. Many phobias usually fall into one category or another but scopophobia can be classified as both. On the other hand, like most phobias, scopophobia usually results from a traumatic event in a person's life. With scopophobia, the person may have been ridiculed as a child. Additionally, a person with scopophobia may be subject to social scrutiny, perhaps because of a physical disability.

Psychoanalytic theories

Building on Freud's perception of the eye as a natural environment, psychologists have linked scopophobia with fear (suppressed) viewing, as well as visual impairment. Freud also referred to scopophobia as "fear of the evil eye" and "the work of looking at and criticizing oneself" during his "eye" research and "I's conversion."

In some definitions, the equation of observation and the feeling of criticism or contempt reveals shame as a motivating force behind scopophobia. In adolescence, with your awareness of More like the appearance of a mirror, embarrassment may increase the feelings of erythrophobia and scopophobia.

There are many options for treating scopophobia. In one way or another, the patient is monitored for a long time and describes his or her feelings. The hope is that the person will be exhausted to be diagnosed or find the root of their scopophobia.

Exposure treatment, another commonly prescribed treatment, has five steps:

· Testing
· Feedback
· Developing fear leadership
· Exposure
· Structure

In the testing phase, a person with a scopophobic can explain his or her fears to a therapist and try to determine when and why this fear started. The response phase is when the therapist offers treatment for phobia. The stage of fear is then developed, when a person creates a list of situations that involve his or her fears, each one getting worse and worse. Exposure involves exposure to the conditions and conditions of their fear category. Finally, construction is where the patient, relaxed in one step, moves on to the next.

Like most health problems, support groups exist for people who like to know nothing. Being around other people who are experiencing similar problems can often create a more comfortable environment.

Other suggested treatments for scopophobia include hypnotherapy, neuro-linguistic programming (NLP), and energy psychology. In severe cases of scopophobia, the subject may be given medication to combat anxiety. Medications may include benzodiazepines, antidepressants, or beta-blockers.

Phobias have a long history. The concept of social phobias was named as far back as 400 B.C. One of the earliest ways to describe the scopophobia of Hippocrates was about a man who was extremely shy, explaining that such a person "loves darkness as light" and "thinks everyone sees him."

The term "social phobia" (phobie sociale) was coined in 1903 by French psychiatrist Pierre Janet. She used the term to describe her patients who showed fear of being watched as they participated in daily activities such as speaking, playing the piano, or writing.

In 1906 the journal Alienist and Neurologist described scopophobia: Then there is the fear of being seen and embarrassed, one sees in the shelters. [...] We called it scopophobia - a terrifying fear of appearance. To a lesser extent, it is a horrible shame, and the patient covers his face with his hands. To a large extent, the patient will avoid the visitor and run away from his or her eyes where possible. Scopophobia is more common in women than in men.

Later in the same paper (page 285), scopophobia is defined as the "fear of seeing people or being seen, especially strange faces"

Social anxiety disorder (formerly referred to as 'social phobia') was officially recognized as a distinct phobic disorder in the mid-1960s (Marks & Gelder, 1965). The term 'social anxiety disorder' reflects current understanding, which includes diagnostic literature, and is used throughout the guide. As set out in the International Classification of Diseases, 10th Revision (ICD-10) (World Health Organization, 1992) and the Diagnostic and Statistical Manual of Mental Disorders, 4th Edition Text Revision (DSM-IV-TR) (American Psychiatric Association). , 2000) Disruption of social anxiety is an ongoing fear of one or more social situations in which embarrassment is possible and the fear or anxiety is greater than the real threat posed by social status as determined by human cultural practices. Ordinary social situations can be grouped into those that involve interaction, observation, and performance. This includes meeting people including strangers, speaking at meetings or groups, initiating conversations, talking to officials, working, eating or drinking in public, going to school, shopping, public appearances, using public toilets, and social activities including talking. . Although anxiety about some of the above is common for most people, people with a social problem may be overly concerned about it and may do so weeks before the expected social status. People with social anxiety are afraid that they will say or do (spontaneously or otherwise) something they think will humiliate or embarrass them (such as nausea, sweating, shivering, looking anxious, or appearing boring, stupid, or inappropriate). Whenever possible, people with a social problems will try to avoid their most frightening situations. However, this does not always happen, and they will have to put up with the situation, often with feelings of the great depression. This condition will often cause serious damage to the community, workplace, or another workplace.

Children may express their concerns differently from adults. As well as the decline in interaction, they may cry out loudly or 'shut up or have behavioral outbursts such as irritability. They may also be less likely to admit that their fears are unfounded when they are away from social status. Some situations that may cause difficulties for troubled children in the community and for young people include participating in-class activities, asking for help in class, activities with peers (such as team sports or attending parties and clubs), participating in school sports, and discussing community challenges.

There are no UK epidemiological surveys that directly report social anxiety data in adults; However, the prevalence of social anxiety disorders has been included in a large population study in some western European countries, the US, and Australia. Frequency ratings vary, with many variations due to differences in the tools used to obtain the diagnosis. However, it is clear that social anxiety disorder is one of the most common causes of all anxiety disorders. Up to 12% of life-long recurrence rates were reported (Kessler et al., 2005a) compared with lifelong recurrence rates in other 6% of anxiety disorders due to general anxiety, 5% panic disorder, and 7% of post-traumatic stress disorder. (PTSD) and 2% obsessive-compulsive disorder (OCD). Twelve monthly rates of up to 7% have been reported due to community concerns (Kessler et al., 2005b). Using strict conditions and face-to-face interviews in the US, lifetime and annual frequency statistics decrease by half to 5% and 3% respectively (Grant et al., 2005b), but they are still more common than severe autoimmune conditions. (rheumatoid arthritis, ulcerative colitis, Crohn's disease, systemic lupus erythematosus, type I diabetes, multiple sclerosis, uveitis, hypothyroidism, and hyperthyroidism) are included (American Autoimmune Related Diseases Association, 2011). Data from the National Comorbidity Survey reveals that social anxiety disorder is the third most common mood after major depression and alcohol dependence (Kessler et al., 2005a).

Women and men have an equal chance of seeking treatment for social anxiety, but social studies indicate that women are more likely to have this condition (Kessler et al., 2005a). Turk and colleagues (Turk et al., 1998) reported that in the clinical sample women feared multiple social conditions and received high scores on a series of social anxiety measures. So it seems that although women are more likely to have social anxiety, men are more likely to seek treatment and do so with worse symptoms.

Social levels of social anxiety disorder in children and adolescents have been investigated in a number of countries. As in adult studies, a variety of diagnostic methods have been used, which may explain a wide range of frequency measurements. A large New Zealand study reported that 11.1% of 18-year-olds experienced conditions of social anxiety (Feehan et al., 1994). However, a large British Epidemiological Survey (Ford et al., 2003) reported that only 0.32% of 5- to 15-year-olds had the disorder, a higher rate than PTSD, OCD and bipolar disorder. , but lower than the severity of anxiety disorders, specific phobia and general anxiety disorders. Diagnosis rates in this British study were higher in men than in women and increased slightly with age. A large US-based study reported very similar rates for 9- to 11-year-olds (Costello et al., 2003), with a German study rate of 4% for 14- to 17-year-olds (Wittchen et al.., 1999b).

Social anxiety disorder usually begins in childhood or adolescence. Among people seeking treatment as adults the first middle years ranged from early to mid-teens when most people first became ill before reaching the age of 20. However, there is a small group of people who improve the situation in later life. Some people may be able to see a time when the social anxiety disorder started and they may associate it with a particular event (for example, moving to a new school or being bullied or teased). Some may describe themselves as always shy and see their social upheaval as a slow, but noticeable, increase in their anxiety as they approach or approach other people. Some may never be able to recall a time when they were free from social anxiety.

Several studies (Bruce et al., 2005; Reich et al., 1994a; Reich et al., 1994b) followed adults with long-term social anxiety disorder. These studies have often found that it is a chronic condition for which there is no treatment. For example, Bruce and colleagues (2005) reported a community study in which adults with various anxiety disorders were followed for 12 years. At the beginning of the study, people had been suffering from social anxiety for 19 years. Over the next 12 years, 37 percent recovered, compared with 58% of GAD and 82% of non-agoraphobia.

Long-term studies with children, although less frequently than in adults, have confirmed that anxiety disorders are more likely to start in adolescence, and this, in particular, is a social anxiety disorder. However, there is evidence that some young people who are anxious in society will overcome this condition (although they maintain a higher risk for other anxiety disorders) (Pine et al., 1998). Putting the lessons together for adults and children, it seems that a large number of people who experience a social anxiety disorder in adolescence may recover before becoming adults. However, if the social anxiety disorder persists into adulthood, the chances of recovery in the absence of treatment are slim compared to other common psychiatric disorders.

Four-fifths of adults with a primary diagnosis of community anxiety will experience at least one mental illness at some point in their lives (Magee et al., 1996). In adults, social anxiety disorders are more likely to be accompanied by other anxiety disorders (up to 70%), followed by any emotional disorders (up to 65%), nicotine dependence (27%), and substance abuse disorders (approximately 20%). %). (Fehm et al., 2008; Grant et al., 2005b). As social anxiety disorders have a very short onset, many of these concomitant conditions develop in the following. Interestingly, comorbid anxiety predicts poor treatment outcomes for people with bipolar affective disorder and major depressive disorder (Fava et al., 2008; Simon et al., 2004) and 25% of people presenting in the first episode of psychosis are social. . anxiety disorder (Michail & Birchwood, 2009), however the link to this in clinical practice has been overlooked. When people experience conditions of social anxiety disorder and other anxiety disorders, social anxiety comes first in 32% of the population; in individuals with social anxiety and related disorders or substance abuse, social anxiety preceded these combined conditions in 71% and 80%, respectively (Chartier et al., 2003); and for people who present with severe depression and social anxiety, the episode of depression may be secondary. This may indicate general etiology or depression about how social anxiety disorders prevent a person from seeing his or her full potential, or it may be an indication of different high-risk events. Another study of adult inpatients who presented treatment for social anxiety found that 53% had a previous episode of depressive disorder, with an average number of episodes being 2.2 in the 33-year-old group. Similarly, problems with drug abuse can arise from people's initial attempts to control their public concern about alcohol and drugs. Of course, the relationship between social anxiety disorder and other clinical conditions can work in a different way. For example, some people with scars and/or other physical problems in a PTSD situation may develop a social anxiety disorder when they worry about how they will appear to other people. Some people who normally have confidence in the community may experience social anxiety during the depression and recover when stress arises. The picture is the same in adolescence: comorbidity is 40% of anxiety disorders, 40% of affective disorders, and 16% of substance abuse (Ranta et al., 2009); in one large German study of young people (up to 24 years) social anxiety preceded an additional diagnosis of anxiety in 64.4% of people, a diagnosis of emotional distress at 81.6% and a diagnosis of substance abuse at 85.2% (Wittchen et al., 1999b).

There is also an important level of comorbidity between social anxiety disorders and certain personality disorders. The most common is avoidant personality disorder (APD), and about 61% of adults seeking treatment for social anxiety also experience behavioral disorders (Sanderson et al., 1994). However, there is controversy over the significance of these findings. There is a significant discrepancy between the processes of social anxiety disorder and APD, and some experts view APD as a difficult variation of social anxiety. As more people develop a social anxiety disorder in childhood, some researchers have argued that most associations with APD are caused by a chronic anxiety disorder. However, research studies have succeeded in identifying a few factors that often distinguish people with a social anxiety disorder from those with social anxiety disorder and APD. These include interpersonal problems, particularly problems of intimacy, increased work disability, and low levels of social support (Marques et al., 2012), although the differences have not been repeated. Whatever the relationship between social anxiety disorder and APD, there is some evidence that effective psychological treatment of social anxiety also reduces the incidence of APD (Clark et al., 2006; McManus et al., 2009a). Similarly, Fahlen (1995) reported that abnormal personality traits decrease with effective drug treatment. With the exception of APD, rates of illness and other personality disorders are lower and not higher than other anxiety disorders or depression.

Among children and adolescents, the comorbidity of anxiety disorders is also very high, as is the comorbidity between anxiety and emotional and behavioral disorders (Ford et al., 2003). The specific comorbidities of social anxiety in this age group are not well investigated, but in a large sample of young people (14- to 24-year-old), Wittchen and colleagues (1999b) found that 41.3% of those with a social status disorder were also diagnosed. had a diagnosis of substance abuse (including nicotine), 31.1% emotional disturbances, and 49.9% other anxiety disorders (compared to 27.9%, 12.1%, and 20.8% of participants without a diagnosis of social disorder, respectively). Social anxiety is a major predictor of nicotine use in adolescence (Sonntag et al., 2000). In some individuals, social anxiety may be expressed as a bias (Viana et al., 2009).

Social anxiety disorders should not be confused with general embarrassment, which can be associated with disability and disruption in many areas of life. Educational achievement can be underestimated, with people at high risk of dropping out of school early and obtaining poor qualifications (Van Ameringen et al., 2003). Another study (Katzelnick et al., 2001) found that people with a general public anxiety disorder had a salary of 10% less than people without a clinic. Naturally, public life is disabled. On average, people with social anxiety disorder have fewer friends and have greater difficulty meeting friends (Whisman et al., 2000). They are less likely to marry, less likely to divorce, and less likely to have children (Wittchen et al., 1999a). Fear of the public can interfere with many daily activities, such as visiting shops, shopping for clothes, cutting hair, and using the telephone. Most people with social anxiety problems are employed; however, they report taking longer days at work and are less productive because of their symptoms (Stein et al., 1999b). People may avoid or leave jobs that involve making presentations or playing games. The proportion of people who receive state benefits is 2.5 times higher than the average adult population. Katzelnick and colleagues (2001) also report that community anxiety disorders are associated with outpatient medical visits.

People with a social anxiety disorder differ greatly in the amount and type of social status they fear and the number and range of outcomes feared. These two factors (feared conditions and feared consequences) may differ independently. For example, some people are afraid of one or two situations but have many feared consequences (such as, 'I will feel bored', 'I will sweat', 'I will look unworthy', 'I will be ashamed', 'I will look stupid' or 'I will look worried'). Some may fear many situations but have only one feared effect (such as 'I will be ashamed'). In view of this diversity, researchers have considered whether it might be helpful to divide social anxiety disorders into subtypes. A few minor typos have been suggested, some of which are described as side effects (fear of blinking, fear of sweating, etc.). The most common differences are between general social anxiety disorders, where people fear multiple social conditions, and rare social anxiety disorder, where people fear moderate conditions (often, but not always, involving activities such as public speaking.); However, some authors have suggested that the differences between these subtypes vary in degree. The typical subtype is associated with severe disability and high levels of comorbidity and other mental disorders (Kessler et al., 1998). A typical subtype with a strong family connection, early years, and a never-ending course. Although many psychiatric therapies are used in both subtypes, drug treatment trials focus on general social anxiety disorders.

Like many mental health disorders, the development of social anxiety disorders is probably best understood as an interaction between several different biopsychosocial factors (Tillfors, 2004).

Genetic factors appear to play a role, but genes may influence the likelihood of developing anxiety or depression rather than improving social anxiety in particular. Higher rates of social anxiety disorder are reported in relatives of people with this condition than relatives of non-patients, and this effect is stronger in the less common type (Stein et al., 1998a). Further evidence of genetic predisposition comes from twin studies. Kendler and colleagues (1992; 1999) found that when one twin was affected, the chances of another twin being affected were higher if the twins were monozygotic rather than sharing only 50% of their dizygotic genes. However, genetic variation is only 25 to 50%, indicating that environmental factors also play a significant role in the development of the condition in most people.

Depressive social events at an early age (e.g., bullying, family abuse, social embarrassment, or a person's empty mind during social work) are often reported by people with a social anxiety disorder (Erwin et al., 2006). Parental modeling of fear and avoidance in social contexts and an extremely protective child-rearing style are both linked to the development of the situation in some studies (Lieb et al., 2000).

The effectiveness of selective serotonin reuptake inhibitors (SSRIs), serotonin and noradrenaline reuptake inhibitors (SNRI), and monoamine oxidase inhibitors (MAOIs) in the treatment of social anxiety disorders suggests that serotonin and dopamine system dysfunction may also affect neurotrans play a role but lessons that. establishing a relationship that causes such disruption in the development of the situation has not yet been reported.

Neuroimaging studies have so far suggested different activation of specific parts of the brain (amygdalae, insulae, and dorsal anterior cingulate - all structures involved in stress management) when threatening motives were introduced compared to healthy volunteers.

Go to:

Recognition of social anxiety disorders in adults, children, and adolescents by general practitioners (GPs) is often poor. The problem of undiagnosed anxiety disorders has recently been highlighted by evidence that the prevalence of PTSD is less pronounced in primary care (Ehlers et al., 2009). In part, this may be due to physicians who do not recognize the disease, a general lack of understanding of its magnitude and complexity, and a lack of clearly defined care options. But it may also be due to the lack of knowledge by service users about its existence, their avoidance of talking about the problem, and discrimination.

The early years and the consequences of academic achievement mean that the recognition of the social anxiety disorder in educational institutions is also problematic. Along with failure, children with a social problems may be victims of bullying and ridicule. Teachers and other education professionals may have limited knowledge of how to identify and supervise the management of this condition.

In primary care, many service users report being misdiagnosed as having a 'pure' depression. Loss of diagnosis may also occur in secondary care if sufficient history has not been taken. This is a huge omission because having comorbidity has treatments and side effects.

Despite the level of suffering and disability, about half of adults with the disease have ever sought treatment, and those who usually seek treatment after 15 to 20 years of symptoms (Grant et al., 2005a). Possible explanations of low levels and delays include people who think social anxiety is part of their personality and cannot be changed (or in the case of children, that they will grow up with it), lack of awareness of the situation by health professionals, discrimination. of mental health services, fear of negative reviews by a health care professional, general lack of information about access to effective treatment, and limited access to services in many areas.

Randomized controlled trials (RCTs) are a key way to determine if a treatment is effective. People diagnosed with community anxiety disorder are randomly assigned to treatment under investigation or in a controlled setting. Tests are performed before treatment / control and after treatment / control. Treatment is considered successful if the most significant improvement is seen in the medical condition rather than the control condition. In order to determine whether treatment-acquired improvement is maintained, participants should be properly monitored long after the end of treatment.

RCTs are the best way to deal with threats to internal fitness (for example, 'is the improvement seen as a result of treatment or does it happen anywhere?'). However, they did not respond well to threats to external eligibility (for example, 'were the results obtained with a selected group of participants who were researched in general RCT for many people with a social anxiety disorder?'). For this reason, it is helpful if data from the RCT is supplemented with data from large groups of relatively unselected individuals receiving the same treatment.

Researchers traditionally distinguish between specific and indirect treatment effects. A particular therapeutic effect refers to the amount of progress that is made from the unique characteristics of a particular treatment. The indirect therapeutic effect refers to the amount of improvement that results from the common features of all (or most) well-functioning therapies.

In RCT intervention interventions the main difference is always between the active drug and the placebo. The placebo controls for the indirect effects of seeing a competent doctor, having regular monitoring symptoms, finding a sound medical basis, and taking a tablet. Thus the comparison between an active drug and a placebo is an indication of the specific therapeutic effect of a particular chemical. Since many chemicals have side effects, some of them serious, it is generally accepted that the drug must show some effect in order to be approved for use. However, it is important to note that users of the service are likely to show significantly greater improvement than the effect of the active drug compared to the size of the placebo effect because providing a placebo also produces another indirect benefit.

Randomized controlled trials (RCTs) are a key way to determine if treatment is effective. People diagnosed with community anxiety disorder are randomly assigned to treatment under investigation or in a controlled environment. Tests are performed before treatment / control and after treatment / control. Treatment is considered successful when significant improvement is seen in the medical condition rather than the control condition. In order to determine whether the treatment-acquired improvement is maintained, participants should be properly monitored long after the end of treatment.

RCTs are the best way to deal with threats to internal fitness (for example, 'does improvement appear as a result of treatment or does it happen anywhere?'). However, they did not respond well to external eligibility threats (for example, 'are the results obtained with a select group of participants routinely evaluated RCT in most people with a social anxiety disorder?'). For this reason, it is helpful if data from the RCT is supplemented with data from large groups of relatively unselected individuals receiving the same treatment.

Researchers traditionally distinguish between specific and indirect treatment effects. A particular therapeutic effect refers to the amount of progress that is made with the unique features of a particular treatment. Indirect treatment effect refers to the amount of improvement that results from the common (or most) of the most effective treatments.

In RCT interventions the main difference is always between the active drug and the placebo. The placebo controls the indirect effects of seeing a competent physician, having regular monitoring symptoms, finding the right medical basis, and taking a tablet. Thus the comparison between an active drug and a placebo is an indication of the specific therapeutic effect of a particular chemical. Since many chemicals have side effects, some of which are very serious, it is generally accepted that the drug must show some effect in order to be approved for use. However, it is important to note that users of the service are likely to show significantly greater improvement than the effect of the active drug compared to the size of the placebo effect because providing a placebo also produces another indirect benefit.

The fact that drug RCTs almost always focus exclusively on evaluating specific treatment outcomes, while psychiatric RCTs may focus on testing a specific type, indirect, or both types of outcome, means that caution should be exercised compared to the findings of such tests. . In a good country, it should be possible to determine the effectiveness of each type of treatment against the controls of certain outcomes and the overall benefit of treatment (compared to non-treatment). The network meta-analysis (NMA) that supports this guideline attempts to provide such information by looking at how medications will be effective without treatment even though most drug RCTs use placebo controls and do not include a waiting list (no treatment).

The following section describes various psychological and drug interventions that have been tested for the effectiveness of community anxiety disorder.

In the mid-1960s, when social anxiety disorder was officially recognized as a distinct phobic disorder (Marks & Gelder, 1965), psychosocial evidence-based interventions for anxiety disorders involved frequent exposure to phobic stimulation in thought. The first RCTs of community-based psychosocial interventions used two alternatives to this method (systemic depression and flooding) and found modest improvement. However, in anxiety disorders often the treatment of perceived exposure was quickly replaced by the treatment that involved addressing a feared motivation in real life. Marks (1975) published a seminal review arguing that real-life ('in vivo') exposure is more effective than hypothetical exposure. This review has had a significant impact on the work of treatment development in all anxiety disorders. Consequential behavioral interventions and consideration of social anxiety disorders have focused on strategies that involve addressing real-life situations and social situations, to a greater or lesser degree.

Exposure in vivo is based on the idea that avoiding dreadful situations is one of the key factors in maintaining social anxiety. Treatment involves creating a series of scary situations (from the smallest to the most feared) and encouraging the person to expose themselves more often, starting with less frightening situations and moving on to more difficult situations as self-esteem grows. Exposure tests include coping with real-life social situations with emerging roles as well as out-of-office tests during treatment sessions and formal home-based activities. Many people with social anxiety find that they are unable to completely avoid social ills and often try to tackle them by holding (for example, by not talking about them, being quiet or being on the edge of a group) or otherwise avoiding the inside. situation. For this reason, exposure therapists spend a lot of time identifying subtle, inherent avoidance patterns (behaviors of seeking safety) and encouraging a person to do the opposite during treatment.

Used rest is a special type of relaxation training aimed at teaching people how to relax in the same social situations. Starting with training on continuous muscle relaxation, treatment takes people through a series of steps that enable them to relax where they feel in everyday situations. The final stage of treatment involves a deep practice in applying relaxation techniques to real-life social situations.

Social skills training is based on the assumption that people are concerned about social conditions in part because they are lacking in their social ethics records and need to develop these songs in order to behave effectively and get positive results in their interactions with others. Treatment involves formal training in non-verbal communication skills (e.g., eye contact, friendly listening posture, etc.) and verbal communication skills (e.g., how to start a conversation, how to give constructive feedback, how to ask questions that encourage conversation, etc.). The skills identified by the therapist are often repeated over and over again by the important role during treatment and home-based activities. Research has failed to support the view that people with social anxiety do not know how to behave in social situations. In particular, there is little evidence that they show a lack of social skills when they are not worried. Any performance deficit appears to be severely limited in cases where they are anxious, suggesting that it is a response to anxiety rather than an indication of a lack of knowledge. However, community-based therapists argue that practicing appropriate skills when you are anxious is a useful way to improve self-confidence in social situations.

Psychological reorganization is an integrated approach to a variety of multidisciplinary therapies and has also occasionally been used alone, although this has often been part of a research study to evaluate the number of different components of complex interventions. The therapist works with the person to identify the fearsome key thoughts they experience in disturbing social situations, as well as other common beliefs about social interactions that may trigger those thoughts. The person is then taught many ways of speaking in order to produce different, less stressful thoughts ('logical answers'), and is encouraged to practice expectations, and during social interactions. To facilitate this process, they regularly fill out records of thoughts, which are discussed with therapists during treatment sessions. Some doctors argue that it is not necessary to fully believe the correct answer before they begin to repeat it in frightening situations (Marks, 1981).

Behavioral interventions include a variety of well-recognized and hand-led methods including behavioral psychotherapy (CBT). However, many psychological behavioral interventions include in vivo exposure and psychological reorganization. Other programs also include specific training in relaxation techniques and/or communication and communication skills training. In recent years, research studies have found a few mechanisms that seem to maintain public concern over avoidance behavior. This includes personal attention, distorted images, and the harmful effects of self-destructive behavior, including how it alters people's behavior. Other psychological interventions include strategies aimed at addressing these additional conservation factors, for example, outdoor focus training and/or work-focused attention, the use of video feedback to correct your distorted images, and the display of unhelpful safety effects. - wanting to behave. CBT can be delivered in individual or group format. When presented in a group format, other team members are often recruited to play roles and exposure tests. Sessions typically take 2 to 2.5 hours with six to eight people in a group and two therapists. If CBT is delivered in each format, therapists may need to identify other people who may occasionally join treatment sessions to play a role.

Cognitive therapy (CT) developed by Clark and Wells (1995) is based on a model of social anxiety disorder that specifically emphasizes: (a) the negative beliefs that people with social anxiety have about themselves and social interactions; (b) misconduct; and (c) problematic cognitive and behavioral processes that occur in social contexts (self-focused attention, safety-seeking behavior). Developed a different type of CT that directly targeted the care features mentioned in the model. The therapies used in the treatment are superior to some of the procedures used in the latest CBT programs, so CT can be officially considered as an alternative to CBT. However, it is distinguished from most CBT programs for community anxiety disorders in that it takes a different approach to exposure (with less emphasis on repetition and so on in increasing inconsistent evidence) and does not use mind records. Instead, the key components of treatment are: building each version of Clark and Wells' (1995) model using user service ideas, images, and behaviors; an exercise experience where self-esteem and safety behaviors are altered to reflect your negative effects; video response, and still images to correct your negative distorted images; observation training without external focused assessment; ethical testing in which a person assesses certain predictions about what will happen in public situations when he or she relinquishes his or her safety behavior; racist training and memory writing to deal with memories of past social ills.

Treatment is usually given individually. However, there is a need for the therapist to be able to invite other people to participate in role-playing games within the session. It is not uncommon for a therapist and a person with a social anxiety problem to also leave the office to check their behavior in the real world during a treatment session. This is easier to do when the times are 90 minutes than the usual 50 minutes.

Interpersonal psychotherapy (IPT) was originally developed as a treatment for depression but was replaced by Lipsitz and colleagues (1997) for use in the community anxiety disorder. Treatment is built within a broad biopsychosocial perspective where climate trends interact with current and post-mortem health to initiate and maintain social anxiety disorders. There are three stages of treatment. In the first stage, a person is encouraged to see the social anxiety disorder as an illness that must be addressed, rather than as a sign of weakness or inadequacy. In the second stage, the therapist works with the individual to solve specific interpersonal problems, especially in the areas of role change and role conflicts, but sometimes with grief. Emphasis is placed on role-playing games that promote emotional expression and effective communication. People are also encouraged to build a social network that includes closer relationships and trust. In the final stage, the therapist and the person review the progress, address the end of the therapeutic relationship, and prepare for challenging situations and information in the future. The duration is usually 50 to 60 minutes for each treatment.

Psychodynamic psychotherapy recognizes the symptoms of social anxiety as a result of a conflict of fundamental relationships based largely on early experiences. Treatment is intended to help a person recognize the link between conflicts and symptoms. The medical relationship is the central vehicle for understanding and change. Specific interventions link symptoms of social anxiety disorder to the underlying theme of human conflict. Leichsenring and colleagues (2009a) consider that in the case of social anxiety the main theme of conflict involves three components: (1) desire (for example, 'I wish to be reassured by others); (2) the expected response from others (e.g., 'others will humiliate me'); and (3) feedback from me (for example, 'I'm scared to reveal myself'). Supportive interventions include suggestions, reassurance, and encouragement. Clients are encouraged to expose themselves to dreaded social situations outside of treatment sessions. Informative internal discussions are also encouraged.

Psychological training is a psychological intervention that has evolved from Buddhist culture and encourages people to find psychological distractions and negative thoughts and feelings, viewing them as observers, rather than focusing on them. Treatment begins with general education about social stress and anxiety. Participants then went to weekly groups where they were taught how to meditate. Formal meditation exercises for at least 30 minutes a day using audio cassettes for guidance are also recommended.

Several different drug interventions have been used to treat community anxiety, many of which were initially developed as antidepressants. The antidepressants used to treat social anxiety disorders come from four different classes: SSRIs, SNRIs, noradrenaline, and selected serotonin antagonists and MAOIs. The fifth class, tricyclic antidepressants (TCAs), were also used in the past but this is no longer the case.

SSRIs began to be marketed in the 1980s, developing as a career-tracking agent for TCAs and MAOIs. They are thought to act by increasing serotonin concentration in the brain and, after obtaining licenses for major depression, many pharmaceutical companies are conducting additional studies showing their effectiveness in social anxiety and other anxiety disorders. The only SNRI that has been extensively studied is venlafaxine and it is possible that its effects on social anxiety disorders are only mediated by changes in serotonin at commonly prescribed doses.

MAOI prevents the breakdown of noradrenaline, dopamine, serotonin, melatonin, tyramine, and phenylethylamine. This effect is not limited to the brain and affects other parts of the body rich in monoamine oxidase (MAO), for example, the intestines. Therapeutic effects on social anxiety disorder are also thought to be related to increased levels of serotonin and dopamine in the brain. However, MAO inhibitors may result in potentially harmful interactions with foods containing tyramine that may result in episodes of dangerously high blood pressure. This risk is greatly reduced by moclobemide as it is 'reversible' - this means that when there are other compounds, moclobemide 'deplets the enzyme'. As a result, the moclobemide prescription book comes with fewer dietary restrictions than older MAOIs, such as phenelzine. MAOIs are now rarely determined because of their perceived risks.

Benzodiazepines are limited by the fact that it is best not to take them for long periods of time due to possible tolerance and dependence. In addition, they may confuse some of the most common illnesses like PTSD with depression.

Finally, alpha2delta calcium gated channel blockers, like pregabalin, reduce neuronal sensitivity but it is not clear at all why these should work when some anticonvulsants do not have known therapeutic effects on social anxiety.

Social anxiety disorder poses significant economic costs to individuals, their families and caregivers, and the community, as a result of work disability, academic failure, job loss, social corruption, severe financial dependence, and quality of life. These costs are much higher for those with depressive disorders, which are more common in people with social anxiety: 50 to 80 percent of people with social anxiety who present to health services have at least one other attitude, often another anxiety disorder, depression, or depression. drug use disorders (Wittchen & Fehm, 2003).

A UK study by Patel and colleagues (2002) examined the economic effects of social anxiety disorders, health services and society as a whole using information from the Adult Psychiatric Morbidity Survey conducted in England in 2000 (Singleton et al., 2001). People with social anxiety were less likely to belong to the highest social and economic group and had lower levels of employment and household income compared to those without mental illness. With regard to the use of health care services and related costs, people with community anxiety are estimated to receive an annual health care cost of approximately £ 609 per person, resulting from GP visits, inpatient and outpatient care, home visits, and counseling. Annual losses due to illness amounted to £ 441 per employee with public concern, while annual social security benefits per person with public concern amounted to £ 1,479. The cost of health care and social benefits were higher for people with social anxiety where the illness situation was higher compared to those with social anxiety problems.

In comparison, people without mental illness receive a typical annual cost per person of £ 379 per health service, £ 595 associated with loss of productivity, and £ 794 related to social security benefits (prices 1997/98).

By relaying information to 100,000 people attending primary care services, Patel and colleagues (2002) estimate that the total cost of health care for social anxiety disorders can be more than £ 195,000 a year, the cost of primary care alone is estimated at £ 49,000. Extensive costs, such as public safety benefit claims, were expected to reach £ 474,000.

Another study from the Netherlands (Acarturk et al., 2009) measured service utilization and costs incurred by individuals with both social and subthreshold anxiety disorders using data from a national mental health survey. Expected costs include direct medical costs associated with mental health services (e.g., GP visits, psychiatric appointments, hospital days), specific non-medical expenses (e.g., transportation for service users, parking, waiting time, and treatment), and production. loss. The annual cost per person with a community anxiety disorder was € 11,952 (2003 prices), much higher than the cost per capita for a person without mental illness at € 2,957. However, when costs are adjusted for stressful situations, the average annual cost of social anxiety is reduced to € 6,100. For those with subthreshold social disorder, the average annual cost is estimated at € 4,687. Other costs that fall into other areas such as education and social services were not considered in the study.

In addition to the deterioration of this condition, social anxiety disorders are often unknown and can be effectively treated with limited information on the impact of the disease on human resources, the health sector, or society (den Boer, 1997; Jackson, 1992; Ross, 1991). Also, given its early onset and incurable condition, the cost of living for an untreated individual is significant due to the negative impact on production (Lipsitz & Schneier, 2000).

A detailed review of the costs of social anxiety disorders has shown that the economic costs associated with poor access to education, social corruption, working disability, and poor quality of life may be greater than the direct costs of direct health care. Every 10 points on the Liebowitz Social Anxiety Scale (LSAS), earnings decreased by 1.5 to 2.9%, and college graduates dropped by 1.8%. However, most of these economic costs have not been calculated on inflation (Lipsitz & Schneier, 2000).

In short, social anxiety disorders are associated with a list of indirect and tangible costs associated with declining productivity, social corruption, and declining quality of life. On the other hand, the general cost of health care incurred by people with a social anxiety disorder compared with those with other anxiety disorders indicates less use of health care services by these individuals. Higher costs compared to other groups are usually caused by compliance with conditions such as depression and alcoholism. Although the costs due to social anxiety disorder vary widely across studies, countries, and groups, they are still significantly lower than the costs associated with other anxiety disorders. This is understandable given the main problem, which is community avoidance.

7 Social Anxiety Disorder-Related Diseases

Comorbidity in Social Anxiety Disorder (SAD) refers to having more illness than SAD. Having SAD increases your risk of developing another disease, and makes treatment more difficult.

Many problems are related to social anxiety disorder (SAD), including other problems of anxiety, depression, and depression.

Avoidant Personality Disorder

If you have avoidant Personality Disorder (APD), you will get many of the same symptoms as someone with SAD. However, your symptoms will be much wider and more severe. There is an overlap between the two disorders, which means you may be diagnosed with APD and social anxiety disorder.

One of the main defining characteristics of avoiding the disorder that often does not occur at the same rate in SAD is the lack of trust in the motives of others.

Panic Disorder

The panic disorder differs from SAD in that it causes panic attacks, the type of symptoms present, and beliefs about the underlying causes. You may be diagnosed with both dementia and social anxiety disorder, and treatment may be the same or different for both diseases.

Although people with panic disorder and social anxiety disorder may share similar patterns of avoidance and experience some of the same types of symptoms, the main difference is that people with panic disorder often feel better in front of a trusted friend, while this may result. those with SAD feel more anxious.

Generalized Anxiety Disorder

If you suffer from Generalized Anxiety Disorder (GAD), your anxiety is often broader and more general, rather than focusing on social or work conditions. You may be concerned about money, your job, global warming, family problems, or many other things. Your anxiety may keep you awake at night and may turn into physical symptoms such as headaches or migraines.

Depression

Depression is an emotional disorder that includes ongoing feelings of sadness and loss of interest. It is different from the mood swings that people experience as a part of life.

Major health events, such as the loss of a job or the loss of a job, can lead to depression in a Reliable Source. However, doctors consider only the feelings of grief as part of the depression if it persists.

Depression is an ongoing problem, not a temporary one. Contains episodes in which the symptoms last for at least 2 weeks. Depression can take weeks, months, or even years.

There is an established link between depression and social anxiety — if you find out you have SAD, you are more likely to develop depression later in life.

In addition, people who suffer from both depression and social anxiety often seek help for depression, although they may have had major social anxiety for many years.

Alcoholism

If you have a social problem, you are more likely to suffer from alcoholism. People with SAD often start drinking to cope — but in the end, drinking becomes a problem in itself. If you have both social anxiety and alcoholism, treatment should be tailored to your unique situation to address both problems.

Alcohol, in general, is any alcohol that leads to significant mental or physical health problems. Because there is disagreement on the meaning of the word alcohol addict, it is not a well-known diagnostic business. The most common diagnostic stages are alcohol use disorder (DSM-5) and alcohol dependence (ICD-11); these are described in their sources.

Excessive alcohol consumption can damage all organs, but it mainly affects the brain, heart, liver, pancreas, and immune system. Alcohol abuse can lead to mental illness, depression, Wernicke-Korsakoff syndrome, irregular heartbeat, immune system function, liver failure, and increased risk of cancer. Drinking during pregnancy can cause damage to the fetus's alcohol spectrum. Women are often more sensitive than men to the harmful effects of alcohol, largely because of their low body weight, low alcohol metabolism, and high body fat content. For a few people, prolonged, severe alcohol abuse ultimately leads to mental retardation and blunt dementia.

Genetics and genetics are two factors in the risk of alcohol addiction, with about half of the so-called risk. Depression and related disorders, including anxiety, are important factors in the development of alcohol as alcohol consumption can temporarily reduce dysphoria. A person with a parent or sibling who has a substance abuse problem has three or four times the risk of developing alcoholism himself, but only a few do. Environmental factors include social, cultural, and moral influences. High levels of stress and anxiety, as well as the low cost of alcohol and easy access, increase the risk. People may continue to drink in part to prevent or improve withdrawal symptoms. After a person stops drinking, he may have a low rate of withdrawal that lasts for months. Medically, alcoholism is considered to be a physical and mental illness. The questionnaire is often used to identify potential intoxication. More information is then collected to confirm the diagnosis.

Prevention of alcohol abuse can be tried by reducing the experience of depression and anxiety in individuals. Attempts can be made to regulate and limit the sale of alcohol (especially for children), to charge alcohol to increase their costs, and to provide education and treatment.

Alcohol treatment may take several forms. Because of possible medical problems during withdrawal, alcohol withdrawal should be carefully controlled. Another common practice involves the use of benzodiazepine drugs, such as diazepam. These can be taken when they are admitted to a health care facility or individually. Medications of acamprosate, disulfiram, or naltrexone may be used to help prevent further drinking. Mental illness or other addictions can be difficult to treat. Different types of individual or group treatments or support groups are used to try to prevent the person from relapsing. One group of supporters is Alcoholics Anonymous.

Prolonged misuse of alcohol can also lead to many mental health problems. Major cognitive problems are common; about 10 percent of all dementia cases are related to alcohol consumption, making it the second leading cause of dementia. Excessive alcohol consumption causes damage to brain function, and mental health can be severely affected over time. Social skills are severely impaired in people with alcoholism due to the neurotoxic effects of alcohol on the brain, especially the prefrontal cortex of the brain. Communication skills affected by alcohol abuse disorders include impaired visual acuity, prosody, vision problems, and mental retardation; the sense of humor is also impaired by people who abuse alcohol. Psychiatric disorders are more common in people with alcoholism, as many as 25 percent also have severe mental disorders. The most common psychological symptoms are anxiety and depression. Psychiatric symptoms are usually worse at the time of cessation of alcohol, but they usually improve or disappear with continued self-control. Psychosis, confusion, and cerebral palsy may be caused by alcohol abuse, which can lead to a misdiagnosis such as schizophrenia. Panic disorder can worsen or worsen as a direct result of long-term alcohol abuse.

The combination of major depressive disorders and alcoholism is well documented. For those with traumatic events, a distinction is often made between depressing episodes of alcohol-induced alcoholism ("substance-indused"), and major depressant and non-self-deprecating episodes ("independent" episodes). Excessive use of certain drugs may increase the risk of depression. Mental illnesses vary according to gender. Women with alcoholism often have a combination of psychological factors such as major depression, anxiety, panic disorder, bulimia, post-traumatic stress disorder (PTSD), or borderline personality disorder. Men with alcohol abuse often have a concomitant diagnosis of narcissistic or antisocial personality disorder, bipolar disorder, schizophrenia, impulse disorder, or attention deficit hyperactivity disorder (ADHD). Women with alcohol abuse are at greater risk of physical or sexual assault, abuse, and domestic violence than women in the community, which can lead to higher levels of mental disorders and alcohol dependence. Attitudes and social attitudes can create barriers to the diagnosis and treatment of alcoholism disorders. This is a bigger barrier for women than men. Fear of discrimination may cause women to deny that they have a health condition, to hide their drinking, and to drink alone. This pattern leads to family, doctors, and others less likely to suspect that a woman they know is having an alcohol problem. Conversely, reducing the fear of stigma may lead men to admit they have a certain disease, show off their drinking in public, and drink in groups. This pattern leads families, doctors, and others to suspect that the man they know is a person with a substance abuse problem.

Eating Disorders

Social anxiety disorders and eating disorders, such as anorexia nervosa, bulimia nervosa, and binge eating disorders can sometimes be found together. Fear of public eating is a common symptom, but the types of behavior and motives are very different.

Eating disorders are serious conditions related to persistent eating habits that negatively affect your health, emotions, and ability to function in important areas of life. The most common eating disorders are anorexia nervosa, bulimia nervosa, and binge-eating disorder.

Many eating disorders include overexertion, weight gain, and diet, which can lead to poor eating habits. These behaviors can greatly affect your body's ability to get proper nutrition. Eating disorders can damage the heart, the digestive system, bones, teeth, and mouth, and cause other diseases.

Dietary disorders are more likely to occur in adolescence and adolescence, although they may also develop into other years. With treatment, you can return to healthy eating habits and sometimes reverse the serious problems caused by eating disorders.

Schizophrenia

Although comorbid SAD and schizophrenia have received little attention, there is some evidence of an increased risk of social anxiety among those with schizophrenia. For those with schizophrenia and SAD, the quality of life can be reduced.

If you are diagnosed with social anxiety and other comorbid disorder, your doctor will determine the best course of treatment to manage the complex interaction between your symptoms.

Schizophrenia is a dangerous mental disorder in which people misinterpret the truth. Schizophrenia may cause a combination of hallucinations, delusions, and extremely disturbed thinking and behaviors that interfere with daily functioning, and may be disabling.

People with schizophrenia need lifelong treatment. Early treatment can help control symptoms before serious problems arise and can help improve long-term vision.

Social Anxiety Disorder is a common mental health condition. Symptoms include intense fear of certain social situations, fear of ridicule, and a strong desire to avoid social situations.

If it is severe or untreated, this condition can be debilitating. However, with effective interventions - which may include oral therapies, medications, or both - people can significantly improve their quality of life.

While the research to better understand the causes of social anxiety disorders is still ongoing, another study involves a small brain structure called the amygdala. The amygdala is believed to be the central nervous system that controls responses to fear.

Social anxiety disorder is diagnosed. In fact, first-degree relatives have two to six times the potential to develop a social anxiety disorder. A study supported by the National Institute of Mental Health (NIMH) also identified genetic predisposition in mice that had been studied. Scientists are exploring the idea that increased sensitivity to dissociation may be based on physical or hormonal support. Some researchers are investigating the influence of the environment on the development of a social phobia. Child abuse and hardship are dangerous aspects of social anxiety disorder.

VI

List of A -Z Most Common Phobias with a brief note

Fear is a dangerous situation that is normal. Phobias, however, transcend common fears and are irrational. Fear can be an animal, an object, a place, or a situation. Often the source of fear does not pose a real threat or danger, but a person is overwhelmed with fear anyway.

People with certain phobias will do everything they can to avoid what causes their fears, even when doing so severely disrupts their daily lives. When confronted with their phobia, they will experience severe anxiety, which is sometimes debilitating.

This article introduces 12 of the most common types of phobias and a list of all the phobias (currently known) that people may experience. Remember that if a person experiences diagnostic procedures for a particular phobia, he or she is living with a mental health condition that may need treatment.

There is no single cause of anxiety disorders like phobias, but experts believe that it is caused by a combination of genes and environmental factors. For example, children with a family history of anxiety disorders and stressful living conditions at an early age are at greater risk for specific phobias. People who develop a particular phobia will show certain symptoms, such as severe anxiety when they face the source of the phobia and go out of their way to avoid it.

There are several categories of phobias that people may be affected by, including phobias related to the environment, animals, conditions, and treatment. Each category has a different set of specifically related phobias. People with these types of phobias may get more than one phobia within a group.

Group 1

ଓ

A -D

A

ଓ

Ablutophobia - Fear of bathing, vomiting, or washing

Ablutophobia is a serious fear of bathing, vomiting, or washing. It is an anxiety disorder that falls under the category of certain phobias. Some phobias are irrational fears centered on a particular situation. They can affect your health.

Acarophobia - Fear of being bitten or small insects that cause itching

irrational or unequal fear of being bitten or attacked by small parasitic insects or worms, which cause crawling or sensation in the skin.

Acerophobia - Fear of sourness

Acerophobia is an irrational fear of sourness. Someone with phobia may find the thought of being sour triggers a bizarre anxiety, not to mention eating something sour. Their fear of being stigmatized may be so disturbing that they do not even touch the facts. While this may not be the case, it is still possible. Acerophobia is a very rare phobia

Achluophobia - Fear of the dark

Achluophobia is a simple phobia, which means it is associated with a dark environment. Some natural conditions do not cause it.

Acousticophobia - Fear of noise

Acousticophobia can refer to a patient's hypersensitivity to hearing and may be part of a migraine diagnosis. It is sometimes called acousticophobia. Phonophobia. Some names. Ligyrophobia, sonophobia, Sonophobia

Acrophobia - Fear of heights

Acrophobia is a state of mental health in which a person feels a great fear of heights. It is a form of anxiety disorder.

Aerophobia - Fear of flying, drafts or fresh air

Fear of flying, also known as aerophobia, is a type of anxiety disorder that involves the feeling of fear and panic that some people experience while flying, or waiting to fly.

Algophobia - Fear of pain

Algophobia is a major fear of physical pain. Although no one wants to feel pain, people with this phobia have deep feelings of anxiety, panic, or depression when they think of pain. Anxiety about algophobia can also make you more sensitive to pain. It is very common in people with chronic pain syndromes

Agoraphobia - Fear of crowds and open spaces

Agoraphobia is a type of anxiety disorder in which you are afraid and avoid places or situations that may make you feel nervous and make you feel trapped, helpless or embarrassed.

Agrizoophobia - Fear of wildlife

From the Greek words αγρός (agrós) meaning camp, ζώo (zoo) meaning animal, and φοβία (fovía or phobia) meaning fear. Agrizoophobia is much clearer than zoophobia, which is the fear of all animals. If you have agrizoophobia, you may be comfortable around pets, such as dogs or cats, or livestock, such as horses and cattle. However, you may be concerned about just animals such as sharks or wolves. The animal does not have to be big or bully to worry about it. Small animals, such as raccoons, mice, squirrels, or bats, can also cause symptoms indiscriminately.

Agyrophobia - Fear of crossing the streets

Fear of crossing the roads, or its terms dromophobia and agyrophobia, is a specific phobia that affects a person's ability to cross a road or a road where cars or vehicles may be located.

Aichmophobia - Fear of sharp objects, such as needles

Aichmophobia is a serious fear of sharp objects. It is a form of anxiety disorder. A person with aichmophobia develops nervousness and anxiety when he or she is in close proximity to sharp objects such as scissors, knives, needles, and pencils. They often avoid situations or places where sharp objects are involved.

Ailurophobia - Fear of cats

Ailurophobia is the fear of cats. People with this particular phobia feel anxious when they think of a cat, see a cat or pictures of a cat, or hear a cat. Many people with cat phobia have had negative experiences with cats. You can overcome cat phobia with exposure therapy, behavioral therapy, hypnotherapy, and other therapies.

Albuminurophobia - Fear of kidney disease

Albuminurophobia is an irrational fear of kidney disease. A person with this condition can expect very high anxiety just by thinking about kidney disease, let alone developing it. In fact, their anxiety may be so great that they may even tolerate panic attacks. Although such a disorder of anxiety may not be common in everyone with albuminurophobia, it is still very likely to occur.

Alektorophobia - Fear of chickens

Alektorophobia is a strong, uncontrollable fear of chickens. People with alelektorophobia have a lot of fear and anxiety around roosters or hens. They do not feel intimidated by any other animal or bird (ornithophobia). The word comes from the Greek word for "phobos," meaning fear, and "alektor," meaning rooster.

Alliumphobia - Fear of garlic

Alliumphobia is an irrational fear of garlic. A person with this condition can expect to experience a very high level of anxiety just by thinking about garlic, let alone seeing it in real life. In fact, their anxiety may be so great that they may even tolerate panic attacks. Although such a state of anxiety may not always be present in everyone with alliumphobia, it is still very likely to occur.

Allodoxaphobia - Fear of ideas

Allodoxaphobia is an irrational fear of ideas. The sufferer may find it extremely difficult to cope with daily life, either because of prejudice or just out of anger. In some extreme cases, they may face a full-blown panic attack that requires hospitalization.

Amathophobia - Fear of dust

Amathophobia is an absurd fear of dust. Someone with a mental illness may be extremely anxious about their condition and may even need to be hospitalized in the event of such anxiety. A person with athophobia may find it very difficult to deal with their daily life and see how dust can be found almost everywhere. In fact, it may not be uncommon for a person with this condition to develop mysophobia (fear of germs).

Amaxophobia – Fear of being in a car

Amaxophobia (Fear of Driving) Amaxophobia (also called hamaxophobia) makes you feel anxious or scared while driving or riding a car, such as a car, bus or plane. With it, you are afraid to drive and you may get anxious about being a passenger. This fear can interfere with work, entertainment, and travel.

Ambulophobia - Fear of walking

Ambulophobia is a type of phobia that involves fear of walking. This phobia mainly affects older people, who prefer not to leave their beds or home to avoid traveling in uneven terrain and reduce the risk of falls.

Amychophobia - Fear of scratching

Amychophobia is an extreme fear of being scratched or scratched, scratched or scratched. Often such fear is related to avoiding animals (cats, dogs, puppies, and cats). In many cases, fear is irrational and exaggerated.

Anablephobia - Fear of looking up

Anablephobia is an irrational fear of looking up. A person with this condition can expect to have very high anxiety due to the mere thought of looking up, not to mention doing so. In fact, their anxiety may be so great that they may have to endure intense panic attacks as a result. Although such a state of anxiety may not always be present in everyone with anablephobia, it is still very likely to occur.

Androphobia - Fear of men

Androphobia is defined as the fear of men. It is considered a phobia because it is a powerful and irrational fear of something - in this case, men - who do not pose a real danger but can still create anxiety and avoid the behavior. Androphobia, like other phobias, lasts a long time and can adversely affect your ability to perform your daily activities, such as work, education, and social relationships.

Anemophobia - Fear of the wind or dizziness

Anemophobia, sometimes called ancraophobia, is a type of catch-all name that includes many types of air-related phobias. Some people are afraid of drafts, others are windy.

Anglophobia - Fear of England or Britain

Anti-Englishsentiment or Anglophobia (from Latin Anglus "English" and Greek φόβος phobos "fear") means opposition, dislike, fear, hatred, or oppression and persecution of the people of England and/or English. In general, the term is sometimes used loosely as a synonym for anti-British ideology. The opposite is Anglophilia.

Anginophobia - Fear of congestion

Anginophobia is defined as an irrational and exacerbated fear of choking, which includes the obvious fear of contracting angina pectoris. Also, the term anginophobia is used to describe the fear or overconfidence of angina inflammation. have you ever experienced an episode when you were a spectator of heartbreak or constipation.

Anthophobia - Fear of flowers

People with anthophobia are very afraid of flowers. The word "Anthos" means Greek flowers. A person with anthophobia may be afraid of any flower or type. Any part of a flower or plant - from the stem to the leaf to the tree - can cause panic.

Antlophobia - Fear of floods

Atlophobia refers to the unreasonable fear of floods. Phobias is a type of anxiety disorder that can affect one's life sadly. It includes panic-like, in which case a person feels sudden breathing, sweating and shivering with the thought of flooding or even seeing flood stories happening in different countries or so.

Anuptaphobia - Fear of staying single

Anuptaphobia is the absurd fear of being single or having no romantic relationship with anyone. People with this condition may be very anxious for fear of being alone. Their anuptaphobia may be so severe that they may never get married.

Apeirophobia - A chronic fear

Apeirophobia (from the Greek άπειρος (ápeiros) "infinite, boundless") is an exaggerated and / or eternal fear, which causes discomfort and sometimes panic attacks. It usually starts in infancy or premature and it is not known how it usually develops over time.

Anthropophobia - Fear of people or society

Anthropophobia is fear of people. It is not an official clinical diagnosis. Many experts consider this condition to be a form of phobia.

Aphenphosmphobia - Fear of intimacy

Aphenphosmphobia is an anxiety disorder characterized by fear of being touched. Other names for Aphenphosmphobia include chiraptophobia, Haphephobia and thixophobia. Contact with strangers even without permission can make many people feel uncomfortable.

Apiphobia - Fear of bees or bees

Fear of bees (or bee stings), technically known as melissophobia (from Ancient Greek: μέλισσα, melissa, "honey bee") and also known as apiphobia (from Latin: apis for "honey bee" + Ancient Greek: φόβος, phobos, "fear"), is one of the most common fears among people and is a form of phobia.

Arachibutyrophobia - Fear of peanut butter sticking to the roof of the mouth

Arachibutyrophobia, derived from the Greek words "arachi" meaning "crushed nut" and "butyr" of butter, is the fear of suffocating peanut butter. Specifically, it refers to the fear of peanut butter sticking to the roof of your mouth

Aquaphobia - Fear of water

Aquaphobia is fear of water. People with this phobia feel anxious when they think or see water. They may avoid bathing, showers, pools, and pools of water. Many people with aquaphobia have had a painful experience in the water.

Arachnophobia - Fear of spiders

Arachnophobia is a specific phobia caused by the irrational fear of spiders and other arachnid-like scorpions.

Arithmophobia - Fear of numbers

Arithmophobia is an extreme fear of numbers. Some people are afraid of certain numbers, such as "bad luck" number 13. Some people are afraid of all the numbers. Arithmophobia can greatly affect daily life. People with phobia may have a difficult time handling certain tasks, paying off debts or managing a budget.

Asthenophobia - Fear of fainting

Asthenophobia is an irrational fear of fainting or weakness. A person with this condition can expect very high anxiety due to the thought of fainting or weakness, not to mention the real deal. In fact, their anxiety may be so great that they may even tolerate panic attacks. Although such a flow of anxiety may not always be the case for everyone with asthenophobia, it is still very rare to occur anyway.

Astraphobia - Fear of thunder and lightning

Astraphobia is a fear of thunder and lightning. It usually affects children, but many adults still face fear of thunderstorms. Astraphobia is one of the most common phobias. Therapies such as speech therapy or medication can help you to control your symptoms and improve your quality of life.

Astrophobia - Fear of the heavenly realm

Astrophobia is a severe and irrational fear of stars and space. It is one of the few phobias associated with a defined object or state. For many, astrophobia is strongly associated with fear of strangers.

Ataxiophobia - Fear of ataxia, which is muscle spasms

Ataxiophobia is an irrational fear of muscle contraction. A person with this condition can expect to have very high anxiety due to just thinking about muscle dysfunction, not to mention dealing with it. In fact, their anxiety may be so great that they may even tolerate panic attacks. Although such a flow of anxiety may not be so common in anyone with ataxiophobia, it is still very likely to occur anyway.

Ataxophobia - Fear of being disturbed or unclean

Ataxophobia is an irrational fear of being disturbed or unclean. A person with this condition can expect very high anxiety due to the thought of being disturbed or unclean, not to mention dealing with it. In fact, their anxiety may be so great that they may even tolerate panic attacks. Although such a flow of anxiety will not always be the case for everyone suffering from ataxophobia.

Atelophobia - Fear of imperfection

Atelophobia is a major fear of imperfection. A person with this condition is afraid to make mistakes. They tend to avoid any situation where they feel they will not succeed. Atelophobia can lead to anxiety, depression and low self-esteem.

Athazagoraphobia - Fear of forgetfulness or neglect

Athazagoraphobia is the fear of forgetting someone or something, and the fear of forgetting. For example, you or someone close to you may have anxiety or fear of Alzheimer's disease or loss of memory. This may result from caring for someone with Alzheimer's disease or dementia.

Atychiphobia - Fear of failure

Atychiphobia is a major fear of failure. It may cause you to postpone or avoid any activity or situation that may have a negative effect. A person with this condition may be afraid to try new things, take risks or accept growth for fear of failure.

Aulophobia - Anxiety Disorders

Aulophobia is an irrational fear of the nerves. A person with this condition can expect to have very high anxiety by just thinking about the flutes, let alone seeing them for real. In fact, their anxiety may be so great that they may even tolerate panic attacks.

Aurophobia - Fear of gold

It may be difficult for many to get involved, but some people suffer from irrational and extreme fears of gold, or sometimes even gold objects - a condition called aurophobia. Seeing or talking about gold can cause nausea, dizziness and panic, among other symptoms.

Auroraphobia - Fear of Aurora, sometimes called northern lights

Auroraphobia is the irrational fear of Northern Lights (aka Aurora Borealis). These beautiful brightly colored curtains can be seen in various places such as Northern Canada, Norway, Greenland, New Zealand, Sweden, and Finland, among others in late November to March. People suffering from auroraphobia may find themselves confronted with a great deal of anxiety when they think only of the Northern lights.

Automatonophobia - Fear of ventriloquist dummies or wax images

Automatonophobia scares human-like figures, such as mannequins, wax figures, statues, dummies, animatronics, or robots. It is a specific phobia, or a certain fear that causes intense and extreme stress and anxiety and can adversely affect a person's quality of life.

Automysophobia - Fear of pollution

Automysophobia is an irrational fear of pollution. A person suffering from this condition can expect to have very high anxiety by just thinking about dirt, let alone dealing with it. In fact, their anxiety may be so great that they may even tolerate panic attacks.

Autophobia - Fear of being alone

Autophobia, or monophobia, makes you feel very anxious when you are alone. This fear of isolation can affect your relationships, community health and work. You may also fear rejection from the traumatic experience of childhood.

Aviophobia - Fear of flying

Aviophobia or aerophobia is the fear of flying. Unlike a terrifying plane that grips the hands of strangers on takeoff and landing, people suffering from aviophobia often have a physical reaction to the thought of flying or the experience itself. In most cases, however, they never let it go that far.

B

❧

Bacteriophobia - Fear of germs

Bacteriophobia Germmaphobia (sometimes spelled germophobia) is a fear of germs. In this "Germs" is generally applied to any micruyhbngb tnujh nb; 'p.oorganism that causes disease - for example, acteria, germs, or parasites. Germaphobia may be called other names, including bacillophobia, Germaphobia (and sometimes spelled germophobia)

Ballistophobia - Fear of arrows or bullets

Ballistophobia is an irrational fear of arrows and bullets. People with Ballistophobia may easily be shocked by loud noises.

Barophobia - Fear of gravity

`People with barophobia are afraid of gravity. They worry that gravity will cause a fall that will lead to more serious injuries or death. Or they may fear that the force of gravity might cause them to drop a heavy object. A person with barophobia may also be afraid of images of outer space where gravity is not present.

Basophobia - Fear of falling

The fear of falling (FOF), also called basophobia (or basiphobia), is a natural and common fear of most people and mammals, with varying degrees of limitation. It is different from acrophobia (fear of heights), although the two fears are closely related.

Bathmophobia - Fear of hills, hills and stairs

Bathmophobia is a fear of the stairs. You may fear falling down stairs or climbing a cliff. A traumatic accident involving a fall, injury or death may cause this special disease.

Bathophobia – fear of Depth

Bathophobia can be described as an irrational fear of depth. One may feel the fear of falling into anything tall, or deep in its physical appearance.

Batrachophobia – Fear of amphibians

Fear of frogs and toads is both a specific phobia, known as frog phobia or ranidaphobia (from ranidae, a family of frogs), and a common superstition in many traditional houses. Specialty psychology books use the simple word "fear of frogs" more than any other special word. The word batrachophobia is also listed in the 1953 dictionary dictionary.

Belonephobia - Fear of pins and needles

Belonephobia is an irrational and modified response to fear of needles. It affects up to 10% of the population and has treatment and follow-up effects, especially in the case of children.

Bibliophobia - Fear of books or reading aloud

Bibliophobia is a major fear of books or reading. It is a form of anxiety disorder. Books are available almost everywhere, and they are hard to avoid. Bibliophobia can cause physical symptoms, disrupt daily life, and affect school and work success.

Bogyphobia - Fear of the bogeyman

Bogyphobia is the fear of bogeys or bogeyman. These fears are influenced by the media and later planted in their minds.

Botanophobia - Fear of plants

Botanophobia is a major plant fear. People with botanophobia may believe that plants are dangerous or dangerous and therefore avoid them. Severe conditions can cause symptoms of anxiety and affect daily life. Treatment includes exposure to exposure, psychotherapy, hypnosis and anti-anxiety medications.

Bovinophobia - Fear of cow or cattle

Cattle fear, or Bovinophobia, is a type of phobia that causes people great anxiety or fear when they are near or thinking of being close to cattle on a farm or farm.

Bromidrosiphobia - Fear of body odor

Bromidrosiphobia is an irrational fear of body odor. A person with this condition can expect to have very high anxiety by just thinking about the body odor, let alone having it. In fact, their anxiety may be so great that they may even tolerate panic attacks. Although such an anxiety disorder may not always be present in everyone with bromidrosiphobia, it is still very likely to occur.

Bufonophobia - Fear of toads

Bufonophobia is an irrational fear of toads. A person with this condition may find himself becoming overly concerned about frogs until he experiences severe anxiety. Their anxiety may be so great that they may be completely overwhelmed by their bufonophobia. While this will vary from person to person, it is very likely that this will happen.

C

ಉ

Cacophobia – Fear of ugliness

Cacophobia is an intense fear of ugliness. People with this anxiety disorder may fear becoming ugly. Or they might have symptoms of panic and anxiety when they think about or see something ugly. Cacophobia is one of only a few phobias that are subjective instead of objective.

Cainophobia – Fear of newness or novelty

Cainophobia is the irrational fear of newness. Someone suffering from this condition can expect to experience a very high amount of anxiety from merely thinking of newness, let alone actually experiencing it. In fact, their anxiety may be so intense that they may even endure a full-blown panic attack as a result of it.

Caligynephobia – Fear of beautiful women

Caligynephobia is the clinical term for an exaggerated or irrational fear of beautiful women. It is also known as venustraphobia; the term gynophobia refers to a fear of women in general. A person may experience caligynephobia because of personal trauma or as part of a larger issue, such as social anxiety disorder. People with phobias like these can find routine social interactions awkward and distressing. Fortunately, many resources both on and off the Internet offer support for sufferers of this not uncommon problem.

Carcinophobia – Feat of developing cancer

Cancer phobia, also known as carcinophobia, is a common phobia and an anxiety disorder characterized by the chronic fear of developing cancer. It can manifest in tremendous feelings of sadness, fear, panic, and distress. In some cases, the phobia can be so extreme that it prevents the individual from living a normal life.

Cardiophobia – Fear of getting heart disease

Cardiophobia is defined as an anxiety disorder of persons characterized by repeated complaints of chest pain, heart palpitations, and other somatic sensations accompanied by fears of having a heart attack and of dying.

Carnophobia – Fear of meat

Carnophobia is the irrational fear of meat. Someone experiencing this condition will find it extremely difficult to be around meat, let alone actually consuming it.

Catagelophobia – Fear of being ridiculed

Catagelophobia is the irrational fear of being ridiculed. Someone suffering from this condition may find the mere thought of being mocked or made fun of to be extremely painful and anxiety provoking. They themselves may already be very self-critical, so when someone else ridicules them or when they perceive that they are being ridiculed by someone else, this may only confirm what they already believe about themselves.

Catapedaphobia – Fear of jumping

Catapedaphobia is the irrational fear of jumping from high and low places. Someone suffering from this condition can expect to experience a very high amount of anxiety from merely thinking of jumping from high and low places, let alone actually doing it. In fact, their anxiety may be so intense that they may even endure a complete panic attack as a result of it. Although such an influx of anxiety will not always be the case for everyone suffering from catapedaphobia, it is still very plausible to occur nonetheless.

Cathisophobia – Fear of sitting

Cathisophobia is the fear of sitting down. The origin of the word cathiso (a.k.a. kathiso) is Greek (meaning to sit or sitting) The causes of this phobia may differ with the age of the sufferer. In elderly people sitting for longer durations can be distressful because of the anticipated pain and discomfort. In children (especially who are rebels) sitting obediently in classroom can cause the feeling of being controlled or being chained down and thus trigger Cathisophobia. For people who have had a past traumatic experience like being held hostage, being tortured by having made to sit on nails, pins or embers; can have this fear. Some people suffer from this phobia only around certain people and situations. For instance the fear of sitting with a celebrity or while waiting for an exam result.

Catoptrophobia – Fear of mirrors or the undead

Spectrophobia, a type of anxiety disorder classified as a specific phobia, is the fear of mirrors and/or the fear of what may be reflected in them. It may also be referred to as eisoptrophobia or catoptrophobia.

Ceraunophobia – Fear of thunder and lightning

Ceraunophobia (from cerauno, Greek for thunder, lightning, thunderbolt) or keraunophobia, is the irrational fear of thunder and lightning, or in other words fear of thunderstorms.

Cetaphobia – Fear of whales

Simply put, cetaphobia is a fear of whales. It's one of many conditions that psychologists commonly refer to as a "specific phobia," which means that it's related to a singular, often very personal, trigger. This particular fear often induces feelings of panic or anxiety at the sight, thought, or mention of whales, whether real or imagined. The phobia isn't well documented in psychological literature and most accounts are anecdotal. Those who fear whales because of specific danger whales have put them in — traditional hunters, for instance, or zoologists who have had bad experiences — are usually thought to be suffering from more generalized trauma than specific phobia. More often, sufferers have never seen a living whale. Scholars have different opinions when it comes to what causes the fear and how many people truly could be diagnosed with any sort of condition, and the manifestations and symptoms vary from person to person in any event. When sought, treatment usually involves talk therapy and positive imaging, and in very severe cases anti-anxiety medications may also be recommended.

Chaetophobia – Fear of hair

Chaetophobia is fear of hair, a type of specific phobia Sufferers fear may be associated with human hair and/or animal hair. They fear people or animals with an excess amount of hair. They may also fear the hair on their own body. Some only fear detached or loose hair and do not mind attached hair. The term *chaetophobia* comes from the Greek χαίτη - *khaitē*, meaning "loose, flowing hair"

Chemophobia – Fear of chemicals or chemistry

Chemophobia literally means "fear of chemicals" and may be used in various ways. It is most often used to describe the assumption that 'chemicals' are bad and that 'natural' things are good. The most usual use of the term 'chemophobia' is analogous to 'homophobia' - a prejudice against something rather than an irrational fear. See Non-clinical uses of 'phobia' and Prejudices described as phobias. In this sense, chemophobia is akin to technophobia.

Cherophobia – Fear of happiness

Cherophobia is a phobia where a person has an irrational aversion to being happy. The term comes from the Greek word "chero," which means "to rejoice." When a person experiences cherophobia, they're often afraid to participate in activities that many would characterize as fun, or of being happy.

Chionophobia – Fear of snow

Chionophobia is an extreme fear of snow and snowy weather. People with this disorder have severe anxiety and panic attacks when they think about or see snow. To avoid snow, they may live in warmer climates or stay indoors during winter.

Chiraptophobia – Fear of being touched

Chiraptophobia is the irrational fear of being touched. Someone suffering from this condition can expect to experience a very high amount of anxiety from merely thinking of being touched, let alone actually experiencing it. In fact, their anxiety may be so intense that they may even endure a full-blown panic attack as a result of it. Although such an influx of anxiety will not always be the case for everyone suffering from chiraptophobia, it is still very plausible to occur nonetheless.

Chirophobia – Fear of hands

Chirophobia is the irrational fear of hands. Someone suffering from this condition can expect to experience a very high amount of anxiety from merely thinking of hands, let alone actually seeing them in real life. In fact, their anxiety may be so intense that they may even endure a full blown panic attack as a result of it. Although such an influx of anxiety will not always be the case for everyone suffering from chirophobia, it is still very plausible to occur nonetheless.

Chiroptophobia – Fear of bats

Chiroptophobia is the irrational fear of bats. Someone experiencing this condition may find themselves enduring intense bouts of anxiety at the mere thought of bats. In fact, their fear may be so intrusive and debilitating that they may even experience full blown panic attacks as a result of their chiroptophobia.

Cholerophobia – Fear of anger, or being afraid of cholera

Phobias are to be taken seriously. If they aren't given proper attention and treatment, might start to limit the sufferers life. In some cases up to the degree of extreme anxiety and depression. Knowing how to manage thoughts and anxiety will not only help a person live or overcome the fear of anger or the fear of cholera.

Chorophobia – Fear of dancing

Defined as an irrational fear of dancing. From the Greek translation, "Choro" means dance. The condition occurs when someone is extremely uncomfortable at the thought of dancing.

Chrometophobia – Fear of money

Chrometophobia is an irrational fear that can make it difficult for you to spend money or pay your bills, even though you may be able to afford it. It's important to seek treatment for this condition as it can affect your health, relationships, overall well-being, and daily life.

Chromophobia – Fear of colors

Chromophobia is **an intense fear of colors**. Most people with this disorder have an extreme aversion to one or two colors in particular — or they may only fear bright colors. People with chromophobia have severe anxiety or panic attacks when they see a color they're afraid of.

Chronomentrophobia – Fear of clocks

Chronomentrophobia is the irrational fear of clocks. Someone suffering from this condition can expect to experience a very high amount of anxiety from merely thinking of clocks, let alone actually experiencing it. In fact, their anxiety may be so intense that they may even endure a full blown panic attack as a result of it.

Cibophobia – Fear of food

Cibophobia is defined as the fear of food. People with cibophobia often avoid food and drinks because they're afraid of the food itself. The fear may be specific to one type of food, such as perishable foods, or it may include many foods. A phobia is a deep, irrational fear about a specific thing or situation.

Chloephobia – Fear of newspapers

Chloephobia is an irrational fear of print newspapers. Its an new term in English.

Chronophobia – Fear of Time

Chronophobia is the extreme fear of time or time passing. It can cause severe anxiety, feelings of dread, obsessive behaviors and depression. People who are elderly, ill or imprisoned are more likely to develop this anxiety disorder.

Claustrophobia – Fear of confined spaces

Claustrophobia (Fear of Enclosed Spaces) Fear of confined spaces (claustrophobia) becomes a phobia when it interferes with your ability to function at work, school, or other daily activities. Common triggers include tunnels, elevators, trains and airplanes. Behavior training is the main treatment.

Cleisiophobia – Fear of being locked in a space that is enclosed

Cleisiophobia is the fear of closed spaces or being locked in an enclosed place. This fear is related to a concern that one will experience panic or significant discomfort, yet will be unable to leave the situation.

Climacophobia – Fear of climbing, especially stairs

Climacophobia, or the fear of the act of climbing, is a relatively unusual phobia. It is known as a specific phobia, just like acrophobia, a fear of heights, as well as bathmophobia, a fear of stairs and slopes.

Clinophobia – Fear of beds or going to bed

Clinophobia causes extreme anxiety and fear around the thought of going to bed. This phobia is also known as hypnophobia, Somniphobia, sleep anxiety, or sleep dread. Sleep disorders can cause some anxiety around sleeping.

Coimetrophobia – Fear of cemeteries

Coimetrophobia is the irrational fear of cemeteries. Someone suffering from this mental illness will find it extremely challenging to even think of cemeteries, let alone to actually be near one. The anxiety they will experience when in the presence of a cemetery will likely have a very strong impact on their behavior as they may avoid driving past cemeteries at all costs.

Contreltophobia – Fear of sexual abuse

Contreltophobia (also called agrophobia; not to be confused with agoraphobia) is the fear or phobia of being sexually abused, assaulted or raped . This fear goes beyond the "normal" fear of this happening, since it is logical to be afraid of being raped or abused. In addition to intense fear, there appears avoidance of situations associated with the feared (or phobic) stimulus or situation (or if not avoided, they are endured with great anxiety), interference in daily life and irrationality or disproportionality of the fear.

Coprastasophobia – Fear of constipation

Coprastasophobia is the irrational fear of constipation. Someone suffering from this condition can expect to experience a very high amount of anxiety when merely thinking about being constipated, let alone actually being constipated in real life. If such a fear were to be left unattended to, someone with coprastasophobia may find themselves enduring a full blown panic attack as a result.

Coprophobia – Fear of feces or defecation

Coprophobia is the irrational fear of feces. Someone suffering from this condition can expect to experience a very high amount of anxiety from merely thinking of feces, let alone actually seeing it. In fact, their anxiety may be so intense that they may even endure a full blown panic attack as a result of it.

Coulrophobia – Fear of clowns

Coulrophobia brings on feelings of fear when you see clowns or clown images. It's a specific phobic disorder that causes anxiety, a racing heart, nausea and profuse sweating. Most people can avoid clowns. Some need exposure therapy, a type of psychotherapy, to help manage their reactions to clowns and clown images.

Cremnophobia – Fear of steep cliffs

Cremnophobia is the irrational fear of precipices. Someone suffering from this condition can expect to experience a very high amount of anxiety from merely thinking of precipices, let alone actually experiencing it. In fact, their anxiety may be so intense that they may even endure a full blown panic attack as a result of it. Although such an influx of anxiety will not always be the case for everyone suffering from cremnophobia, it is still very plausible to occur nonetheless.

Cryophobia – Fear of extreme cold

Cryophobia, or the irrational fear of extreme cold, is a relatively complex phobia. Some people are afraid only of cold weather while others fear touching cold objects. In addition, the definition of cold varies widely among individuals.

Crystallophobia – Fear of crystals or glass

Crystallophobia is the irrational fear of crystals or glass. Someone suffering from this condition can expect to experience a very high amount of anxiety from merely thinking of crystals or glass, let alone actually seeing it. In fact, their anxiety may be so intense that they may even endure a full blown panic attack as a result of it. Although such an influx of anxiety will not always be the case for everyone suffering from crystallophobia.

Cyberphobia – Fear of computers

Cyberphobia refers to the fear or rejection of computers, the Internet, and other related technology. Several factors can contribute to cyberphobia, including the prospect that many jobs will be replaced by automated systems. A general lack of knowledge regarding computers can also influence this fear.

Cyclophobia – Fear of bicycles

A strong dislike or fear of bicycles. Riding a bike is fun and exhilarating for most of us but can be extremely scary for one who has cyclophobia or the irrational and persistent fear of bicycles.

Cynophobia – Fear of dogs

Cynophobia is the overwhelming fear of dogs. People with this anxiety disorder feel intense fear and anxiety when they think about, see or encounter a dog. In severe cases, this phobia can cause people to avoid places where dogs might be.

D

❧

Decidophobia – Fear of making decisions

The fear of making the wrong decision, or "decidophobia" — a term coined by Princeton University philosopher Walter Kaufmann in his book Without Guilt and Justice — can affect people even when it comes to the smallest choices, such as what to have for lunch or what to wear.

Defecaloesiophobia – Fear of painful bowel movements

Defecaloesiophobia is the irrational fear of painful bowel movements. Someone suffering from this condition can expect to experience a very high amount of anxiety from merely thinking of painful bowel movements, let alone actually experiencing them. In fact, their anxiety may be so intense that they may even endure a full blown panic attack as a result of it. Although such an influx of anxiety will not always be the case for everyone suffering from defecaloesiophobia.

Deipnophobia – Fear of dining with others

Deipnophobia is a type of social anxiety disorder wherein the individual feels anxious while dining in public or engaging in dinner conversations. Social anxiety disorder is common in the general population, with a lifetime prevalence of around 12%. However, the exact prevalence of deipnophobia is unknown.

Dementophobia – Fear of going insane

Dementophobia is a type of phobia that involves the fear of madness or insanity. People who have this fear are afraid that they are going insane or losing touch with reality. The fear may be triggered by a family history of mental illness or periods of severe stress.

Demonophobia – Fear of demons

An abnormal and persistent fear of evil supernatural beings in persons who believe such beings exist and roam freely to cause harm. Those who suffer from this phobia realize their fear is excessive or irrational.

Dendrophobia – Fear of trees

Dendrophobia is a fear of trees. People with this specific phobia feel anxious when they think about or see a tree. Many people with tree phobia have had negative experiences with trees.

Dentophobia – Fear of dentists

Dentophobia is a fear of the dentist. People with this specific phobia feel anxious when they think about going to the dentist or actually visit the dentist. Past negative experiences, family history or feeling a loss of control can lead to dentophobia.

Dermatophobia – Fear of skin lesions or skin disease

Dermatophobia is the irrational fear of skin disease. Someone suffering from this condition can expect to experience a very high amount of anxiety from merely thinking of skin disease, let alone actually developing it. In fact, their anxiety may be so intense that they may even endure a full blown panic attack as a result of it.

Dextrophobia – Fear of having objects to your right

Dextrophobia is the irrational fear of having objects at the right side of the body. Someone experiencing this condition may endure extremely intrusive bouts of anxiety as a result of their mental illness. Their near compulsive behavior is reminiscent of that of someone with obsessive compulsive disorder (OCD) as they may become obsessed with their "inability" to have objects to the right of them.

Didaskaleinophobia – Fear of going to school

Didaskaleinophobia (fear of going to school). School avoidance, school refusal and school phobia are more common terms interchangeably used to describe a constellation of behaviors occurring among 1-5% of school aged children.

Dikephobia – Fear of justice

Dikephobia is the irrational fear of justice. Someone suffering from this condition can expect to experience a very high amount of anxiety from merely thinking of justice, let alone actually experiencing it. In fact, their anxiety may be so intense that they may even endure a full blown panic attack as a result of it. Although such an influx of anxiety will not always be the case for everyone suffering from dikephobia, it is still very plausible to occur nonetheless.

Dinophobia – Fear of dizziness

Dinophobia is the irrational fear of dizziness or whirlpools. Someone suffering from this condition can expect to experience a very high amount of anxiety from merely thinking of dizziness or whirlpools, let alone actually experiencing it. In fact, their anxiety may be so intense that they may even endure a full blown panic attack as a result of it.

Diplophobia – Fear of double vision

Diplophobia is the irrational fear of double vision. Someone suffering from this condition will find it extremely anxiety provoking to even think of double vision, let alone actually experiencing it. In fact, in some extreme cases of diplophobia, someone's fear of double vision may be so intrusive and intense that they themselves may even endure full blown panic attacks as a result of it. Although this is not always the case for everyone suffering from this condition, it is still very plausible for it to occur nonetheless.

Dipsophobia – Fear of drinking alcohol

Dipsophobia is the irrational fear of alcohol. Someone experiencing this mental disorder may find that they become extremely anxious when around alcohol or when around people drinking alcohol. They may find the idea of them drinking it to be dreadful. In some extreme cases, someone with dipsophobia may need to be hospitalized if they endure an intense enough panic attack.

Dishabiliophobia – Fear of undressing in front of another person

Dishabiliophobia is the irrational fear of undressing in front of someone. Someone suffering from this condition can expect to experience a very high amount of anxiety when undressing in front of someone, even in front of someone whom they are in a romantic relationship with. Such a fear can pose a lot of abysmal problems, especially in such relationships, among other situations.

Domatophobia – Fear of houses

Domatophobia is the abnormal, extreme, and persistent fear home, houses, or being inside a house.

Doraphobia – Fear of animal fur or skins

Doraphobia is the irrational fear of fur or skins of animals. Someone suffering from this condition can expect to experience a very high amount of anxiety from merely thinking of fur or skins of animals, let alone actually seeing it.

In fact, their anxiety may be so intense that they may even endure a full blown panic attack as a result of it.

Dromophobia – Fear of crossing streets or wandering

The fear of crossing streets, or its terms dromophobia and agyrophobia, is a specific phobia that affects a person's ability to cross a street or roadway where cars or vehicles may be present. The term dromophobia comes from the Greek dromos, meaning racetrack.

Dysmorphophobia – Fear of deformity

Body dysmorphic disorder (BDD) previously known as 'dysmorphophobia' is defined as a preoccupation with an imagined defect in one's physical appearance. The preoccupation is associated with many time-consuming rituals such as mirror gazing or constant comparing.

Dystychiphobia – Fear of accidents

Dystychiphobia is a fear of accidents. With this specific phobia, you may feel anxious when you think about or see a place where you fear an accident may happen. Many people with this fear have had past traumatic experiences with accidents.

Group 2

ଛଓ

E – K

E

ଛଓ

Ebulliophobia – Fear of bubbles

Ebulliophobia (from Latin ebullio, "bubble", "boil") is the fear of bubbles. People suffering this fear would avoid looking at liquids and soap that might bubble, as well as bubblewrap, chewing gum, and even foods that are prone to bubble.

Ecclesiophobia – Fear of church

Ecclesiophobia, or the fear of churches, refers to either of two separate fears: A fear of the building itself. A fear of what the church represents.

Ecophobia – Fear of one's home

Ecophobia is the irrational fear of home. Someone suffering from this condition can expect to experience a very high amount of anxiety when merely thinking of home, let alone actually being home. In fact, their ecophobia may be so severe that they may even endure full blown panic attacks as a result of it.

Eisoptrophobia – Fear of mirrors or seeing oneself in a mirror

Eisoptrophobia is an unhealthy fear of mirrors. Some people fear mirrors due to self-image issues. People may also avoid mirrors because they distort the way an object looks. This phobia leads to lifestyle changes that enable people to avoid mirrors.

Electrophobia – Fear of electricity

Electrophobia is the irrational fear of electricity. Someone suffering from this condition can expect to experience a great deal of anxiety when when they are around electricity in some capacity. For example, merely being in a room with the light switched on may give someone with electrophobia an influx of painful anxiety.

Eleutherophobia – Fear of freedom

Eleutherophobia is the fear of freedom. The origin of the word eleuthero is Greek (meaning free or freedom)

Emetophobia – Fear of vomiting

A phobia of vomiting, or emetophobia, is a condition characterized by a disproportionate fear of vomiting or other people vomiting, and is generally associated with an overwhelming sense of losing control, becoming very ill, or that others will find them repulsive.

Enetophobia – Fear of pins

Enetophobia is the irrational fear of pins. Someone suffering from this condition can expect to experience a very high amount of anxiety from merely thinking of pins, let alone actually seeing them. In fact, their anxiety may be so intense that they may even endure a full blown panic attack as a result of it. Although such an influx of anxiety will not always be the case for everyone suffering from enetophobia, it is still very plausible to occur nonetheless.

Enochlophobia – Fear of crowds

Enochlophobia refers to a fear of crowds. It's closely related to agoraphobia (a fear of places or situations) and ochlophobia (a fear of mob-like crowds). But enochlophobia has more to do with the perceived dangers posed by large gatherings of people you might encounter in your daily life.

Enosiophobia – Fear of criticism or committing an unpardonable sin

Enosiophobia is the irrational fear of criticism or committing a sin. Someone suffering from this condition can expect to experience a very high amount of anxiety from merely thinking of criticism or committing a sin, let alone actually experiencing it. In fact, their anxiety may be so intense that they may even endure a full blown panic attack as a result of it. Although such an influx of anxiety will not always be the case for everyone suffering from enosiophobia, it is still very plausible to occur nonetheless.

Entomophobia – Fear of insects

Entomophobia is a **fear of insects**. People with this specific phobia feel anxious when they think about or see an insect. Many people with insect phobia have had traumatic experiences with insects.

Eosophobia – Fear of dawn or daylight

Eosophobia is the irrational fear of dawn or daylight. Someone suffering from this condition can expect to experience a very high amount of anxiety from merely thinking of dawn or daylight, let alone actually seeing it. In fact, their anxiety may be so intense that they may even endure a full-blown panic attack as a result of it.

Ephebiphobia – Fear of adolescents or youth

Ephebiphobia is the fear of youth. First coined as the "fear or loathing of teenagers", today the phenomenon is recognized as the "inaccurate, exaggerated and sensational characterization of young people" in a range of settings around the world. Studies of the fear of youth occur in sociology and youth studies. It is distinguished from pedophobia by being more so focused on adolescents than prepubescent children.

Epistaxiophobia – Fear of nosebleeds

Epistaxiophobia is the irrational fear of nosebleeds. Someone suffering from this condition can expect to experience a very high amount of anxiety from merely thinking of nosebleeds, let alone actually experiencing them. In fact, their anxiety may be so intense that they may even endure a full blown panic attack as a result of it.

Epistemophobia – Fear of knowledge

Epistemophobia is the irrational fear of knowledge. Someone suffering from this disorder will find the mere thought of knowledge to be very anxiety provoking. In some societies, knowledge of certain aspects of life or of the world may be deemed to be dangerous. Interestingly enough, the aforementioned three phobias are all something that most people deeply desire to have.

Equinophobia – Fear of horses

Equinophobia is a fear of horses. A scary experience with a horse — such as falling off a horse, or being stepped on, kicked or bitten by a horse — may cause this phobia. You may also have a fear of donkeys, mules and ponies. Psychotherapies like exposure therapy can help you gradually overcome a fear of horses.

Eremophobia – Fear of being oneself

Also known as autophobia, isolophobia, or eremophobia, monophobia is the fear of beingisolated, lonely, or alone. As a phobia, this fear isn't necessarily a realistic one.

Erythrophobia– Fear of blushing

Erythrophobia is a specific phobia that causes the excessive, irrational fear of blushing. People with erythrophobia experience severe anxiety and other psychological symptoms over the act or thought of blushing.

Ergophobia – Fear of work

An abnormal and persistent fear of work. Sufferers of ergophobia experience undue anxiety about the workplace environment even though they realize their fear is irrational.

Erotophobia – Fear of sex or sexual intimacy

Fear of sex or sexual intimacy is also called "genophobia" or "erotophobia." This is more than a simple dislike or aversion. It's a condition that can cause intense fear or panic when sexual intimacy is attempted. For some people, even thinking about it can cause these feelings.

Euphobia – Fear of hearing good news

Euphobia (from Greek eu, meaning good) is the fear of good news. This phobia is usually a result of getting disappointed by good news .

Eurotophobia – fear of female genitalia

Eurotophobia is the aversion to or dislike of female genitalia.

F

⁝

Febriphobia – Fear of fever

There are a large variety of reasons that cause or trigger the fear of fever. But the most prominent ones are are:

Upbringing – People who are raised by people that either are afraid, or have transmitted a sense of uncertainty or danger related to fever, might experience Febriphobia or Fibriphobia or Fibriophobia most commonly.

Past Experience – It might be also induced, or suggested from people that might have had bad past experiences with/in fever.

Genetics – A persons ancestors that have been fearful of fever were probably more likely to survive and pass down these fearful genes to their children and so on.

Francophobia – Fear of France or French people

The hatred or fear of France, its people and culture. The hatred or fear of the presence of the French language and its native speakers.

Frigophobia – Fear of becoming too cold

Frigophobia is a condition in which patients report coldness of extremities leading to a morbidfear of death. It has been reported as a rare culture-related psychiatric syndrome in Chinese populations.

G

⁝

Gamophobia – Fear of marriage

a fear of commitment or fear of marriage — can keep you from enjoying meaningful relationships. A painful breakup, divorce or abandonment during childhood or adulthood may make you afraid to commit to someone you love.

Geliophobia – Fear of laughter

Geliophobia is the irrational fear of laughter. Someone suffering from this condition can expect to experience a very high amount of anxiety from merely thinking of laughter, let alone actually laughing. In fact, their anxiety may be so intense that they may even endure a full blown panic attack as a result of it. Although such an influx of anxiety will not always be the case for everyone suffering from geliophobia, it is still very plausible to occur nonetheless.

Geniophobia – Fear of chins

Geniophobia is the irrational fear of chins. Someone suffering from this condition can expect to experience a very high amount of anxiety from merely thinking of chins, let alone actually seeing them. In fact, their anxiety may be so intense that they may even endure a full blown panic attack as a result of it

Genuphobia – Fear of knees

People with genuphobia, a fear of knees, may be repulsed by how knees look. Or they may worry about their vulnerability to knee injuries, like ACL tears and knee dislocations. They may experience anxiety when seeing or touching knees, crossing legs or having to kneel.

Gerascophobia – Fear of growing old

Gerascophobia is a fear of growing or aging . Fear is an unpleasant emotion that occurs in response to a source of danger, whether real or imaginary, and has cognitive, behavioral, and physiological components

Globophobia – Fear of balloons

Balloon phobia or globophobia is a fear of balloons. The source of fear may be the sound of balloons popping. Generally, people with globophobia will refuse to touch, feel, or go near a balloon for fear it will burst. This is a form of phonophobia.

Glossophobia – Fear of public speaking

Glossophobia isn't a dangerous disease or chronic condition. It's the medical term for the fear of **public speaking**. And it affects as many as four out of 10 Americans. For those affected, speaking in front of a group can trigger feelings of discomfort and anxiety.

Gymnophobia – Fear of nudity

Gymnophobia, or the fear of nudity, is a highly personalized phobia. Some people with this fear are afraid only of being naked in public, as is the case in communal showers or changing rooms. However, some people also fear being naked while they're with their partner or even when they're on their own.

Gynophobia – Fear of women

Gynophobia or gynephobia is an abnormal fear of women, a type of specific social phobia. In the past, the Latin term horror feminae was used.

H

&

Hadephobia – Fear of hell

The word *hadephobia* is derived from two Greek words, *Hades* ("hell" or "the underworld") and *phobos* ("fear"). Thus, hadephobia is "the fear of hell."

Hagiophobia – Fear of holy people, places and things, like saints

Hagiophobia is the irrational fear of saints or holy things. Someone suffering from this condition can expect to experience a very high amount of anxiety

Harpaxophobia – Fear of being robbed

Harpaxophobia is the Fear of Being Robbed. This may involve either being 'mugged' or alternatively being burgled in the safety of your own home.

Hedonophobia – Fear of feeling pleasure

An irrational fear of pleasure or joy, especially engaging in pleasurable or joyful activities while others are experiencing depression, illness, pain, economic hardship, or other grief.

Heliophobia – Fear of the sun

Heliophobia refers to intense, sometimes irrational fear of the sun. Some people with this condition are also afraid of bright, indoor light. The word heliophobia has its root in the Greek word helios, which means sun. For some people, heliophobia may be caused by extreme anxiety about getting skin cancer.

Hemophobia – Fear of blood

While some people may feel uneasy about blood from time to time, hemophobia is an extremefear of seeing blood, or getting tests or shots where blood may be involved. This phobia can have a serious impact on your life, especially if you skip important doctor appointments as a result.

Herpetophobia – Fear of reptiles

Herpetophobia is a fear of reptiles. People with herpetophobia are most often afraid of reptiles like snakes and lizards. However, they may also be afraid of other reptiles, such as turtles, alligators, and crocodiles. Herpetophobia is a specific phobia, which is a kind of anxiety disorder.

Heterophobia – Fear of heterosexuals

Irrational fear of, aversion to, or discrimination against heterosexual people As in so many areas of our society, divisions are drawn in black and white; there are no shades of gray. Homophobia is countered by heterophobia; the empty answer to gay-bashing is a vow to bash back.

Hippopotomonstrosesquippedaliophobia – Fear of long words

Hippopotomonstrosesquippedaliophobia is one of the longest words in the dictionary — and, in an ironic twist, is the name for a fear of long words. Sesquipedalophobia is another term for the phobia. The American Psychiatric Association doesn't officially recognize this phobia.

Hodophobia – Fear of travel

Hodophobia is an irrational fear, or phobia, of travel. Hodophobia should not to be confused with travel aversion. Acute anxiety provoked by travel can be treated with anti-anxiety medication. The condition can be treated with exposure therapy, which works better when combined with cognitive behavioral therapy.

Homichlophobia – Fear of fog or humidity

Homichlophobia, also known as Nebulaphobia, is the fear of fog.

Homilophobia – Fear of sermons

Homilophobia is the irrational fear of sermons. Someone suffering from this condition can expect to experience a very high amount of anxiety from merely thinking of sermons, let alone actually hearing them. In fact, their anxiety may be so intense that they may even endure a full blown panic attack as a result of it. Although such an influx of anxiety will not always be the case for everyone suffering from homilophobia, it is still very plausible to occur nonetheless.

Homophobia – Fear of homosexuality

Homophobia encompasses a range of negative attitudes and feelings toward homosexuality or people who are identified or perceived as being lesbian, gay, bisexual or transgender (LGBT). It has been defined as contempt, prejudice, aversion, hatred or antipathy, may be based on irrational fear, and is also related to religious beliefs.

Homophobia is observable in critical and hostile behavior such as discrimination and violence on the basis of sexual orientations that are non-heterosexual. Recognized types of homophobia include *institutionalized* homophobia, e.g. religious homophobia and state-sponsored homophobia, and *internalized* homophobia, experienced by people who have same-sex attractions, regardless of how they identify.

Negative attitudes toward identifiable LGBT groups have similar yet specific names: lesbophobia is the intersection of homophobia and sexism directed against lesbians, gayphobia is the dislike or hatred of gay men, biphobia targets bisexuality and bisexual people, and transphobia targets transgender and transsexual people and gender variance or gender role nonconformity. According to 2010 Hate Crimes Statistics released by the FBI National Press Office, 19.3 percent of hate crimes across the United States "were motivated by a sexual orientation bias. Moreover, in a Southern Poverty Law Center 2010 *Intelligence Report* extrapolating data from fourteen years (1995–2008), which had complete data available at the time, of the FBI's national hate crime statistics found that LGBT people were "far more likely than any other minority group in the United States to be victimized by violent hate crime.

Hoplophobia – Fear of firearms

Hoplophobia (from Greek hoplo, meaning "weapon") is the fear of weapons, specifically firearm. Hoplophobia is a common phobia as weapons are deadly.

Hydrophobia – Fear of water

Aquaphobia, a psychological fear of water, Hydrophobia, a historic name for rabies, a term used in chemistry to describe chemical "aversions" of a molecule, or part of a molecule, to water

Hylophobia – Fear of forests

Hylophobia is an irrational fear of wooded areas. It is also known as Xylophobia. Some people find that their fear is worse at night, while others are equally afraid at all times of the day. Xylophobia is sometimes connected to other phobias, such as animal fears, but may also occur alone.

Hypegiaphobia – Fear of responsibility

Hypegiaphobia refers to the irrational fear of responsibility. Phobias are a type of anxiety disorder that can disturb a person's life miserably.

Hypochondria – Fear of illness

Illness anxiety disorder, sometimes called hypochondriasis or health anxiety, is worryingexcessively that you are or may become seriously ill. You may have no physical symptoms.

I

Iatrophobia – Fear of doctors

Iatrophobia causes you to fear doctors or medical tests. You may avoid seeking medical care even when you're very sick because you have extreme anxiety or panic attacks. The thought of getting medical tests also causes fear. Therapy can help ensure you get the medical care you may need.

Ichthyophobia – Fear of fish

Fear of fish or ichthyophobia ranges from cultural phenomena such as fear of eating fish, fear of touching raw fish, or fear of dead fish, up to irrational fear (specific phobia). Selachophobia, or galeophobia, is the specific fear of sharks. Ichthyophobia. Other names. Galeophobia.

Ideophobia – Fear of new ideas or thoughts

Ideophobia is the morbid fear of new ideas or thoughts. The word originates from Greek Idées meaning ideas

Illyngophobia – Fear of vertigo

Those who suffer from illyngophobia, the fear of vertigo (dizziness), are not afraid of the height itself, but of developing vertigo when looking down.

Insectophobia – Fear of insects

Entomophobia, sometimes known as *insectophobia*, Entomophobia is a fear of insects. People with this specific phobia feel anxious when they think about or see an insect. Many people with insect phobia have had traumatic experiences with insects.

Iophobia – Fear of poison

Iophobia is the irrational fear of poison. Someone suffering from this condition may find themselves enduring extremely intense amounts of anxiety at the mere thought of poison. In fact, their fear of poison may be so intrusive and severe that they may even experience full blown panic attacks which may require them to be hospitalized. Though such an occurrence may not be the norm, it is still very plausible for someone to be on such a severe end of the mental illness spectrum.

Isolophobia – Fear of isolation

Also known as autophobia, isolophobia, or eremophobia, monophobia is the fear of being isolated, lonely, or alone. As a phobia, this fear isn't necessarily a realistic one.

Ithyphallophobia – Fear of an erection

Ithyphallophobia in its narrower sense is a fear of the erect penis and in a broader sense an excessive aversion to masculinity. Alternative terms for this condition include Phallophobia or medorthophobia. An individual who has the condition is a *phallophobe.* The term is derived from the word *phallo* in Greek meaning penis and at times denoting masculinity, coupled with the suffix phobia. Medomalacuphobia, the fear of losing an erection or acquiring erectile dysfunction, is its antonym. At its most extreme, phallophobia when coupled with a psychiatric condition may result in issues such as Klingsor Syndrome or ederacinism.

J

❧

Japanophobia – Fear of Japanese people

Japanophobia (also known as Anti-Japanese Sentiment, Nipponophobia and Anti-Japanism) refers to racism, prejudice, negative feelings and discrimination directed towards Japanese people or people of Japanese descent.

Judeophobia – Fear of Jews

Judeophobia encompasses greatly varying degrees of hatred, contempt, scorn, and fear vis-à-vis Jewish people; in one form or other, it was an unfortunate constant of all of pre-1945 European history, a social condition of virtually any era.

K

❧

Kainolophobia – Fear of novelty

It is said that variety is the spice of life, and that every day and practically every moment the things, people and events which surround us are evolving and changing. This evolutionary change is beneficial in the main, and certainly, unavoidable as life is in a continual state of flux. However, there are people who loathe and fear change, they will do whatever it takes to attempt to keep all aspects of their lives exactly the way they are right now. People who suffer from this anxiety are said to have kainolophobia or kainophobia.

Kakorrhaphiophobia – Fear of failure

Kakorrhaphiophobia is an abnormal, persistent, irrational fear of failure. In clinical cases, it's debilitating: the fear of even the most subtle failure or defeat is so intense that it restricts a person from doing anything at all.

Katagelophobia – Fear of ridicule

katagelophobia An irrational dread of being ridiculed, "put down", and embarrassed in social situations.

Kathisophobia – Fear of sitting down

Kathisophobia means fear of sitting down, and the other means fear of thinking—and she's overtaxing her brain trying to devise a combination meaning fear of sitting down to think.

Kenophobia – Fear of empty spaces

Kenophobia is an intense fear of empty spaces or voids. It is a specific situational phobia, in which the individual experiences an irrational response to a situation that does not pose any actual threat."Keno" is from the Greek word for "empty" or "blank,"

Kinemortophobia – Fear of zombies

Kinemortophobia, or the fear of zombies,1 is surprisingly common. Zombies play a major role in horror fiction from novels to Hollywood films and are a staple at most major Halloween events. The term "zombie apocalypse," which refers to a pandemic in which zombies take over the planet, is a relatively new concept.

Kinetophobia – Fear of motion

Kinetophobia is the Fear of Motion or of movement, usually in a vehicle of some sort which may cause them to feel sick (motion sickness). It is perfectly conceivable that if the 'sick' feeling is intense enough, that some people would develop an aversion to motion which might evolve into a fear at some later point.

Kleptophobia – Fear of theft

Kleptophobia (also known as cleptophobia) involves the fear of theft. This phobia can actually be used to describe two distinct fears. The first is a fear of being stolen from or robbed. The second is a fear of stealing from someone else.

The two fears are often related and may exist simultaneously.

Koinoniphobia – Fear of rooms that are full of people

Koinoniphobia is a fear of rooms or people in rooms. People with this phobia often go out of their way to avoid being in a room, especially a room full of people.

Kopophobia – Fear of fatigue

Kopophobia is the irrational fear of fatigue. Someone suffering from this condition can expect to experience a very high amount of anxiety from merely thinking of fatigue, let alone actually experiencing it. In fact, their anxiety may be so intense that they may even endure a full blown panic attack as a result of it. Although such an influx of anxiety will not always be the case for everyone suffering from kopophobia, it is still very plausible to occur nonetheless.

Koniophobia – Fear of dust

Fear of dust: An abnormal and persistent fear of dust. Sufferers of this fear experience anxiety even though they realize dust poses no threat.

Group 3

ಬ

L – N

L

ಬ

Lachanophobia – Fear of vegetables

Lachanophobia is an unwarranted or an irrational fear of vegetables. The word originates from Greek Lachno meaning vegetables. Many people dislike vegetables and avoid eating them; however, in case of Lachanophobes, the dislike or hatred actually turns into a full blown panic attack at the mere sight or thought of vegetables.

Leprophobia – Fear of leprosy

Leprophobia is a pathological fear of leprosy that may be expressed as a delusion that one is actually suffering from leprosy.

Leukophobia – Fear of the color white

Leukophobia is an intense fear of the color white. It's a specific phobia, which occurs when you face or think of a particular situation.

Ligyrophobia – Fear of loud noises

Fear of loud noise is referred to as phonophobia, sonophobia, or ligyrophobia. This condition is not caused by hearing loss, or any type of hearing disorder. Phonophobia is a specific phobia. Specific phobias are an extreme, irrational fear of situations or objects that do not warrant that intense a reaction.

Lilapsophobia – Fear of tornadoes and hurricanes

Lilapsophobia is an unhealthy fear of tornadoes or hurricanes. Exposure therapy is the most common treatment. It can help lessen the impact of lilapsophobia on your daily life.

Limnophobia – Fear of lakes

Limnophobia is the irrational fear of lakes. Someone experiencing this condition may find it virtually impossible to be near lakes or to even see them from a far distance. Depending on the intensity of their limnophobia, they may even experience full blown panic attacks that may require them to be hospitalized. However, this may not be the case for everyone.

Linonophobia – Fear of string

Linonophobia is the abnormal fear of string; and that means string of all colors and fibers, including yarn, thread and even sometimes rope.

Liticaphobia – Fear of lawsuits

Liticaphobia is an intense fear of facing a lawsuit, therefore they get their legal advice thoroughly and try to be prompt in their payments as well as their dealings with people. are afraid that they may have to face jail time or have to pay money they do not have to defend themselves or to pay for bail.

Lockiophobia – Fear of childbirth

Lockiophobia, also known as Tokophobia, Maieusiophobia and Parturiphobia is an abnormal andpersistent fear of childbirth usually caused by a negative past experience. Sufferers from lockiophobia experience undue anxiety about giving birth. The phobia can become quite irrational if left untreated.

Logophobia – Fear of words

an irrational or disproportionate fear of words: Children with learning disorders or logophobia may still cultivate a love for books with graphic novels, comics, or picture books.

Luiphobia – Fear of syphilis

luiphobia An exaggerated horror of having lues, which is a synonym for syphilis. Lues is derived from the Latin word for "infection" or "plague".

Lutraphobia – Fear of otters

Lutraphobia is the irrational fear of otters. Someone suffering from this condition can expect to experience a high amount of anxiety when merely thinking of otters, let alone actually being in the presence of one in real life. Someone with this condition may believe otters to be very dangerous, so much so that they may try their best to avoid seeing them as best they can.

Lygophobia – Fear of darkness

an age-inappropriate fear of darkness that can prompt someone to limit their activities, avoid certain situations, and experience anxiety in anticipation of there being no light. The fear may not be related to darkness itself but unknown dangers hidden in the darkness (which is why horror and suspense movies often use darkness as a way to scare viewers).

M

&

Mageirocophobia – Fear of cooking

Mageirocophobia is an extreme fear of cooking. It's a specific phobia, meaning that it causes fear of a particular situation. Mageirocophobia may stem from other mental health issues, including: Obsessive-compulsive disorder (OCD), known for its repetitive thoughts and urges.

Malaxophobia – Fear of love play

Malaxophobia is the irrational fear of love play. Someone suffering from this condition can expect to experience a very high amount of anxiety from merely thinking of love play, let alone actually experiencing it. In fact, their anxiety may be so intense that they may even endure a full blown panic attack as a result of it. Although such an influx of anxiety will not always be the case for everyone suffering from malaxophobia, it is still very plausible to occur nonetheless.

Mastigophobia – Fear of punishment

Mastigophobia is the irrational fear of punishment. Someone suffering from this condition can expect to experience a very high amount of anxiety when merely thinking of being punished. In some extreme cases, their anxiety may be so extreme and intrusive that they may even endure full blown panic attacks as a result of their mastigophobia. However, this will vary from person to person, as well as how severe their mastigophobia is.

Mechanophobia – Fear of machines

Mechanophobia is the irrational fear of machines. Someone who suffers from this condition may find it extremely difficult to operate or even be around machines. For someone suffering with mechanophobia, they need only be in the presence of machines for them to feel intense dread and anxiety.

Megalophobia – Fear of large things

Megalophobia is the irrational fear of large things. This can include large airplanes, large ships, large buildings, and virtually any other arbitrary object someone perceives to be large. Their fear of large things will cause them a great amount of anxiety. Due to the fact that what one person deems to be large someone else may not, there is a lot of nuance with regards to trying to pinpoint specifically what it is that people with megalophobia fear.

Melanophobia – Fear of the color black

Melanophobia is the irrational fear of the color black. Someone suffering from this condition will find the mere thought of this color to be very anxiety provoking, let alone actually seeing the color in real life. In some extreme cases, their fear of the color black may so extreme that they may even experience full blown panic attacks. However, this will vary greatly from person to person.

Melophobia – Fear of music

Melophobia is the irrational fear of music. Someone suffering from this condition can expect to experience a very high amount of anxiety from merely thinking of music, let alone actually hearing it. In fact, their anxiety may be so intense that they may even endure a full blown panic attack as a result of it. Although such an influx of anxiety will not always be the case for everyone suffering from melophobia, it is still very plausible to occur nonetheless.

Menophobia – Fear of menstruation

Menophobia is the irrational fear of menstruation. Menstruation, also called a woman's "menstrual cycle" or "period" is the process in a woman of discharging blood and other substances from the lining of the uterus at different intervals of about once a month from the moment of puberty until menopause. The only exception to this is during pregnancy where a woman will not experience menstruation.

Merinthophobia – Fear of being tied up

Merinthophobia is the irrational fear of being bound or tied up. Someone suffering from this condition can expect to experience a very high amount of anxiety from merely thinking of being bound or tied up, let alone actually experiencing it. In fact, their anxiety may be so intense that they may even endure a full blown panic attack as a result of it.

Metathesiophobia – Fear of changes

Metathesiophobia is the irrational fear of change. People suffering from this condition may find change that naturally occurs in their life to be unacceptable and dreadful to the point to where they may even experience a full blown panic attack because of it.

Methyphobia – Fear of drinking alcohol

Methyphobia is the Fear of Alcohol or, probably more accurately, the fear of getting drunk on alcohol. For some people the idea of not being in 'control' can be a major cause of anxiety and this may be the main reason why people develop methyphobia. Methyphobia is more likely to be a fear of the 'consequences' of drinking alcohol rather than a fear of alcoholic beverages in themselves.

Metrophobia – Fear of poetry

Metrophobia, or the fear of poetry, is surprisingly common. Many people first develop this phobia in school, when overzealous teachers encourage them to rank poems according to artificial scales, break them down, and search for esoteric meanings.

Microphobia – Fear of small things

Microphobia is an intense fear of small things, like germs and insects. Trying to avoid little things can lead to negative thoughts and behaviors that affect daily life.

Mnemophobia – Fear of memories

Mnemophobia is the fear of memories, either by remembering past events or fearing memory loss duringmental diseases like Alzheimer's. Like most other phobias, this is traced from memorable traumatic experiences in the past.

Motorphobia – Fear of automobiles

Fear or dislike of automobiles or riding in one. Sometimes referred to as amaxophobia, the fear of driving is incredibly common and may be mild or severe. Some people fear only specific driving situations, such as driving in storms or on freeways, while others are afraid of simply sitting behind the wheel.

Musophobia – Fear of mice

Fear of mice and rats is one of the most common specific phobias. It is sometimes referred to as musophobia (from Greek μῦς "mouse") or murophobia (a coinage from the taxonomic adjective "murine" for the family Muridae that encompasses mice and rats, and also Latin *mure* "mouse/rat"), or as suriphobia, from French *souris*, "mouse". The phobia, as an unreasonable and disproportionate fear, is distinct from reasonable concern about rats and mice contaminating food supplies, which may potentially be universal to all times, places, and cultures where stored grain attracts rodents, which then consume or contaminate the food supply.

Mycophobia – Fear of mushrooms

Mycophobia is defined as the irrational fear of fungus and mold. Essentially it is based on the idea that any fungus, and its environment, is toxic. It's easy to understand why someone would suffer from mycophobia in our society, as we've left mushrooms in the dark corners of our culture. Sure, some are toxic, but fearing ALL mushrooms, and then remaining uneducated about their values as well as their risks, is a tragedy.

Myrmecophobia – Fear of ants

Myrmecophobia is the inexplicable fear of ants. It is a type of specific phobia. It is common for those who suffer from myrmecophobia to also have a wider fear of insects in general. Such a condition is known as entomophobia. This fear can manifest itself in several ways, such as a fear of ants contaminating a person's food supply, or fear of a home invasion by large numbers of ants. The term *myrmecophobia* comes from the Greek μύρμηξ, *myrmex*, meaning "ant"

Mysophobia – Fear of dirt and germs

Mysophobia is an extreme fear of germs. You may go out of your way to avoid situations that expose you to germs. The phobia and steps you take to avoid it worsen over time. You may find yourself stuck in a cycle of repetitive behaviors that affect your quality of life, similar to obsessive-compulsive disorder (OCD).

Myxophobia – Fear of slime

Myxophobia can be described as a persistent and sometimes irrational fear of gooey, icky, or slippery slime that occurs in certain individuals. Slime can literally be found in almost all corners of the earth. Slime can occur naturally or it can be man-made. It's typically transparent, viscous and sticky. This fear can be triggered by the notion that the slime is smelly or has a lot of germs.

N

❦

Necrophobia – Fear of death, dying and dead things

Necrophobia is a specific type of phobia that involves a fear of dead things and things that areassociated with death. A person with this type of phobia may be afraid of dead bodies as well as things such as coffins, tombstones, and graveyards.

Neopharmaphobia – Fear of new drugs

Neopharmaphobia is the irrational fear of new drugs. Someone suffering from this condition can expect to experience a very high amount of anxiety from merely thinking of new drugs, let alone actually experiencing it. In fact, their anxiety may be so intense that they may even endure a full blown panic attack as a result of it.

Neophobia – Fear of anything new

Neophobia is the characteristic fear of novel foods, and ensures that animals ingest only small quantities of new foodstuffs. If no illness results from consumption of the new food, and assuming that the food is reasonably palatable, animals will increase their intake on subsequent exposures.

Nephophobia – Fear of clouds

Nephophobia is the irrational fear of clouds. Someone suffering from this condition can expect to experience a very high amount of anxiety from merely thinking of clouds, let alone actually seeing them. In fact, their anxiety may be so intense that they may even endure a full blown panic attack as a result of it. Although such an influx of anxiety will not always be the case for everyone suffering from nephophobia, it is still very plausible to occur nonetheless.

Noctiphobia – Fear of the night

Noctiphobia is the irrational fear of the night. Someone suffering from this condition can expect to experience a very high amount of anxiety from merely thinking of the night, let alone actually being outside during the night. In fact, their anxiety may be so intense that they may even endure a full blown panic attack as a result of it.

Nomatophobia – Fear of names

Nomatophobia is the fear of names. As unbelievable as it may seem, some people actually have an irrational fear of names. Names are like tags that we use to identify ourselves and other people or things. It is what makes it easy for us to address individuals that we meet in order to help other people know when we are referring to them and not just addressing the group.When a person becomes afraid of names, they are said to suffer from Nomatophobia.

Nomophobia – Fear of losing or being without your mobile phone

Nomophobia is the irrational fear of being without your phone. Someone suffering from this condition can expect to experience a very high amount of anxiety from merely thinking of being without their phone, let alone actually experiencing it. In fact, their anxiety may be so intense that they may even endure a full blown panic attack as a result of it.

Nosocomephobia – Fear of hospitals

Nosocomephobia is the irrational fear of hospitals. Someone suffering from this condition can expect to experience a very high amount of anxiety from merely thinking of hospitals, let alone actually being inside of one. In fact, their anxiety may be so intense that they may even endure a full blown panic attack as a result of it. Although such an influx of anxiety will not always be the case for everyone suffering from nosocomephobia, it is still very plausible to occur nonetheless.

Nostophobia – Fear of returning home

Nostophobia is the irrational fear of returning home. Someone suffering from this condition can expect to experience a very high amount of anxiety from merely thinking of returning home, let alone actually doing it. In fact, their anxiety may be so intense that they may even endure a full blown panic attack as a result of it. Although such an influx of anxiety will not always be the case for everyone suffering from nostophobia, it is still very plausible to occur nonetheless.

Novercaphobia – Fear of stepmothers

Novercaphobia is the irrational fear of one's step-mother. Someone suffering from this condition can expect to experience a very high amount of anxiety from merely thinking of their step-mother, let alone actually seeing her. In fact, their anxiety may be so intense that they may even endure a full blown panic attack as a result of it.

Numerophobia – Fear of numbers

Numerophobia is the irrational fear of numbers. Someone experiencing this mental disorder may find it extremely difficult to be around numbers or to see depictions of numbers. Though they may realize that their fear of numbers is completely irrational, they simply aren't able to logically convince themselves of this in the midst of a panic attack. Their inability to achieve this task is a significant cause of their distress.

Nyctophobia – Fear of the dark

Nyctophobia is the irrational fear of darkness. Someone who has this mental disorder may find it extremely difficult or nearly impossible to be in the dark. They may go to painstaking efforts to stay indoors once it gets dark outside regardless of the situation. This may force them to isolate themselves from others in an attempt to ensure that they won't be in any sort of darkness.

Group 4

৪৩

O – R

O

♋

Obesophobia – Fear of gaining weight

Obesophobia is the irrational fear of becoming obese or gaining weight. Someone with this condition may also suffer from other mental illnesses such as anorexia or bulimia. Someone with obesophobia may take their body to the extreme by starving themselves or by working out excessively in hopes that they will never become obese or gain weight.

Ochophobia – Fear of vehicles

Ochophobia is the irrational fear of automobiles. Someone suffering from this mental illness may experience intense bouts of anxiety and dread when inside of a vehicle or when merely being around them. In fact, the mere thought of an automobile may give them painstaking anxiety. They may find it quite difficult to go through their day to day lives not only due to their anxiety, but also due to their difficulty with traveling.

Octophobia – Fear of the number 8

Octophobia is the irrational fear of the number 8. Someone suffering from this condition can expect to experience a very high amount of anxiety from merely thinking of the number 8, let alone actually seeing it. In fact, their anxiety may be so intense that they may even endure a full blown panic attack as a result of it. Although such an influx of anxiety will not always be the case for everyone suffering from octophobia, it is still very plausible to occur nonetheless.

Odontophobia – Fear of dental surgery

Odontophobia is the irrational fear of teeth or dental surgery. Someone suffering from this condition can expect to experience a very high amount of anxiety from merely thinking of teeth or dental surgery, let alone actually experiencing it. In fact, their anxiety may be so intense that they may even endure a full blown panic attack as a result of it. Although such an influx of anxiety will not always be the case for everyone suffering from odontophobia, it is still very plausible to occur nonetheless.

Odynophobia – Fear of pain

A pathological fear of pain. is an extreme fear of physical pain. While nobody wants to experience pain, people with this phobia have intense feelings of worry, panic or depression at the thought of pain. The anxiety of algophobia can also make you more sensitive to pain. It's most common in people with chronic pain syndromes.

Oenophobia – Fear of wines

Oenophobia is the irrational fear of wines. Someone suffering from this condition can expect to experience a very high amount of anxiety from merely thinking of wine, let alone actually being near it. In fact, their anxiety may be so intense that they may even endure a full-blown panic attack as a result of it.

Oikophobia – Fear of home

Oikophobia is the irrational fear of home. Someone suffering from this condition can expect to experience a very high amount of anxiety when merely thinking of home, let alone actually being home. In fact, their Oikophobia may be so severe that they may even endure full blown panic attacks as a result of it. A

Olfactophobia – Fear of odors

Olfactophobia is the irrational fear of smells. Someone suffering from this condition can expect to experience a very high amount of anxiety from merely thinking of smells, let alone actually smelling something. In fact, their anxiety may be so intense that they may even endure a full-blown panic attack as a result of it.

Ombrophobia – Fear of rain

Ombrophobia is the irrational fear of rain. Someone suffering from this condition can expect to experience a very high amount of anxiety from merely thinking of rain, let alone actually seeing it. In fact, their anxiety may be so intense that they may even endure a full-blown panic attack as a result of it. Although such an influx of anxiety will not always be the case for everyone suffering from ombrophobia, it is still very plausible to occur nonetheless.

Ommetaphobia – Fear of eyes or eye care

Ommetaphobia is the irrational fear of eyes. Someone suffering from this condition can expect to experience a very high amount of anxiety from merely thinking of eyes, let alone actually seeing them. In fact, their anxiety may be so intense that they may even endure a full-blown panic attack as a result of it.

Omphalophobia – Fear of belly buttons

Omphalophobia is the irrational fear of belly buttons. Someone experiencing this disorder may endure very intense bouts of anxiety when merely thinking of belly buttons. They may in fact realize that their fear is very irrational, but when they are in the presence of a belly button, they are typically unable to realize this. In extreme cases, they may experience anxiety that is so intense that they will have a full blown panic attack which will require them to be hospitalized.

Onomatophobia – Fear of certain words or names

An abnormal dread of certain words or names because of their supposed significance. *Onomatophobia* (from Greek onoma meaning "word" or "name") a branch of logophobia

Ophidiophobia – Fear of snakes

Ophidiophobia is the irrational fear of snakes. Someone suffering from this condition can expect to experience a very high amount of anxiety from merely thinking of snakes, let alone actually seeing them in real life. In fact, their anxiety may be so intense that they may even endure a full blown panic attack as a result of it. Although such an influx of anxiety will not always be the case for everyone suffering from ophidiophobia, it is still very plausible to occur nonetheless.

Ophthalmophobia – Fear of being stared at

Scopophobia, scoptophobia, or ophthalmophobia is an anxiety disorder characterized by a morbid fear of being seen in public or stared at by others. Similar phobias include erythrophobia, the fear of blushing, and an epileptic's fear of being looked at, which may itself precipitate such an attack.

Opiophobia – Fear of opioids

Opiophobia is the irrational fear of opioids. Someone suffering from this condition can expect to experience a very high amount of anxiety from merely thinking of opioids, let alone actually seeing them. In fact, their anxiety may be so intense that they may even endure a full blown panic attack as a result of it. Although such an influx of anxiety will not always be the case for everyone suffering from opiophobia, it is still very plausible to occur nonetheless.

Optophobia – Fear of opening one's eyes

Optophobia is a fear of opening one's eyes. This fear can be extremely debilitating, as it is hard for an individual to carry out daily activities without opening their eyes. People with optophobia may prefer to stay indoors or in dimly lit areas. This phobia is usually associated with a generalized anxiety disorder.

Ornithophobia – Fear of birds

Ornithophobia is the irrational fear of birds. Someone suffering from this condition may endure anxiety that is so intense and painstakingly intrusive that the mere thought of birds may immediately put them into a fight or flight state of mind, and in some extreme cases they may even experience full blown panic attacks as a result of it.

Osphresiophobia – Fear of smells

An extreme fear of bodily odors, either one\'s own or that of others. A pathological fear of (bad) odors or of being contaminated by them.

Ostraconophobia – Fear of shellfish

Ostraconophobia is the irrational fear of shellfish. Someone experiencing this disorder my experience a great deal of anxiety when in the presence of a shellfish. They may find them to be extremely repulsive and grotesque. Depending on the severity of their condition, they may even experience full-blown panic attacks as a result of their ostraconophobia. Their intense fear of shellfish will typically involve all sorts of shellfish such as lobsters, crabs, shrimp, crayfish, etc. Their anxiety may even be so severe that they may find it virtually impossible to even be near someone else eating shellfish.

Ouranophobia – Fear of heaven

Ouranophobia is the irrational fear of heaven. Someone suffering from this condition can expect to experience a very high amount of anxiety from merely thinking of heaven, let alone actually seeing a depiction of it. In fact, their anxiety may be so intense that they may even endure a full blown panic attack as a result of it

P

❧

Pagophobia – Fear of ice or frost

Pagophobia (from Greek pago, "ice") is the fear of ice or frost. Some might have developed this fear because they might have had a near death experience or traumatic experience with ice or snow.

Panophobia – Fear of an unknown evil

Panphobia, omniphobia, pantophobia, or panophobia is a vague and persistent dread of some unknown evil. Panphobia is not registered as a type of phobia in medical references.

Papaphobia – Fear of the Pope

papaphobia (uncountable) the pathological fear of the pope or the papacy.*Papaphobia* is also related to Hierophobia (fear of holy people or sacred things)

Papyrophobia – Fear of paper

Papyrophobia is the irrational fear of paper. Someone suffering from this phobia may find that they are extremely anxious at the mere thought of paper. Someone who has a deep fear of paper may in fact be able to realize that their fear is very irrational, but when in the midst of heightened anxiety, they may be unable to think logically enough to realize this. So, they will often be left feeling extremely anxious.

Parasitophobia – Fear of parasites

Parasitophobia is the irrational fear of parasites. Someone suffering from this condition can expect to experience a very high amount of anxiety from merely thinking of parasites, let alone actually seeing them in real life. In fact, their anxiety may be so intense that they may even endure a full blown panic attack as a result of it. Although such an influx of anxiety will not always be the case for everyone suffering from parasitophobia, it is still very plausible to occur nonetheless.

Pathophobia – Fear of disease

Morbid fear of disease Other terms for nosophobia include disease phobia, *pathophobia* and hypochondria. A related and fairly new phobia is cyberchondria.

Peccatophobia – Fear of sinning

Peccatophobia is the irrational fear of sinning or imaginary crimes. Someone suffering from this condition can expect to experience a very high amount of anxiety from merely thinking of sinning or imaginary crimes, let alone actually experiencing it. In fact, their anxiety may be so intense that they may even endure a full blown panic attack as a result of it. Although such an influx of anxiety will not always be the case for everyone suffering from peccatophobia, it is still very plausible to occur nonetheless.

Pediophobia – Fear of dolls

Pediophobia is a fear of dolls or inanimate objects that look real, and pedophobia is a fear of actual children. People can suffer from both phobias, so someone who fears children (pedophobia) may also fear the childlike features of dolls (pediophobia), and someone with pediophobia may also have pedophobia.

Pedophobia – Fear of children

People with pedophobia develop an irrational fear of babies and small children. The word pedophobia stems from "paida," the Greek word for children. "Phobos" is the Greek word for fear. Someone who has pedophobia may take extreme measures to avoid being around small children.

Pentheraphobia – Fear of your mother-in-law

Pentheraphobia is the fear of your mother-in-law. The origin of the word penthera is Greek (meaning mother-in-law). Pentheraphobia is considered to be a specific phobia.

Phalacrophobia – Fear of going bald

phalacrophobia refers to an irrational fear of baldness: it´s a phobia caused by the fear of going bald, that becomes an uncontrollable obsession. People with fear of bald men or women can feel that uncontrollable fear even when they are not losing hair at all and there are no signs indicating that they may suffer from alopecia in the future. In addition, their condition may not be limited only to baldness itself; on the contrary, they can also feel fear of bald men, even hate about those with baldness.

Pharmacophobia – Fear of medicines

Pharmacophobia is a fear of medication and a negative attitude toward drugs in general. The aim of this study was to determine predictors of pharmacophobia. 700 participants participated in the study, of which 80.9% were female. The age of the participants ranged from 19 to 62 years (M=26.5, SD=7.41).

Phasmophobia – Fear of ghosts

Phasmophobia is an intense fear of ghosts. For people with a ghost phobia, the mere mention of supernatural things — ghosts, witches, vampires — can be enough to evoke the irrational fear.

Philemaphobia – Fear of kissing

Philemaphobia, or philematophobia, is the fear of kissing. It is common among young and inexperienced kissers who are afraid of doing something wrong. In these cases, the anxiety is generally mild to moderate and dissipates quickly as the person gains experience.

Philophobia – Fear of love

People who have philophobia have a fear of love. This fear is so intense that they find it difficult, sometimes impossible, to form and maintain loving relationships. "Philos" is the Greek word for loving or beloved.

Phobophobia – Fear of phobias

Phobophobia is an intense fear of being afraid. Some people might be terrified of the physical symptoms that come with fear, such as rapid breathing or dizziness. Others are scared of developing another phobic disorder.

Phonophobia – Fear of loud noises

Phonophobia is defined as a persistent, abnormal, and unwarranted fear of sound. Often, these are normal environmental sounds (e.g., traffic, kitchen sounds, doors closing, or even loud speech) that cannot under any circumstances be damaging.

Photophobia – Fear of light

Photophobia is eye discomfort in bright light. The cornea allows light to enter the eye. As light passes through the eye the iris changes shape by expanding and letting more light through or constricting and letting less light through to change pupil size.

Phthisiophobia – Fear of tuberculosis

An irrational or exaggerated fear of tuberculosis. Late 19th century; earliest use found in The Lancet. From phthisio- + -phobia, perhaps after French phthisiophobie.

Placophobia – Fear of tombstones

Placophobia is the irrational fear of tombstones. Someone suffering from this condition can expect to experience a very high amount of anxiety from merely thinking of tombstones, let alone actually seeing them in real life. In fact, their anxiety may be so intense that they may even endure a full blown panic attack as a result of it. Although such an influx of anxiety will not always be the case for everyone suffering from placophobia, it is still very plausible to occur nonetheless.

Plutophobia – Fear of money or wealth

Plutophobia is the irrational fear of wealth. Someone with this phobia may be extremely terrified of people who are wealthy and powerful. They may also be immensely fearful of becoming wealthy themselves. Though most people would probably not find much of an issue with becoming rich, some people are truly afraid of it. Thus, someone with plutophobia may purposely sabotage their potential in their career by putting forth mediocre efforts each day to ensure they never become wealthy.

Podophobia – Fear of feet

Podophobia is an overwhelming fear of feet. People with this condition might be scared of their own feet or other people's feet. They may avoid places where people are barefoot, such as beaches or pools.

Pogonophobia – Fear of beards

The term *pogonophobia* is derived from the Greek words *pogon* (πώγων) for beard. Its antonym would be "pogonophilia", that is the love of beards or bearded persons.

Poinephobia – Fear of punishment

An abnormal fear of punishment. which is also referred to as Mastigaphobia, can be defined as the irrational fear of getting punished.

Porphyrophobia – Fear of the color purple

Porphyrophobia is the irrational fear of the color purple. Someone suffering from this condition can expect to experience a very high amount of anxiety from merely thinking of the color purple, let alone actually seeing it. In fact, their anxiety may be so intense that they may even endure a full blown panic attack as a result of it. Although such an influx of anxiety will not always be the case for everyone suffering from porphyrophobia, it is still very plausible to occur nonetheless.

Proctophobia – Fear of rectums

Abnormal apprehension in those suffering from rectal disease. Intense fear of a man anus. This fear is generated from obsessive filching.

Pteridophobia – Fear of ferns

Pteridophobia is the fear of ferns which is a type of plant that is often used in food. Examples include matteuccia struthiopteris (ostrich fern) and osmundastrum cinnamomeum (cinnamon fern).

Pteromerhanophobia – Fear of flying

Fear of flying is a fear of being on an airplane, or other flying vehicle, such as a helicopter, while in flight. It is also referred to as flying anxiety, flying phobia, flight phobia, aviophobia, aerophobia, or pteromerhanophobia (although the penultimate also means a fear of drafts or of fresh air).

Pupaphobia – Fear of puppets

Pupaphobia is the fear of puppets and marionettes. People who suffer from this phobia experience great amounts of anxiety and dread if in the same room with a puppet. Their fear of puppets is extremely irrational and can be very debilitating. Pupaphobia, as well as pediophobia (fear of dolls) is somewhat common among children, but this doesn't limit the fear of puppets to this demographic only.

Pyrophobia – Fear of fire

"Pyrophobia" is the term for a fear of fire that's so intense it affects a person's functioning and daily life. Pyrophobia is one of many specific phobias, which are a type of anxiety disorder.

Q

❧

Quadraphobia – Fearing the number four

Quadraphobia is the irrational fear of the number four. Someone suffering from this condition can expect to experience a very high amount of anxiety from merely thinking of the number four, let alone actually seeing it in real life. In fact, their anxiety may be so intense that they may even endure a full blown panic attack as a result of it. Although such an influx of anxiety will not always be the case for everyone suffering from quadraphobia, it is still very plausible to occur nonetheless.

Quintaphobia – Fearing the number five

Quintaphobia is the irrational fear of the number five. Someone suffering from this condition can expect to experience a very high amount of anxiety from merely thinking of the number five, let alone actually seeing it in real life. In fact, their anxiety may be so intense that they may even endure a full blown panic attack as a result of it. Although such an influx of anxiety will not always be the case for everyone suffering from quintaphobia, it is still very plausible to occur nonetheless.

Quadriplegiaphobia – Fearing becoming a quadriplegic or being afraid of quadriplegics

Quadriplegiphobia is the irrational fear of quadriplegics or of becoming a quadriplegic. Someone suffering from this condition can expect to experience a very high amount of anxiety from merely thinking of quadriplegics or of becoming a quadriplegic, let alone actually seeing one in real life. In fact, their anxiety may be so intense that they may even endure a full blown panic attack as a result of it.

R

ಬ

Radiophobia – Fear of radiation, X rays

Radiophobia is the irrational fear of radiation. Someone experiencing this condition will have a very difficult time thinking about radiation, let alone being subjected to it. There are not many instances in people's lives were they are directly exposed to radiation in high amounts. Such instances are getting x-rays or getting radiation therapy for cancer. People suffering from radiophobia may refuse to accept either.

Ranidaphobia – Fear of frogs

Ranidaphobia is an intense fear of frogs and toads. People with ranidaphobia may believe frogs and toads are harmful or dangerous. Or they may believe the amphibians are cursed. Specific fears such as ranidaphobia can cause nightmares and other symptoms of anxiety.

Rhabdophobia – fear of Magic

Rhabdophobia, or the fear of magic, is a highly personalized phobia that means different things to different people. Some people are afraid only of magic, the purportedly real version in which spellcasters make things happen according to their will.

Rhypophobia – Fear of defecation

Rhypophobia or Belonephobia is the fear or phobia of defecation or of its product feces. These might include needles or knives. Although the second aspect of the definition is more correctly labelled coprophobia

Rhytiphobia – Fear of getting wrinkles

Rhytiphobia is the irrational fear of wrinkles. Someone experiencing this mental illness may find that they have extreme amounts of anxiety at the mere thought of them having wrinkles or of showing any sort of age. Due to their intense and intrusive fear, they may go to painstaking efforts to try and preserve their youth. They may do this by purchasing hundreds if not thousands of dollars worth of beauty products.

Rupophobia – Fear of dirt

Rupophobia is the irrational fear of dirt. Someone suffering from this condition will find it extremely anxiety provoking to just think about dirt, let alone physically being near it. In fact, the amount of anxiety they can expect to experience as a result of their rupophobia may be so intrusive and extreme that they may even experience full blown panic attacks as a result of it. Although this may not be the case for everyone, it is still plausible to occur, especially if their rupophobia is severe.

Russophobia – Fear of Russians

Russophobia is the irrational fear of Russia, Russian culture, and Russian people. Much of this fear is likely to be the result of what occurred during the Cold War (1947–1991) when the Union of Soviet Socialist Republics (USSR) aka the Soviet Union was in power. The Cold War was a state of geopolitical tension between the Soviet Union (Present day Russia) and the United States, along with several other states and allies after World War II.

Group 5

ॐ

S – Z

S

ॐ

Samhainophobia – Fear of Halloween

Samhainophobia is the irrational fear of Halloween. People who suffer from this illness may find it extremely difficult to think about Halloween, let alone participate in it. The convictions they withhold about Halloween give them extreme amounts of anxiety and stress.

Sarmassophobia – Fear of love play

Sarmassophobia (or malaxophobia) is the fear of love play. It is weakly considered a branch of philophobia, fear of love. This phobia is often associated with the persistent fear of situations, objects, activities or persons that involves love play, like unwittingly getting kissing by them a lot.

Satanophobia – Fear of Satan

Satanophobia is the irrational fear of Satan. Someone with this condition may find day to day life to be quite difficult as their fear of Satan may be at the forefront of their thoughts. This is especially true for those who consider themselves to be very religious. Someone suffering from satanophobia who is also religious will not merely have an aversion to Satan, but will be so paralyzed by their fear that they may even experience a full blown panic attack because of it.

Scabiophobia – Fear of scabies

Scabiophobia is the irrational fear of scabies. Someone suffering from this condition can expect to experience a very high amount of anxiety from merely thinking of scabies, let alone actually experiencing it. In fact, their anxiety may be so intense that they may even endure a full blown panic attack as a result of it. Although such an influx of anxiety will not always be the case for everyone suffering from scabiophobia, it is still very plausible to occur nonetheless.

Scelerophobia – Fear of bad men, burglars

Scelerophobia is the irrational fear of bad men or burglars. Someone suffering from this condition can expect to experience a very high amount of anxiety from merely thinking of burglars, let alone actually seeing one. In fact, their anxiety may be so intense that they may even endure a full blown panic attack as a result of it. Although such an influx of anxiety will not always be the case for everyone suffering from scelerophobia, it is still very plausible to occur nonetheless.

Sciophobia – Fear of shadows

Sciophobia is the irrational fear of shadows. Someone experiencing this condition may experience extremely intense amounts of anxiety as a result of their fear. Their sciophobia may dictate major decisions they make in their day to day life such as choosing to not go outside in the daylight much in fear that they may come across a shadow. They may also be hyper-aware of shadows and may consciously look for them as opposed to them only having a subconscious "knee-jerk" reaction to them.

Scoleciphobia – Fear of worms

Scoleciphobia is the irrational fear of worms. Someone suffering from this condition will find it extremely difficult to even think about worms, let alone to actually see one in real life. Seeing one would likely give them an immense influx of unwanted anxiety that may even cause them to experience a panic attack insofar as they have the genetics to do so.

Scolionophobia – Fear of school

Scolionophobia is the irrational fear of school. Someone suffering from this mental illness may experience a great deal of anxiety at the mere thought of school. It is important to note that merely having a distaste for school or not liking to study is not intimation of having scolionophobia. This is a mental illness that is likely due to a chemical imbalance in the brain, though more research is needed to know for sure.

Scotomaphobia – Fear of blindness

Scotomaphobia is the irrational fear of blindness. Someone suffering from this condition can expect to experience a very high amount of anxiety from merely thinking of blindness, let alone actually experiencing it. In fact, their anxiety may be so intense that they may even endure a full blown panic attack as a result of it. Although such an influx of anxiety will not always be the case for everyone suffering from scotomaphobia, it is still very plausible to occur nonetheless.

Scriptophobia – Fear of writing in public

Scriptophobia is the irrational fear of writing in public. Someone suffering with this phobia will find it extremely difficult to write in public or even think about writing in public. Doing so will likely give them intense amounts of anxiety. In some cases, their anxiety will be so extreme that they may even experience full blown panic attacks because of it. Though this is not likely to be common, it is definitely plausible to occur nonetheless.

Selenophobia – Fear of the moon

Selenophobia is the irrational fear of the moon. Someone with this condition may especially be fearful of full moons due to the countless folklore tales and movie depictions of werewolves reacting hostile and violently when in the presence of a full moon. People with full blown selenophobia may find it so unbearably difficult to be outside when the moon is visible that they may even experience full blown panic attacks.

Seplophobia – Fear of decaying matter

Seplophobia is the fear of decaying matter. Phobias are to be taken seriously. If they aren't given proper attention and treatment, might start to limit the sufferers life. In some cases up to the degree of extreme anxiety and depression. Knowing how to manage thoughts and anxiety will not only help a person live or overcome the fear of decaying matter. But also manage to live will all phobias in general.

Sesquipedalophobia – Fear of long words

Sesquipedalophobia is the fear of long words. The irony is clear as the word itself is ridiculously long. People who suffer from sesquipedalophobia may find it very difficult to read articles, novels, or even be out in public due to the chances of them seeing a very long word displayed on a billboard or sign somewhere. In fact, This illness was actually the inspiration for the well known funny song titled "Hippopotomonstrosesquippedaliophobia" by Bryant Oden.

Siderodromophobia – Fear of trains

Siderodromophobia is the irrational fear of trains/railroads. People who suffer from this mental disorder find it extremely difficult being near trains, and virtually impossible to be inside of one. Their intense fear of trains may alter their behavior and dictate certain decisions in their day to day life.

Siderophobia – Fear of stars

a strong dislike or fear of stars. Of the many types of irrational phobias that exist out there, one of the most obscure ones is the fear of stars, which is also known as siderophobia.

Sinistrophobia – Fear of left-handedness

Sinistrophobia is the fear of things at the left side or left-handed people. Sufferers may avoid using their left hand, touching someone else's left hand, or touching an object which has come into contact with a left hand.

Spectrophobia – Fear of mirrors or the undead

Spectrophobia, a type of anxiety disorder classified as a specific phobia, is the fear of mirrors and/or the fear of what may be reflected in them. It may also be referred to as eisoptrophobia or catoptrophobia.

Spheksophobia – Fear of wasps

Spheksophobia is the irrational fear of wasps. Someone suffering from this condition can expect to experience a very high amount of anxiety from merely thinking of wasps, let alone actually seeing them in real life. In fact, their anxiety may be so intense that they may even endure a full blown panic attack as a result of it.

Social Phobia – Fear of social evaluation

Social anxiety disorder (or social phobia) is a mental illness in which social interactions cause intense fear and anxiety, especially if the situations calls for the possibility for the individual to be publicly scrutinized by others. Constant worry thoughts about their appearance, the way they are speaking to others, the way they walk, how other people are looking at them, constantly analyzing and judging other people's body language and facial expressions is a normal occurrence for someone suffering from social phobia.

Somniphobia – Fear of sleep

Somniphobia is the irrational fear of sleep. Someone suffering from this condition can expect to experience a very high amount of anxiety from merely thinking of sleep, let alone actually experiencing it. In fact, their anxiety may be so intense that they may even endure a full blown panic attack as a result of it.

Staurophobia – Fear of the crucifix

Staurophobia is the irrational fear of crosses or the crucifix. Someone suffering from this condition can expect to experience a very high amount of anxiety from merely thinking of crosses or the crucifix, let alone actually seeing one in real life.

Stenophobia – Fear of narrow places

Stenophobia is the irrational fear of narrow things or places. Someone suffering from this condition can expect to experience a very high amount of anxiety from merely thinking of narrow things or places, let alone actually seeing it. In fact, their anxiety may be so intense that they may even endure a full blown panic attack .

Symbolophobia – Fear of symbolism

Symbolophobia is the irrational fear of symbolism. Someone suffering from this condition can expect to experience a very high amount of anxiety from merely thinking of symbolism, let alone actually seeing it. In fact, their anxiety may be so intense that they may even endure a full-blown panic attack.

Symmetrophobia – Fear of symmetry

Symmetrophobia is the irrational fear of symmetry. This phobia is not nearly as common as more notable phobias such as the fear of the number 13, the fear of flying, and the fear of staying single. Nevertheless, symmetrophobia is still viable enough to inflict anxiety and trepidation within the individual suffering from it. In fact, their anxiety may be so intrusive that they may even need to be hospitalized if an intense enough panic attack were to ensue.

Syngenesophobia – Fear of relatives

Syngenesophobia is the irrational fear of relatives. Someone suffering from this condition can expect to experience a very high amount of anxiety from merely thinking of relatives, let alone actually seeing them. In fact, their anxiety may be so intense that they may even endure a full-blown panic attack as a result of it.

Syphilophobia – Fear of syphilis

Syphilophobia is the irrational fear of syphilis. Someone suffering from this condition can expect to experience a very high amount of anxiety from merely thinking of syphilis, let alone actually getting it. In fact, their anxiety may be so intense that they may even endure a full-blown panic attack as a result of it. Although such an influx of anxiety will not always be the case for everyone suffering from syphilophobia, it is still very plausible to occur nonetheless.

T

ℭ

Tachophobia – Fear of speed

Tachophobia is the irrational fear of speed. Someone with this condition may find it extremely difficult to move at a fast rate. In fact, their anxiety may be so intrusive and intense that they may even experience full blown panic attacks that may require them to be hospitalized. Though this may not be the norm, it is definitely possible to occur.

Taphephobia – Fear of being buried alive

Taphophobia (from Greek τάφος - *taphos*, "grave, tomb") is an abnormal (psychopathological) fear of being buried alive as a result of being incorrectly pronounced dead.

Tapinophobia – Fear of being contagious

Tapinophobia is the irrational fear of being contagious. Someone suffering from this condition can expect to experience a very high amount of anxiety from merely thinking of being contagious, let alone actually experiencing it in real life. In fact, their anxiety may be so intense that they may even endure a full-blown panic attack.

Taurophobia – Fear of bulls

Taurophobia is the irrational fear of bulls. Someone suffering from this condition can expect to experience a very high amount of anxiety from merely thinking of bulls, let alone actually seeing them

Technophobia – Fear of technology

Technophobia is the irrational fear of technology. Someone suffering from this condition can expect to find themselves extremely fearful of computers, artificial intelligence (A.I.), or any other software or hardware that they deem to be advanced. Technophobia is different from mechanophobia as the former is more of broad fear of technology in general, while the latter is an even more specific fear of machines only.

Teleophobia – Fear of definite plans

the fear of making definite plans;fear of things ending. Reluctance or refusal to ascribe purpose to natural phenomena.

Testophobia – Fear of taking tests

Testophobia is the irrational fear of taking tests. Someone experiencing this condition may find it extremely difficult to take tests and may perform very poorly on them due to the intense anxiety and stress that they feel when taking them. The may have convinced themselves that they are "bad test takers". Such a conviction may reinforce the fear they have about taking tests.

Thalassophobia – Fear of the sea

Thalassophobia is the irrational fear of the sea. Someone suffering from this condition may find it extremely difficult to be in or near the sea. Their fear may also include being fearful of large lakes, ponds, and rivers too. Essentially, any relatively large body of water with a significant depth that comes with it the risk of drowning or of being home to carnivorous creatures may spawn fear and terror in the mind of someone with thalassophobia.

Thanatophobia – Fear of death or dying

Thanatophobia is an intense fear of death or the dying process. Another name for this condition is "death anxiety." You might be anxious about your own death or the death of someone you care about.

Theatrophobia – Fear of theaters

Theatrophobia is the irrational fear of theaters. Someone suffering from this disorder will find it extremely anxiety provoking to even be near a theater, let alone to actually be inside of one. Their fear of theaters may stem from a combination of other conditions, such as claustrophobia (fear of confined spaces), agoraphobia (fear of crowded places), and/or nyctophobia (fear of the dark), for example. However, this will depend on many factors such as genetics and environment.

Thermophobia – Fear of heat

Thermophobia is the irrational fear of heat. Someone suffering from this condition can expect to experience a very high amount of anxiety from merely thinking of heat, let alone actually experiencing it. In fact, their anxiety may be so intense that they may even endure a full blown panic attack as a result of it.

Tocophobia – Fear of childbirth

Tokophobia or Tocophobia is a pathological fear of pregnancy and can lead to avoidance of childbirth. It can be classified as primary or secondary. Primary tokophobia is morbid fear of childbirth in a woman, who has had no previous experience of pregnancy. The dread of childbirth may start in adolescence or early adulthood.

Tonitrophobia – Fear of thunder

Tonitrophobia is the irrational fear of thunder. Someone suffering from this phobia may find day to day life to be quite challenging, especially if they live in an area where stormy weather is commonplace. In such a circumstance, someone suffering with tonitrophobia may take extreme measures such as being indoors when it is merely cloudy outside for example. Such an action would be meant to help relieve some of the painstaking anxiety this disorder will inflict on them.

Toxiphobia – Fear of poison

Toxiphobia in non-human animals is rejection of foods with tastes, odors, or appearances which are followed by illness resulted from <u>toxins</u> found in these foods. In human animals, toxiphobia is fear of poisons and being poisoned.

Traumatophobia – Fear of injury

Traumatophobia is the irrational fear of having an injury. Someone suffering from this phobia may find that they have extreme amounts of anxiety at the mere thought of having an injury. They may go to painstaking efforts to avoid becoming injured. In extreme cases of traumatophobia they may stay home-bound to reduce their risk. In such an extreme case, they may even become self-loathing and depressed.

Tremophobia – Fear of trembling

Tremophobia is the irrational fear of trembling. Someone suffering from this condition can expect to experience a very high amount of anxiety from merely thinking of trembling, let alone actually experiencing it.

Trichopathophobia – Fear of hair disease

Trichopathophobia (uncountable). A fear relating to the colour, growth or disorders of hair.

Trichophobia – Fear of loose hair

Phobias are extreme fears of certain objects or situations. The term trichophobia comes from the Greek words that mean "hair" (trichos). A person who has trichophobia has a persistent fear of hair, particularly seeing or touching loose hairs on the body, clothing, or elsewhere. This fear can lead to a number of symptoms that may interfere with everyday life.

Triskaidekaphobia – Fear of the number 13

Triskaidekaphobia is the irrational fear of the number 13. People who suffer form this phobia may find it extremely difficult or utterly impossible to do anything that has to do with the number 13. For example, they may make sure that all of the "like items" in their home are either less than 13 or more than 13 in quantity. For instance, if they realize that they own 13 shirts or have 13 items in their refrigerator, then they may simply throw one item away so to make the total number of times 12 instead of 13.

Trypanophobia – Fear of needles or injections

Trypanophobia is the irrational fear of needles or injections. Someone suffering from this condition may find it extremely difficult to cope with very strong emotions such as the dread they will inevitably experience as a result of their fear of needles. This inability to cope with their fear will likely reassure them that their fear is justified.

Turophobia – Fear of cheese

Turophobia - fear of cheese For some people, the smell, sight, taste or even thought of cheese is enough to send them into a cold sweat. Some think that it can be related to a traumatic experience associated with cheese, although there are links with those who are lactose intolerant too.

U

ॐ

Uranophobia – Fear of heaven

Uranophobia or Ouranophobia is the irrational fear of heaven. Someone suffering from this condition can expect to experience a very high amount of anxiety from merely thinking of heaven, let alone actually seeing a depiction of it. In fact, their anxiety may be so intense that they may even endure panic attack.

Urophobia – Fear of urine or urinating

Urophobia is the irrational fear of urine. Someone suffering from this condition can expect to endure a very high amount of anxiety at the mere thought of urine or of someone urinating. Someone with urophobia may be fearful of urine in general, including their own, or they may only be fearful of other people's urine. Their fear may be rooted in a deep concern of getting contaminated or getting the other person's germs in some way.

V

Vaccinophobia – Fear of vaccinations

A fear of or aversion to the practice of vaccination. **Vaccine hesitancy:**is the delay in acceptance or refusal of vaccination despite the wide availability of vaccination services

Venustraphobia – Fear of beautiful women

Venustraphobia is the irrational fear of beautiful women. People who suffer from this illness find it extremely difficult to be around attractive women and may feel intense anxiety and dread when in the company of one. Beauty or attractiveness is a subjective, superficial characteristic that humans have glamorized throughout history.

Verbophobia – Fear of words

Verbophobia is the fear of words. It is also called Logophobia and can be categorized as fear of long words and fear of hearing a certain word or names. The causes for such a phobias are external, can be genetic as well as hereditary.

Verminophobia – Fear of germs

Mysophobia, also known as germophobia, germaphobia, verminophobia, and bacillophobia, is the fear of contamination and germs.

Vestiphobia – Fear of clothing

Vestiphobia is the irrational fear of clothing. Someone suffering from this condition can expect to experience a very high amount of anxiety from merely thinking of clothing, let alone actually wearing it. Someone suffering from vestiphobia may find themselves avoiding that which they fear. They may take this to the extreme by ensuring that they cannot be exposed to clothing in any way. For example, someone with this condition may refuse to wear clothing, regardless of the particular situation that they are in. Such excessive worry and irrational thinking is likely to be one of the main causes of their mental anguish.

Virginitiphobia – Fear of rape

Virginitiphobia refers to the fear of rape or being raped. This is an irrational fear which creates anxiety and even panic attacks with a mere thought of being around people and being raped. People suffering from this find it difficult to be around people as the constant thought of rape and being raped scares the person. Although the number of people suffering from Virginitiphobia is less it affects women more than men. Women fear men around them, the constant fear of getting raped doesn't let them even interact with anyone.

Vitricophobia – Fear of stepfathers

Fear of one's step-father is called Vitricophobia. Normally, children fear their step-fathers because for them, a step-father is a replacement of their real father. Some children feel fearful of them because he's an entirely unknown person, living with their mother as her husband and as their father. For children who have seen and have lived with their real father, adjusting with a new one makes them feel uncomfortable. Maybe because they miss their father or the negative perception society has of this new relationship.

W

Walloonophobia – Fear of the Walloons, an ethnic group native to Belgium

An irrational fear for the Walloons. The Walloons are just a group of people who speak the French language, live in the neighboring region of France, or lives in the southern or eastern part of Belgium.

Wiccaphobia – Fear of witches and witchcraft

Wiccaphobia is the irrational fear of witches and witchcraft. Someone suffering from this condition can expect to experience a very high amount of anxiety from merely thinking of witches and witchcraft. Someone suffering from wiccaphobia may find themselves avoiding that which they fear. They may take this to the extreme by ensuring that they cannot be exposed to witches and witchcraft in any way.

X

❧

Xenophobia – Fear of strangers or foreigners

Xenophobia is the irrational fear of strangers or foreigners. Someone suffering from this condition can expect to experience a very high amount of anxiety from merely thinking of strangers or foreigners, let alone actually seeing them in real life. Someone experiencing a panic attack as a result of their xenophobia can expect to have an increased heart rate, an increased rate of breathing, higher blood pressure, muscle tension, trembling, and excessive sweating, among several other symptoms.

Xanthophobia – Fear of the color yellow

Xanthophobia is the irrational fear of the color yellow. Someone suffering from this condition can expect to experience a very high amount of anxiety from merely thinking of the color yellow, let alone actually seeing it in real life. In fact, their anxiety may be so intense that they may even endure a panic attack as a result of it.

Xerophobia – Fear of dryness

Xerophobia is the irrational fear of dryness. Someone experiencing this condition may find it extremely difficult to be in a dry area or to experience dryness of the skin or to feel parched. In fact, the mere thought of this may give them an immense amount of anxiety that is so intrusive and extreme that they may even experience a panic attack because of it. However, this will vary from person to person.

Xylophobia – Fear of forests

Xylophobia is the irrational fear of wooden objects or forests. Someone suffering from this condition can expect to experience a very high amount of anxiety from merely thinking of wooden objects or forests, let alone actually seeing them in real life. In fact, their anxiety may be so intense that they may even endure a panic attack as a result of it. Although such an influx of anxiety will not always be the case for everyone suffering from xylophobia, it is still very plausible to occur nonetheless.

Xenoglossophobia - Fear of Foreign Languages

Xenoglossophobia is the irrational fear of foreign languages. Someone experiencing this condition may find it extremely difficult to be around people who speak a different language than the one they speak. As a result of this, their anxiety may be so intrusive and abysmal that they may even experience full blown panic attacks which may only reassure them of their fear of foreign languages. Someone suffering with xenoglossophobia does not also mean that they are xenophobic (fear of foreign people). They may simply be extremely fearful of someone who speaks a foreign language.

Xyrophobia - Fear of Razors

Xyrophobia is the irrational fear of razors. Someone suffering from this condition can expect to experience a high amount of anxiety when merely thinking about razors, let alone actually being near one in real life. If someone were to experience a panic attack from their xyrophobia, then they can expect to experience a plethora of different symptoms, such as sharper senses, higher blood pressure, and an increase in stress hormones such as cortisol and adrenaline, among others. If someone with xyrophobia experiences an influx of anxiety due to their fear of razors and is unable to effectively cope with the strong emotions that they will inevitably experience, then a panic attack may occur.

Y

❧

Ymophobia – Fear of being contrary or contrariety in general

Ymophobia is the irrational fear of contrariety. Someone suffering from this condition can expect to experience a very high amount of anxiety from merely thinking of contrariety, let alone actually experiencing it. Someone experiencing a panic attack as a result of their ymophobia can expect to have an increased heart rate, an increased rate of breathing, higher blood pressure, muscle tension, trembling, and excessive sweating, among several other symptoms. Although panic attacks may not always be the case for everyone experiencing symptoms of ymophobia, it is still possible to occur, especially if their symptoms are very severe. There are no definitive causes of ymophobia. Nevertheless, genetics and one's environment may both play very significant roles in the development of this condition. For example, if someone has a family history of mental illness, especially anxiety disorders or specific phobias, then they may have a higher chance of developing ymophobia. This may be due to them having a genetic predisposition to developing mental illness in general.

Z

Zelophobia – Fear of jealousy

Zelophobia is the irrational fear of jealousy. Someone suffering from this condition can expect to experience a very high amount of anxiety from merely thinking of being jealous, let alone actually experiencing it. As is the case with virtually every other phobia that exists, someone with zelophobia can expect anxiety to be the most prominent symptom of their condition. Depending on the severity of their panic attack, they may even need to be hospitalized. However, this will vary from person to person and will be dependent on many factors.

Zemmiphobia – Fear of the great mole rat

Zemmiphobia is the irrational fear of the great mole rat. Someone suffering from this condition can expect to experience a very high amount of anxiety from merely thinking of the great mole rat, let alone actually seeing it in real life. In fact, their anxiety may be so intense that they may even endure panic attack as a result of it.

Zeusophobia – Fear of God or gods

Zeusophobia is the irrational fear of God or Gods. Someone suffering from this mental disorder may experience extreme amounts of anxiety as a result of their condition. In some severe cases, they may even have full-blown panic attacks that require hospitalization. Religion is all around us and it is more common in some countries as opposed to others. So, the country someone lives in may be a pertinent factor as to how much anxiety they will inevitably experience. Someone who has zeusophobia may also be suffering from scrupulosity as well. Scrupulosity is characterized by someone having deep religious guilt or fear of sinning. Depending on how severe their zeusophobia is, they may very well develop scrupulosity, which will inevitably make them feel even more guilty and shameful about themselves. There are many different symptoms of zeusophobia that can make life quite distressing. Someone suffering from this phobia can expect to endure long bouts of anxiety, stress, guilt, and shame. They may feel as though they are worthless and that nothing they do matters or has meaning. Their fear of God may also evoke strong irrational fears of the number 666 and of hell as well. They may feel that their zeusophobia has damned them to rot in hell for all eternity.

Zoophobia – Fear of animals

Zoophobia is the irrational fear of animals. Someone suffering from this condition will find it extremely difficult to be around other animals. In fact, in some extreme cases, they may even experience full-blown panic attacks as a result of their zoophobia, though this will vary from person to person. People suffering from zoophobia may find it extremely difficult to go out to certain places due to their intense, irrational fear of animals. This may cause them to become a recluse which may increase their risk of developing major depressive disorder. There are no known causes of zoophobia. However, genetics and one's environment may play very pertinent roles. For example, someone who has a family history of mental illness, especially anxiety disorders may have a higher chance of developing an irrational fear of animals. This may be due to them also having a higher chance of being genetically predisposed to developing mental illness.

BIBLIOGRAPHY

LeBeau, R. T., Glenn, D., Liao, B., Wittchen, H.-U., Beesdo-Baum, K., Ollendick, T., & Craske, M. G. (2010). Specific phobia: A review of DSM-IV specific phobia and preliminary recommendations for DSM-V.Depression and Anxiety, 27(2), 148-167. doi: http://dx.doi.org/10.1002/da.20655

Van Houtem, C. M. H. H., Laine, M. L., Boomsma, D. I., Ligthart, L., van Wijk, A. J., & De Jongh, A. (2013). A review and meta-analysis of the heritability of specific phobia subtypes and corresponding fears.Journal of Anxiety Disorders, 27(4), 379-388. doi: http://dx.doi.org/10.1016/j.janxdis.2013.04.007

Hofmann, S. G., Alpers, G. W., & Pauli, P. (2008). Phenomenology of panic and phobic disorders. In M. M. Antony & M. B. Stein (Eds.),Oxford handbook of anxiety and related disorders(pp. 34-46). New York, NY: Oxford University Press,.

Hood, H. K., & Antony, M. M. (2012). Evidence-based assessment and treatment of specific phobias in adults. In T. E. Davis III, T. H. Ollendick & L-G. Öst (Eds.),Intensive one-session treatment of specific phobias(pp. 19-42). New York, NY: Springer Science + Business Media.

McCabe, R. E., Ashbaugh, A. R., & Antony, M. M. (2010). Specific and social phobia. In M. M. Antony & D. H. Barlow (Eds.),Handbook of assessment and treatment planning for psychological disorders(2nd ed., pp. 186-223). New York, NY: Guilford Press.

Wolitzky-Taylor, K. B., Horowitz, J. D., Powers, M. B., & Telch, M. J. (2008). Psychological approaches in the treatment of specific phobias: A meta-analysis.Clinical Psychology Review, 28(6), 1021-1037. doi: http://dx.doi.org/10.1016/j.cpr.2008.02.007

Cisler, J., Lohr, J., Sawchuk, C., & Olatunji, B. (2010). Specific Phobia. In J. C Thomas & M. Hersen (Eds.),Handbook of Clinical Psychology Competencies(pp. 697-722). New York: Springer

Abramowitz JS, Moore EL, Braddock AE, Harrington DL. Self-help cognitive-behavioral therapy with minimal therapist contact for social phobia: a controlled trial. Journal of Behavior Therapy and Experimental Psychiatry. 2009;40:98–105.

Acarturk C, de Graaf R, van Straten A, Have MT, Cuijpers P. Social phobia and number of social fears, and their association with comorbidity, health-related quality of life and help seeking: a population-based study. Social Psychiatry and Psychiatric Epidemiology. 2008;43:273–9. [PubMed]

Acarturk C, Smit F, de Graaf R, van Straten A, Ten Have M, Cuijpers P. Economic costs of social phobia: a population-based study. Journal of Affective Disorders. 2009;115:421–9.

Adler LA, Liebowitz M, Kronenberger W, Qiao M, Rubin R, Hollandbeck M, et al. Atomoxetine treatment in adults with attention-deficit/hyperactivity disorder and comorbid social anxiety disorder. Depression and Anxiety. 2009;26:212–21.

Kendler KS, Neale MC, Kessler RC, Heath AC, Eaves LJ. The genetic epidemiology of phobias in women. The interrelationship of agoraphobia, social phobia, situational phobia, and simple phobia. Archives of General Psychiatry. 1992;49:273–81.

Allgulander C, editor. Efficacy of paroxetine in social phobia – a single-center double-blind study of 96 symptomatic volunteers randomized to treatment with paroxetine 20–50mg or placebo for 3 months; 11th European College of Neuropsychopharmacology Congress; 1998 31 October – 4 November; Paris, France.

Almlöv J, Carlbring P, Källqvist K, Paxling B, Cuijpers P, Andersson G. Therapist effects in guided internet-delivered CBT for anxiety disorders. Behavioural and Cognitive Psychotherapy. 2011;39:311–22.

Alonso J, Angermeyer MC, Bernert S, Bruffaerts R, Brugha TS, Bryson H, et al. Disability and quality of life impact of mental disorders in Europe: results from the European Study of the Epidemiology of Mental Disorders (ESEMeD) project. Acta Psychiatrica Scandinavica Supplementum. 2004:38–46.

American Psychiatric Association. Diagnostic and Statistical Manual of Mental Disorders – Text Revision (DSM-IV-TR). Washington, DC: American Psychiatric Association; 2000.

Andersson G, Carlbring P. Commentary on Berger, Hohl, and Caspar's (2009) internet-based treatment for social phobia: a randomized controlled trial. Journal of Clinical Psychology. 2009;65:1036–38.

Andersson G, Carlbring P, Holmström A, Sparthan E, Furmark T, Nilsson-Ihrfelt E, et al. Internet-based self-help with therapist feedback and in vivo group exposure for social phobia: a randomized controlled trial. Journal of Consulting and Clinical Psychology. 2006;74:677–86.

Andrews G, Davies M, Titov N. Effectiveness randomized controlled trial of face to face versus internet cognitive behaviour therapy for social phobia. Australian and New Zealand Journal of Psychiatry. 2011;45:337–40.

Asakura S, Tajima O, Koyama T. Fluvoxamine treatment of generalized social anxiety disorder in Japan: a randomized double-blind, placebo-controlled study. International Journal of Neuropsychopharmacology. 2007;10:263–74.

Atmaca M, Kuloglu M, Tezcan E, Unal A. Efficacy of citalopram and moclobemide in patients with social phobia: some preliminary findings. Human Psychopharmacology. 2002;17:401–05.

Aune T, Stiles TC, Svarva K, Aune T, Stiles TC, Svarva K. Psychometric properties of the Social Phobia and Anxiety Inventory for Children using a non-American population-based sample. Journal of Anxiety Disorders. 2008;22:1075–86.

Baer S, Garland E. Pilot study of community-based cognitive behavioral group therapy for adolescents with social phobia. Journal of the American Academy of Child and Adolescent Psychiatry. 2005;44:258–64.

Baker SL, Heinrichs N, Kim HJ, Hofmann SG. The Liebowitz Social Anxiety Scale as a self-report instrument: a preliminary psychometric analysis. Behaviour Research and Therapy. 2002;40:701–15.

Baldwin DS, Bobes J, Stein DJ, Scharwächter I, Faure M. Paroxetine in social phobia/social anxiety disorder. Randomised, double-blind, placebo-controlled study. Paroxetine Study Group. The British Journal of Psychiatry. 1999;175:120–26.

Baldwin DS, Cooper JA, Huusom AK, Hindmarch I. A double-blind, randomized, parallel-group, flexible-dose study to evaluate the tolerability, efficacy and effects of treatment discontinuation with escitalopram and paroxetine in patients with major depressive disorder. International Clinical Psychopharmacology. 2006;21:159–69.

Becker ES, Rinck M, Turke V, Kause P, Goodwin R, Neumer S, et al. Epidemiology of specific phobia subtypes: findings from the Dresden Mental Health Study. European Psychiatry. 2007;22:69–74.

Beidel DC, Turner SM, Morris TL. Psychopathology of childhood social phobia. Journal of the American Academy of Child and Adolescent Psychiatry. 1999;38:643–50.

Berger T, Hohl E, Caspar F. [Internet-based treatment for social phobia: a 6-month follow-up]. Zeitschrift fur Klinische Psychologie und Psychotherapie: Forschung und Praxis. 2010;39:217–21.

Birmaher BB. Psychometric properties of the screen for child anxiety related emotional disorders (SCARED): a replication study. Journal of the American Academy of Child and Adolescent Psychiatry. 1999;38:1230–36.

Blomhoff S, Haug TT, Hellstrom K, Holme I, Humble M, Madsbu HP, et al. Randomised controlled general practice trial of sertraline, exposure therapy and combined treatment in generalised social phobia. British Journal of Psychiatry. 2001;179:23–30.

Boettcher J, Berger T, Renneberg B. Internet-based attention training for social anxiety: a randomized controlled trial. Cognitive Therapy and Research. 2011;36:522–36.

Cabrera J, Emir B, Dills D, Murphy K, Whalen E, Clair A. Characterizing and understanding body weight patterns in patients treated with pregabalin. Current Medical Research and Opinion. 2012;28:1027–37.

Den Boer JA, van Vliet IM, Westenberg HG. A double-blind placebo controlled study of fluvoxamine in social phobia. Clinical Neuropharmacology. 1992;15:615.

den Boer JA. Social phobia: epidemiology, recognition, and treatment. BMJ. 1997;315:796–800.

Caldwell DM, Ades AE, Higgins JP. Simultaneous comparison of multiple treatments: combining direct and indirect evidence. BMJ. 2005;331:897–900.

Carlbring P, Gunnarsdóttir M, Hedensjö L, Andersson G, Ekselius L, Furmark T. Treatment of social phobia: randomised trial of internet-delivered cognitive-behavioural therapy with telephone support. British Journal of Psychiatry. 2007;190:123–28.

Carlbring P, Nordgren LB, Furmark T, Andersson G. Long-term outcome of internet-delivered cognitive-behavioural therapy for social phobia: a 30-month followup. Behaviour Research and Therapy. 2009;47:848–50.

Cartwright-Hatton S, McNally D, Field AP, Rust S, Laskey B, Dixon C, et al. A new parenting-based group intervention for young anxious children: results of a randomized controlled trial. Journal of the American Academy of Child and Adolescent Psychiatry. 2011;50:242–51.

Chartier MJ, Walker JR, Stein MB. Considering comorbidity in social phobia. Social psychiatry and psychiatric epidemiology. 2003;38:728–34.

Chung YS, Kwon JH. The efficacy of bibliotherapy for social phobia. Brief Treatment and Crisis Intervention. 2008;8

Clark DM. A controlled trial of cognitive therapy and pharmacotherapy in the treatment of social phobia. National Research Register. 1998

Clark DM, Wells A. A cognitive model of social phobia. In: Heimberg RG, Liebowitz M, Hope DA, Schneier FR, editors. Social Phobia: Diagnosis, Assessment and Treatment. New York: Guildford Press; 1995. pp. 69–93.

Clark DM, Ehlers A, McManus F, Hackmann A, Fennell M, Campbell H, et al. Cognitive therapy versus fluoxetine in generalized social phobia: A randomized placebo-controlled trial. Journal of Consulting and Clinical Psychology. 2003;71:1058–67.

Connor KM, Davidson JR, Churchill LE, Sherwood A, Foa E, Weisler RH. Psychometric properties of the Social Phobia Inventory (SPIN). New self-rating scale. The British Journal of Psychiatry. 2000;176:379–86.

Cottraux J, Note I, Albuisson E, Yao SN, Note B, Mollard E, et al. Cognitive behavior therapy versus supportive therapy in social phobia: a randomized controlled trial. Psychotherapy and Psychosomatics. 2000;69:137–46.

Curtis GC, Magee WJ, Eaton WW, Wittchen HU, Kessler RC. Specific fears and phobias. Epidemiology and classification. The British Journal of Psychiatry. 1998;173:212–7.

Davidson JR, Foa EB, Huppert JD, Keefe FJ, Franklin ME, Compton JS, et al. Fluoxetine, comprehensive cognitive behavioral therapy, and placebo in generalized social phobia. Archives of General Psychiatry. 2004;61:1005–13.

Davis TE, Jenkins WS, Rudy BM. Empirical status of one-session treatment. In: Davis TE, Ollendick TH, Öst LG, editors. Intensive One-Session Treatment of Specific Phobias. New York: Springer; 2012.

De Los Reyes A, Alfano CA, Beidel DC. The relations among measurements of informant discrepancies within a multisite trial of treatments for childhood social phobia. Journal of Abnormal Child Psychology. 2010;38:395–404.

Fahlen T. Personality traits in social phobia, II: Changes during drug treatment. Journal of Clinical Psychiatry. 1995;56:569–73.

Fraser J, Kirkby KC, Daniels B, Gilroy L, Montgomery IM. Three versus six sessions of computer-aided vicarious exposure treatment for spider phobia. Behaviour Change. 2001;18:213–23.

Furmark TT. Common changes in cerebral blood flow in patients with social phobia treated with citalopram or cognitive-behavioral therapy. Archives of General Psychiatry. 2002;59:425–33.

Gallagher HM, Rabian BA, McCloskey MS. A brief group cognitive-behavioral intervention for social phobia in childhood. Journal of Anxiety Disorders. 2004;18:459–79.

Gilroy LJ, Kirkby KC, Daniels BA, Menzies RG, Montgomery IM. Controlled comparison of computer-aided vicarious exposure versus live exposure in the treatment of spider phobia. Behavior Therapy. 2000;31:733–44.

GlaxoSmithKline. A randomized, double-blind, fixed dose comparison of 20, 40, and 60 mg daily of paroxetine and placebo in the treatment of generalized social phobia. GSK Clinical Study Register. 1997

Gould R, Buckminster S, Pollack M, Otto M, Yap L. Cognitive-behavioral and pharmacological treatment for social phobia: a meta-analysis. Clinical Psychology Science and Practice. 1997;4:291–306.

Hoffart A, Borge FM. Psychotherapy for social phobia: how do alliance and cognitive process interact to produce outcome? Psychotherapy Research. 2012;22

Kendler KS, Karkowski LM, Prescott CA. Fears and phobias: reliability and heritability. Psychological Medicine. 1999;29:539–53.

Liebowitz MR, Schneier F, Campeas R, Gorman J, Fyer A, Hollander E, et al. Phenelzine and atenolol in social phobia. Psychopharmacology Bulletin. 1990;26:123–25.

Magee WJ, Eaton WW, Wittchen HU, McGonagle KA, Kessler RC. Agoraphobia, simple phobia, and social phobia in the National Comorbidity Survey. Archives of General Psychiatry. 1996;53:159–68.

Marks IM, Kenwright M, McDonough M, Whittaker M, Mataix-Cols D. Saving clinicians' time by delegating routine aspects of therapy to a computer: a randomized controlled trial in phobia/panic disorder. Psychological Medicine. 2004;34:9–17.

Smith KL, Kirkby KC, Montgomery IM, Daniels BA. Computer-delivered modeling of exposure for spider phobia: relevant versus irrelevant exposure. Journal of Anxiety Disorders. 1997;11:489–97.

Stinson FS, Dawson DA, Patricia Chou S, Smith S, Goldstein RB, June Ruan W, et al. The epidemiology of DSM-IV specific phobia in the USA: results from the National Epidemiologic Survey on Alcohol and Related Conditions. Psychological Medicine. 2007;37:1047–59.

Tillfors M, Carlbring P, Furmark T, Lewenhaupt S, Spak M, Eriksson A, et al. Treating university students with social phobia and public speaking fears: internet delivered self-help with or without live group exposure sessions. Depression and Anxiety. 2008;25:708–17.

Tortella-Feliu M, Botella C, Llabrés J, Bretón-López JM, del Amo AR, Baños RM, et al. Virtual reality versus computer-aided exposure treatments for fear of flying. Behavior Modification. 2011;35:3–30.

Marks IM. Fears and Phobias. London: Heinemann; 1975.

Müller BH, Kull S, Wilhelm FH, Michael T. One-session computer-based exposure treatment for spider-fearful individuals: efficacy of a minimal self-help intervention in a randomised controlled trial. Journal of Behavior Therapy and Experimental Psychiatry. 2011;42:179–84.

Mulkens S, Bögels SM, de Jong PJ, Louwers J. Fear of blushing: effects of task concentration training versus exposure in vivo on fear and physiology. Journal of Anxiety Disorders. 2001;15:413–32.

Nardi AE, Lopes FL, Valenca AM, Freire RC, Nascimento I, Veras AB, et al. Double-blind comparison of 30 and 60 mg tranylcypromine daily in patients with panic disorder comorbid with social anxiety disorder. Psychiatry Research. 2010;175:260–5.

Schneider AJ, Mataix-Cols D, Marks IM, Bachofen M, Schneider AJ, Mataix-Cols D, et al. Internet-guided self-help with or without exposure therapy for phobic and panic disorders. Psychotherapy and Psychosomatics. 2005;74:154–64.